A GODDESS IN THE STONES

NORMAN LEWIS

A GODDESS IN THE STONES

Travels in India

A John Macrae Book

HENRY HOLT AND COMPANY
NEW YORK

Library of Congress Cataloging-in-Publication Data
Lewis, Norman.
A goddess in the stones : travels in India / Norman Lewis.
—1st American ed.
p.   cm.
Originally published: London : J. Cape, 1991.
"A John Macrae book."
Includes index.
1. India—Description and travel—1981–   . I. Title.
DS414.2.L48   1992
915.404'52—dc20   91-31039
                                                    CIP

ISBN 0-8050-1959-6

Henry Holt books are available at special discounts for bulk purchases
for sales promotions, premiums, fund-raising, or educational use. Special
editions or book excerpts can also be created to specification.
For details contact:
Special Sales Director,
Henry Holt and Company, Inc.,
115 West 18th Street,
New York, New York 10011.

First American Edition—1992

Printed in the United States of America
Recognizing the importance of preserving the written word,
Henry Holt and Company, Inc., by policy, prints all of its first
editions on acid-free paper. ∞

1   3   5   7   9   10   8   6   4   2

Contents

Preface

IT WAS NOT the best of times in which to explore the attractions of what may appear to many of us as the most glamorous of the countries of the East. India is frequently referred to as 'the greatest democracy on earth', but immediately prior to my arrival greatness had been diminished by general elections conducted in an atmosphere of outrage and fraud. The characteristic Indian cheerfulness had been overtaken by the savagery of local politics. The Indian press described 'booth-capturing' by armed thugs hired by all parties alike who drove off the police and stuffed the boxes with their candidates' votes. Despite the intervention of paramilitary forces 'backward areas' were reported where sixty percent of the electorate were deprived of their votes by intimidation or outright violence.

In May 1991 the shock-waves of Rajiv Gandhi's assassination were felt round the world. Apart from the briefest of interludes, the dynasty founded by Nehru, and carried on by his daughter Indira Gandhi and her son, Rajiv, had held power since Independence in 1947, and its Congress party had developed into an efficient, if somewhat relentless, machine. It had created a middle class and fostered industrialization, but after four decades in control many observers saw the country as more lawless and corrupt than ever before.

The density and darkness of this metaphorical jungle was deepened at the time of my visit in 1990 by a worsening caste-war in the North. Religious fanaticism was on the upsurge, and ten thousand fundamentalist zealots, manipulated by a political conspiracy, set out to destroy a Muslim holy place, the ancient mosque of Ayodhia. They were repelled by the police, but 200 died in the fighting, thus touching off nationwide reprisals, largely against small, isolated Muslim communities. Death by fire is an all-too-frequent feature of these ultimate acts·of violence. Burnings have become part of the ritual of Indian dissent, as in the case of the protesters angered by governmental support for the 'untouchable' cause who set themselves alight.

The worst of these atrocities took place in the State of Bihar, strategically chosen as the starting point for the journey that lay ahead. In Bihar feudalism in its most blatant form remains, nevertheless it is an area of supreme beauty and outstanding historic interest. Little is written about it apart from depressing newspaper reports. It is far away from the well-beaten itineraries of the North offering the justly famous attractions of Agra and the monumental towns of Rajasthan.

Through a shortage of information about the accessibility of regions, my journey was of necessity loosely planned. Moving on southwards from Bihar I proposed to travel in what were once known as the Central Provinces – now largely Orissa and Madhya Pradesh. Certainly, very little had appeared in print about this area in recent years, although it was of great interest to me since it contained the greater part of the Indian tribal population, numerically exceeding that of any other region of the world. Astonishingly, according to accounts furnished largely by anthropologists, many of these tribal groupings, despite all the pressures put upon them by the times, had been successful in retaining much of their aboriginal culture.

According to the latest census, 7 per cent of India's total population of 773 millions – roughly 54 millions – comprises tribal peoples. These are spread in innumerable pockets all over central and northern India, largely in mountainous areas into which they withdrew following the Aryan invasions from the north immediately preceding the Christian era. Some are classified as Proto-Australoid, having a supposed racial affinity with the Aborigines of Australia. Others, the Dravidians, are regarded by the anthropologists as of Asian origin. In addition there are Mongoloid tribes who have reached India by way of Burma and China. Although a proportion of them still carry bow and arrows, it would be a very great mistake to label them primitive, for their culture, although strikingly diverse from that of the Hindu minority, has developed its own forms of sophistication, notably in the widespread practice and appreciation of the arts. Above all, the descendents of the original inhabitants of the sub-continent are free of the burden of caste.

When, shortly after the war, I travelled through Indo-China and Burma, I went there spurred on by the conviction that much of what I would see and hoped to record was shortly destined to vanish forever. In *A Dragon Apparent* I discovered that, despite the fairly recent French occupation, a most refined and ancient culture had survived in Indo-China in which magnificence was tempered by good taste. Prestige went to the composer of acceptable poetry. People dressed not according to the dictates of fashion but to be in harmony with their environment, and there were mass excursions to admire the effects of moonlight on lakes, or to paint flowering trees, or simply to admire them. It was a country whose miracles of grace I felt impelled – almost from a sense of duty – to chronicle as best I could, so that not all memory of them should be lost. Burma, too, was heir to a great and little-known civilisation, doomed, as I saw it, to effacement through incurable civil war. In *Golden Earth* I attempted once again to put on paper what I could of scenes and ceremonies so soon to be obliterated.

In India – reservoir of endless colour, pageantry, and interest – the pace of transformation, by comparison, has been slow, but it is happening, and at an increasing tempo. India, once dependent upon agriculture, has become a major industrial power, and the unhappy processes accompanying the drive for growth are only too familiar. Here, as elsewhere, the forests are vanishing – in India almost as fast as in Brazil. Hundreds of miles of river valleys are being flooded to provide more water for industries, and tens of thousands of once self-sufficient tribesmen, thus displaced, now furnish low-paid labour for factories and mines. Thirty years ago there were elephants and tigers within a few miles of the centre of Bilaspur in Madhya Pradesh. This is now the scene of the largest open-cast coalmine in the world, which is said to employ 100,000 miners. All round, the industrial wilderness stretches to the horizon.

The great palaces, the monuments and the tombs of the North will endure. India's jungles and all that they contain are to be swept away. It was a thought that increased my feelings of urgency in writing this book.

Norman Lewis, 1992

EAST INDIA

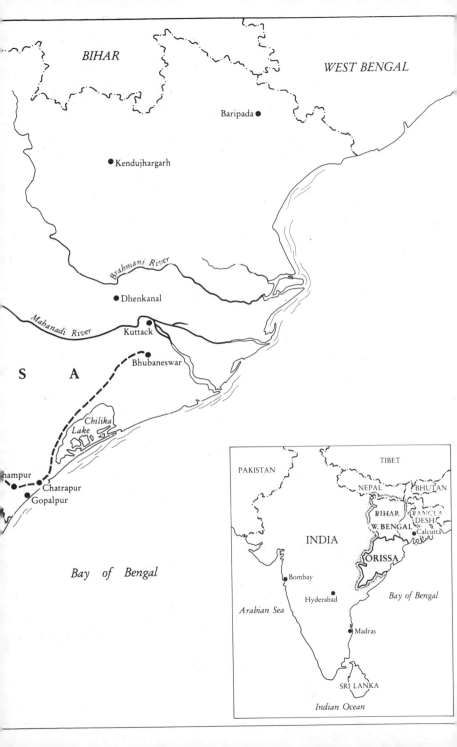

BIHAR

WEST BENGAL

Baripada ●

●Kendujhargarh

Brahmani River

●Dhenkanal

Mahanadi River

Kuttack ●

S   A

●Bhubaneswar

*Chilika
Lake*

hampur

Chatrapur
Gopalpur

Bay of Bengal

PAKISTAN   TIBET

NEPAL   BHUTAN

BIHAR   BANGLA
W. BENGAL   DESH
                  ●Calcutta

INDIA

ORISSA

●Bombay

Arabian Sea

Hyderabad ●

Bay of Bengal

● Madras

SRI LANKA

Indian Ocean

THROUGH THE
BADLANDS OF BIHAR

ONE

MY RICKSHAW JOINED the stream of traffic at the end of the airport road and turned in the direction of the city of Patna. The scene was one not to be forgotten. Three taxis from the airport bumped through the potholes and the fog into the distance and out of sight. After that we were part of a great fleet of rickshaws, of which there were possibly fifty in view, all keeping up with each other, while the pullers – as they were still called – pedalled along as if under the orders of an invisible captain. No sound came from them but the dry grinding of bicycle chains, the rattle of mudguards and the horse-like snort with which they cleared dust and mucus from their nasal passages. Muffled against the cold and fog, the pullers looked like Henry Moore's shrouded shelterers in the wartime Tube, or like Ethiopian refugees with only their stick-thin legs showing below their tattered body wrappings, or like Lazaruses called from the dead. The single change in this prospect wrought by modern times was the presence of towering advertisement hoardings, closing off both sides of the road to form continuous ramparts for mile after mile. Floodlit faces radiating joy through the twilight and thickening fog praised Japanese stereos, Scotch whisky, wise investments, luxury footwear and packaged food. Nearing the city the gap left between the bottom of the hoardings and the earth provided glimpses of the homeless, scattered like the victims of a massacre, singly and in groups, who had claimed these uncontested spaces to settle for the night. In the Indian context there would have been nothing exceptional in this apart from the advertisements, and it was these that added a brush stroke of the macabre.

A power failure had cancelled out the city's centre and added it to suburbs glutted with shadows, with sleepers picked out by the headlights who had dumped themselves among the rubbish, and the stealthy inscrutable movements of those who chose to remain awake. From this obscurity the Mauriya Patna hotel, rescued by its generators, stood apart in an oasis of light. Patna had fallen into a coma. The Mauriya overbrimmed with almost unnatural vivacity. There were big events afoot. WELCOME TO THE BALLOONISTS said a large notice in the lobby, and a small one on the reception counter warned that, since the next day was a public holiday, the hotel palmist would not be on duty as usual. It regretted the inconvenience that patrons might suffer. In the absence of separate public rooms a small area to the rear held two long opulent settees upon which rows of guests sat facing each other in a kind of expectant silence. While waiting for the reception clerk to cope with the lengthy formalities involved in checking in I took my seat here. Indians are not necessarily outgoing with their own people, but often fall spontaneously into an easy and informal relationship with foreigners. It came as no surprise to be asked by the man sitting next to me, quite courteously and without preamble, who I was, where I was from, and what were my immediate plans. 'I am Mr

Mandhar Chawra,' he said, 'Inspector of Works. You will be here to see the balloon?'

When I said I was not, he was surprised. He was a small, neat man with a pleasant expression and thick black hair, and nostrils drawn back as if to sniff the odour of cooking of which he approved. 'It is an event', he said, 'to break the monotony of our life. Something we are all looking to. Have you ever been in Patna before?'

I said I had not, and Mr Chawra said, 'Oh, you will like it. In our country we call it the City of Kings. It is having a bad press, but do not believe half you hear.'

The key was handed over and Mr Chawra and I parted company in the hope, as we assured each other, of watching the arrival of the balloon together on the morrow. I went up to my room for a shower in a lift that warbled soft Hindu music at me as soon as the door closed. The view through the bedroom window was of a swimming pool lightly feathered by fog and with what appeared as a dark bulk afloat in it. Accounts of happenings in this town during the recent election made this at the time seem a little sinister, although by morning it had gone.

The fog was slow to lift next day. The neighbourhood people were still swaddled voluminously in African style, or wearing ragged ponchos like those to be seen in the depressed cities of Latin America. I braced myself for a reconnaissance. The hotel had been built with an optimistic vista of the park, Gandhi Maidan, but, turning with some reluctance away from this in the direction of the business centre, I was plunged instantly into a slum. Patna is the capital of Bihar, unanimously recognised by Indians as the most atrociously governed of the Indian states, thus the metropolis of civic abuse. A minor official in Delhi had mentioned that one fifth of the population slept on the streets, and at the moment of my arrival the mass daily resurrection of these multitudes was in progress, although those with any reason to get up were already pitched into the business of survival.

Perhaps the medieval warrens of Europe were like this. This was the place where an empty beer-bottle had its price, where a worn-out lorry tyre provided material for a dozen pairs of shoes, and tea in the bottom class of teashop was swilled from hollowed-out gourds. Men practised their crafts in workshops like enormous rabbit hutches raised upon wooden posts above the cluttered one-man factories at street level. Every square foot of earth was put to one commercial use or another, with occasional lanes patrolled by cows splashed liberally with their dung. The cows fascinated me; clean, sensitive, delicately stepping animals that dealt so effortlessly with the maelstrom of traffic and coped with all the imperatives of urban civilisation. I had observed in India before how easily they fall into a routine. Here they were doing the rounds of the town in search of food, gobbling up windfalls of wood-shavings, packaging materials and old newspapers, although quietly nuzzling aside the plastic.

Families lived under sheets of plastic stretched in every angle of the walls, in burrowings among collapsed masonry, on the roofs of houses about to crumble, in dried-up wells, sections of drainpipes (although there were no drains), and in the husks of crashed cars after every utilisable part had been stripped away. There was no room here for the luxury of privacy in the movement of the bowels. Men defecated candidly, without effort or concealment. Five citizens stood in line to piss on or around the feet of the film actor Ramarao, shown in a large poster in the part of a god who looked down with aversion as the yellow trickles joined a black mainstream drawing its tributaries of fermenting liquid from the piled-up rubbish. Perhaps the men did this in token of their displeasure at his performance – there was no way of knowing.

The advertisements were everywhere: great, gloating faces adding their surrealism to those scenes of famine, barely contained, of bodies like cadavers awaiting dissection, of excrement, urine, mucus and phlegm. ALWAYS A STEP AHEAD WITH LIBERTY SHOES . . . FOR THEM ONLY THE BEST . . . THE TRUE FLAVOUR OF THE GLEN . . . LET'S PLAY THE FUTURE TOGETHER. On whom were these inducements and appeals targeted?

A Mr Singh, an insurance claims adjuster down on a flying visit from the capital whose acquaintance I had made in the hotel bar, was happy to reveal what he believed was the trickery involved. 'The people who are spending their money in this way may be under the misapprehension that they are buying prime space in Delhi,' he said, 'where it happens that there is a street of the same name.'

Back in the Mauriya, the news was disappointing. A notice had gone up:

> *WILLS CIGARETTES BALLOONING*
> *ACROSS INDIA EXPEDITION 1990*
> The Wills balloon 'Indra Dharnust' will take
> off between 14.30 and 15.30 hours subject to
> favourable weather conditions instead of
> 11.30 hours as announced earlier.

Mr Chawra was at my elbow. 'I see we will be wasting

time,' he said. 'This is problem of weather. We must only hope that there will be no further delay.'

The balloon was to take off from a spot marked by a small circle of whitewash on the grass of the Maidan about 200 yards from the hotel, all of whose rooms overlooking the scene had long since been reserved. The last of the fog, still adhering here and there like tufts of wool to the grimy façades of the city, was clearing away, and the sun shafting through the clouds haloed a patient group of early arrivals. I would have expected a crowd of those who had not been notified of the postponement to have gathered by now, but the Maidan was surprisingly empty. I mentioned this to Mr Chawra, who said, 'Actually many are not attending in the belief that they have nothing suitable to put on.'

Suddenly the hotel staff seemed to have disappeared. At the reception only the lurking figure of a man whose sole job appeared to be to hand out and receive keys was to be seen. The travel bureau was closed. The porter had slipped away. At the back of the lobby two lines of guests faced each other on the settees, and no one stirred. An out of order notice had been fastened to the lift door. A card left on the palmist's desk held promise. 'On this day the horoscope for all of us is favourable.'

'The thing is what to do with myself,' I said to Mr Chawra.

'Understandably so,' he said. 'Normally in Patna there are many things to occupy the time. When we are holiday-making it is different.'

He was from Gaya he told me, describing it as a provincial hole, and seemed to be happily stimulated by the mere knowledge that he was now in the capital. 'Patna', he said, 'is the centre of my little world. There are people who come to Patna to drive over the bridge to the middle of river. Here they are stopping to make a wish. This is lucky.'

'Isn't there a museum?' I asked.

'There is none better. It is famous for its archaeological sculptures from Maurya and Gupta periods.'

'In that case I may as well give it the once over.'

'Today it is shut,' Chawra said. 'There is also the famous Khudabaksh Library containing many unique volumes. This, too, is closed for holiday. Continually I am arguing that all these places must remain open when there is opportunity for the public to see them.'

'What about the famous grain store?'

'You are referring to the Gholgar built by your Warren Hastings? It is a must, but unfortunately at this moment the only view is of outside as the interior is under reconstruction.'

'Any suggestions, then?' I asked.

'Yes,' he said. 'You should visit the burning ghats here. This is my word of advice. They are very interesting.'

'In what way, would you say?'

'Because they a natural sight to be seen. In Gaya also we have such ghats, but in Patna they are more select. Today is Sankranti, which for us is first festival of the year. Many people will be coming to immerse their bodies in river, also there will be many burnings. As a foreigner this is interesting for you to see.'

The driver of the taxi I took had no more than four or five words of English. Mr Chawra, who had decided to stay in the hotel in case some freak of the weather brought the balloon in to land earlier than expected, told him to take me to the ghats. The driver nodded in confirmation.

'Crematorium,' he said. 'This is a new word they are all using,' Chawra explained. 'He will take you to the ghats.' At the end of the short ride, nevertheless, I found myself shoved through a gate into a dismal shed. This was the new electric crematorium which, had I known, could have been avoided by a nearby path leading down to the river. Here a scarecrow human figure materialised in the gloom, signalling to me with desperate gestures to accompany him. I found myself staring up at what appeared to be a bundle of rags stuffed into a niche in the wall. This was some funerary goddess. An offering was clearly expected. I handed over five rupees, had paste smeared upon my forehead as equivalent of a receipt, then, taken off my guard, found myself peering through an oven door which had suddenly been flung open to reveal a shapeless carbonised mass. Seconds later, reaching daylight and fresh air once again, I found myself holding a leaflet in Sanskrit characters and in English. *Low rate burning for families. Discount satisfaction. Ashes for river in 45 minutes.*

What was on offer was a cut-price although ritually unsatisfactory passage through the portals of this life into the reincarnation appropriate to the state of the dead man's karma. All those who could raise the money saw to it that they were burned with proper ceremony on a pile of freshly cut and fragrant wood at the edge of the great river into which their remains would be most carefully stirred.

At Patna the Ganges, fed by important tributaries, becomes very wide, a placid unruffled flood, green and opaque in the shallows, then lightening to the milky aquarelle of the distant shore, with its line of palms, on this occasion, sketched in on a ribbon of mist. I noted that a few patches of pinkish scum floating at the water's edge were mixed with straw and ash from a recent burning. On the ghat the scene was a lively one devoid even of token solemnity. Children in their holiday best romped noisily up and down the long flights of steps to the water. A few dogs, even, had slipped past the guards posted at the gates to discourage intrusion by persons of the scheduled castes, previously known as untouchable. Funeral parties entered the enclosure by a separate gate and thus, distanced from the holiday crowd, carried their bier to the music of horns and flutes down to the readied pyres they had been allotted. A hundred or two yards upstream those who hoped to refurbish their spiritual lives by a simple process poured water over their heads, torsos and arms, before immersion. These operations conducted with some grace appeared almost as a ballet, in slow motion. Midway between the groups concerned with this life and those with the next, a man who had arrived on a bicycle unstrapped a large vacuum flask from its carrier, and clambered down the slope to fill it with holy water, evidently for drinking purposes.

The most notable burning that afternoon was of a man whose impressive cortège included a portly Brahmin priest and a photographer with an assistant carrying a battery of cameras. The dead man could have been in his forties, and such had been the mortician's artistry that the semblance of a face flushed with health suggested a man taking a nap after a good meal rather than one that would never rise again. A bed had been made up on piled tree-trunks and on this the corpse dressed in white pyjamas was laid. A flowered coverlet, brought along seemingly as an afterthought, was removed from its plastic wrapping and spread in position. An English-speaking mourner, spotting a European face, came over eager for a chance to speak well of a friend. 'We were all admiring this man for his positive attitudes,' he said. 'Yesterday he announced that he proposed to depart this world on this day, and this he did.' The English speaker was called away to take his place in the group gathering at the head of the bier. The photographer crouched, Pentax levelled, the priest raised a hand to signify that all was ready and the shot was taken. With this, to my surprise, the party broke up, turned their backs and began to walk away. Someone snatched off the coverlet and pushed it back into its plastic envelope. The body was covered with light, combustible material and the dead man's son, abandoned by the rest, approached to apply the match.

On the circuitous stroll back to the centre I paused to study the work in progress on a new building going up at tremendous speed. The building was destined to become a block of flats, and when finished was certain to be outwardly indistinguishable from a similar construction in any city of the West, yet at first glance it was no more than an enormous example of cottage industry.

Although elsewhere in the city all work appeared to have come to a stop, here this was not the case. The first floor, unfinished, sprouted a forest of spindly tree-trunks upon which the one above would be supported, and this teemed with busily occupied figures. A load of bricks had been dumped by the roadside and a team of girls who appeared to be between fifteen and eighteen years of age were carrying these into a position within easy reach of the bricklayers. Each girl, assisted by another, stacked eleven bricks on the platform on her head – a burden which she carried with unfaltering step and even a kind of absent-minded dignity for twenty yards or so to the waiting bricklayer, before returning to be laden as before. I picked up a brick and estimated its weight as at least five pounds. Thus the total load would have been over fifty pounds. I knew that it was one I could never have carried. These tribal girls were contract or (illegally) bonded labourers, recruited in all probability from destitute families who had lost their land and were now prisoners of a system to which many millions of Indians are subjected and from which there is no escape. There is no secret about the abuses to which they are exposed, and the current number of the *Illustrated Weekly of India*, reporting on a seemingly immutable situation, revealed nothing that was new. 'They are ruthlessly exploited', said the newspaper, 'by labour contractors who are hand in glove with officials. Men are paid 12 rupees (42p) and women 10 rupees (35p) for a 10-hour day.'

The feudal state of Bihar is the principal source of supply of female and child labour. In this case the choice would have been the building site or starvation, and the girls endured their fate with customary stoicism.

Some hours later I arrived back at the Mauriya where Mr Chawra awaited me in a state of consternation.

'Mr Lewis, where have you been missing? The balloon has come and gone. I am sorry for you. It has been an experience of much joy to us all. We were all on the look-out for you, but you were nowhere to be found.'

'I'm sorry. I got rather held up.'

'And you were interested by the burnings?'

'Very much so.'

'I am glad. There has been a press conference given at the hotel by Mr Gupta who is leading the expedition to outline his objectives. I have kept for you one press-release.'

I took the paper and read. 'Soaring above the Gangetic plains of Bihar and West Bengal, Mr Gupta asseverated that the Wills Balloon Indra would sail into the clouds amidst the Himalayan heights of Darjeeling and Gangtok before crossing the rolling hills of Assam prior to touching down in the plain of Padman in Bangladesh. Explaining his choice of Patna as the expedition's starting point, Mr Gupta said it would help popularize this adventure sport in this part of the country. "Anyone who is willing to set up a ballooning club here is welcome to get in touch with us. The Ballooning Club of India will extend all possible help." Asked to sum up the philosophy behind the sport, Mr Gupta said, "Sky is the limit, press on regardless."'

'For me the philosophy to be included is that sport is an instrument of peace,' Mr Chawra said.

TWO

NEXT MORNING MR CHAWRA went off to spend the
last day of his holiday with a party of friends visiting a
nearby shrine where there was a spring and a pool in
which they would swim; the water being most beneficial,
Chawra said, for the condition of the skin from which he
suffered.

In his absence Mr Singh provided companionship. The
two men were poles apart. Where Chawra was on the
whole sanguine, Singh was invaded by doubt. He was
tall, lantern-jawed, and one day would be cadaverous. 'I
have chosen the wrong profession,' he said. 'It is not
good to lose faith in one's fellow men, and in the
insurance business this is possible.'

Most of the people who had come to see the balloon
had gone home. The travel bureau was open, and the
pretty girl in charge was polishing everything in sight for
the second time. A woman was discussing her problems
with the palmist, who had used a magnifying glass to
examine the fine creases of her hand. She looked up at my
approach to inspect and evaluate me with her fine oracular eyes. The fog was back, and according to the weather
forecast could not be expected to disperse before mid-
morning.

'May I know the nature of the business you are conducting?' Mr Singh asked.

'I'm not in business,' I told him.

'But clearly you are not a tourist,' Singh said. 'There are no foreign tourists in Bihar. Did you come here of your own accord? Willingly?'

'It was largely a matter of curiosity. There was quite a lot about Bihar in our papers at the time of the election. It sounded like a place not to be missed.'

Singh shook his head in amazement. 'No one is wishing to come to Patna. I am only here because I am the victim of office politics. In Bihar there are always problems for us, but in my office in Delhi they are ganging up on me so that I am the one who is sent.'

The explanation I had given Mr Singh for my presence was not the whole truth. In the autumn of 1989 my friend John Hatt had visited the great annual fair at Sonepur, just across the Ganges from Patna, in which many hundreds of elephants change hands, most of them being bought by zamindars – the feudal landlords who outside of industrial areas or cities are in reality in control of the state. John took tea with one of these, who had an elephant for sale. 'Two gunmen attended him on either side,' he wrote in *Harpers & Queen*. 'When being photographed, he insisted on adjusting his dress in order to ensure a clear view of the pistol at his waist. When I asked my host if his elephant had ever killed anyone, he replied, "Only three mahouts and a labourer." One notorious animal is known to have dispatched eight of its mahouts . . . at last year's fair one of these killed a visitor. Life in Bihar is cheap indeed.'

John thought that there was a book to be written about this state alone, although far too much of it would be little more than a relation of atrocity. 'A large number of persons', said the *Indian Express* in a leading article, 'die in police custody ... the favourite police excuse is suicide, or that they run away.' News of the abundant trivial violences of India rarely filter through to the foreign press. Although several years back the methods used by the police of the terrible town of Bhagalpur in East Bihar to deal with recalcitrant bonded labourers proved an exception. A dozen or so were blinded in the police station there by thrusting bicycle spokes into their eyeballs, after which pads soaked in acid were applied to the wounds. Considerable international coverage was also given to the autumn elections in 1989 in which numerous voters were done to death, and in some cases buried in mass graves. In Bihar a television team arrived at a village where an unexpectedly large vote had been polled by the Congress Party and the zamindar who had conducted the polling explained, 'First we bribed them, then we beat them, and after that we killed them.'

'Welcome to hell,' was the greeting of a newspaperman when Trevor Fishlock visited him in Patna. A few days later this man, too emphatic in his defence of the freedom of the press, was beaten unconscious.

On his outward journey from Delhi Mr Singh's plane had left five hours later than the scheduled departure time and now on the return flight there was a long delay with talk of cancellation. At worst he was faced with another day in Patna, where the hours passed slowly.

We sat in the bar over slightly scented soft drinks of local manufacture while Singh spoke of the reason for his presence in the city. Head office in Delhi had been subjected to a spate of claims arising from what was described as accidental and flood damage to the largest of the housing estates, which consisted of 3,000 flats and was one of the biggest in the country. When Singh was packed off down to Patna to go into the case he had an inkling, he said, of what he would find. His suspicions were confirmed by an interview with the company's local agent, who for all that he was a Bihari, Singh said, was a very nice man. Mr Patel, the agent, showed his cuttings from a local newspaper; he had checked on the report and found it to be accurate.

The story was that the Bihar State Housing Board had designed the flats for occupancy by deserving and respectable applicants of middle and low income groups, and a majority of these had been on the waiting list for up to seventeen years. Ninety per cent of the accommodation was found to have been taken over by persons who had been able to grease the palms of officials of the board, or secure the backing of what the newspaper described as unscrupulous politicians. Many tenants possessed criminal records, and Mr Patel, who had thought fit to take bodyguards when he went to inspect the building, concluded that the claims of accidental damage arose through the wilful stripping away for sale of fixtures and fittings of every kind, even of cisterns and doors, and the flooding had been caused through the removal of lengths of piping and damage to the mains. The report added that there were 3,000 illegal power connections in the colony and the number of genuine consumers was only 150. Patel had arrived to find a complete breakdown of the sewage system, with night soil everywhere afloat in the shallow lake surrounding the colony. There was no secret about these facts at any time, Singh said. They were common knowledge, provoking laughter rather than indignation.

Singh had an idea. We had been talking about zamindars. 'If you are interested, Patel is the man you should
see,' he said. 'He is knowing everybody. Maybe he can
take you to see one of these people.' 'Wouldn't it be an
intrusion?' I asked. 'An intrusion?' he laughed. 'All these
men are looking to find someone to talk to about
themselves.' He got on the phone and in a few minutes
Mr Patel appeared. He was small and lively, and full of
over-energetic movement, reminding me in a way of Mr
Chawra, and I was surprised that he should be wearing a
battle blouse, muffler and gloves. 'On account of a
vitamin deficiency I am feeling the cold,' he explained.
'Mr Singh tells me that you are wishing to see Mr Kumar.
There is no problem. Mr Kumar is very happy to
welcome any visitor we may bring to his house. This is a
nice man. He is our very good friend.'

Singh excused himself from accompanying us, feeling
unable to leave the hotel in the absence of news of his
flight, and we set out in Patel's Ambassador, arriving in a
matter of minutes at the zamindar's village up a side-
turning off the Gaya road. This was a cluster of hutments, appearing as hardly more than the outbuildings of
the house of many architectural styles in which the
zamindar and his family lived. Basically this was a
grey-stone porticoed dwelling based upon early Victorian English models to which had been added a cast-iron
first-floor balcony, recently sprayed with aluminium
paint, and later ground-floor extensions of concrete,
having typical factory windows. We crossed a courtyard
full of bullock carts and stunted, scuttling little men,
strangely like Breughel peasants, to reach a flight of steps
at the head of which in a doorway flanked by stone

cobras with numerous heads, the zamindar waited to greet us.

He was an imposing figure, a good head and shoulders taller than any of the members of his work force in sight, with a fine up-sweep of moustaches divided by a great aquiline beak of a nose. There was something to be learned of him from his attire: a respect for tradition illustrated by the dhoti, the expansive individualism of the Edwardian fancy waistcoat, the devil-may-care confidence of the Astrakhan cap worn at a jaunty angle, and the in-step-with-the-times display of the big wrist-watch with over-complicated dial. Above all, I took note of the easy, good-natured, immutable smile that advertised peril in the land of the straight-faced.

The zamindar led the way into a roomful of blurred family portraits from the beginning of photography. An enormous grandfather clock let out a single sonorous chime as he kicked it with a bare foot in passing, and a jolly papier-mâché Ganesh enthroned in a corner among frangipani blossom, its trunk dangling in a wisp of incense smoke.

We settled ourselves side by side on a wide divan. The zamindar drew his feet up under him, and Mr Patel, who up to this point had been vigorously chewing a vitaminised betel substitute (which he either disposed of, or managed to swallow), did his best to explain an acceptable purpose of the visit.

The zamindar nodded agreeably, rolling his head from side to side at whatever was said. There was a quick outpouring of Hindi. When this was directed at me the zamindar's eyes bulged in emphasis, and he spoke more slowly and in a louder voice, as if in the hope of demolishing the language barrier.

'Mr Kumar is saying that his family is living here two hundred years,' Mr Patel said. 'His great-grandfather was in this place with two goats and one cow. He was very much liking hard work and made a whopping amount of money. Mr Kumar is also liking work. If other people will work in this manner they also may be rich.'

A door opened on a not unpleasant farmyard smell, mixed with the waftings of curry. A little man shuffled in carrying three glasses of tea on a tray held at shoulder height, as if to lower it in the manner of a yoke over the necks of his oxen.

'Mr Kumar is a very religious man,' Patel said. 'Each morning he is going with offerings to the temple. One teaspoonful of his own urine he is drinking. With his own hands he is feeding cows with vegetables gathered in his garden. In this house no meat may be eaten.'

The zamindar's eye was constantly on me. He gave the impression, perhaps through a kind of animal instinct, of following what was being said, appearing at one moment to be illustrating Patel's account of his pieties with hand movements like those of a dancer. I sipped the milky, spice-flavoured tea and the zamindar nodded and smiled his encouragement.

'Does Mr Kumar own all the land in the village?' I asked.

The question was put, and the zamindar laughed musically.

'He says that is not possible. The government's maximum is forty acres. He laughs because this is no problem. His family is very numerous. Between all members they are cultivating much land. Here they are very grateful to Mr Kumar because he is giving work. Rice, lentils and crops of many kinds he is growing. All these he is sending to market in Calcutta where prices are better.'

'Can I ask about rates of pay?' I asked.

'You may ask him, but I can tell you. For a strong man he is paying ten rupees [36p a day]. If he is weak he will be asking eight.'

'Is that a bit lower than usual?'

Mr Patel translated, and Mr Kumar replied with such theatrical fluency of gesture that Mr Patel's help was almost superfluous.

'You see he is paying not only with money,' Patel said, 'but with kindness. If a man comes to him to ask for a bag of grain he is giving him that grain. Mr Kumar is the father of all these people. When a daughter must be married he will tell some boy who has no job, "Take this girl and there will be work for you on my farm. This is my dowry for her. Treat her thankfully."'

There was a moment of silence. In the guise of scratching his nose Patel had managed to sneak fresh vitaminised betel into his mouth and, with a sidelong glance at Mr Kumar, was chewing surreptitiously behind his hand.

'Who do the people here vote for?' The question caught him off guard, and he replied from a corner of the mouth. 'They are voting for Congress Party.'

'All of them?'

'All. Here there are no problems with voting. "I am your father," Mr Kumar is telling them. "If you vote for Rajiv Gandhi you are voting for me." They are one hundred per cent thankful for his fatherliness, and this they do.'

The meeting was at an end and Mr Kumar dismissed us with a graceful wave of the hand. On the way back to

Patna I asked, 'Does everybody in Bihar vote for Gandhi?'

'No, not everybody. Some are refusing to give their vote.'

I put the point-blank question. 'Do you?'

'What you are asking me is very much a secret,' he said. 'Perhaps better not even to tell my wife. I only tell you because you are a foreigner and tomorrow you will be going. No, I do not vote for this man.'

THREE

MUCH OF INDIA'S wealth is drawn from the mining and steel towns and the industries of a black country extending 500 miles through Bihar. Yet quite a short distance to the south of this, in the mountains of Bastar and Orissa where there are no minerals to be mined, the old India precariously survives. In 1947 the anthropologist Verrier Elwin, who had spent ten years in the field in the region, published a book about a tribe living in Bastar which, in so far as any scientific book could, produced a stir among the general public.

The Murias Verrier Elwin lived among and described occupied – and still occupy – an area only just over 100 miles south of the steel town of Bhilai. It remains purely tribal, with 65 per cent of forest cover, and mountains hardly even surveyed. *The Muria and Their Ghotul* describes the complex and artistic life-style of an exceptionally interesting group, 'the most beautiful and most interesting of all the people of Bastar', Elwin called them, adding, 'it was always with heavy heart that I bid farewell to these children of the foothills.' In those days he thought there might have been about 100,000 of these Proto-Australoid aboriginals, established in this location long before the Aryo-Indian invasion from the north.

They were short in stature; their skin colour was dark chocolate, their hair and eyes black, and they were vivacious and poetic in temperament. The Murias, Elwin reported, would eat almost anything: monkeys, red ants, even crocodile. They amused themselves with theatrical performances, dancing, marriage games, cock-fighting, falconry, quizzes, riddles, folk tales and recitations, and ceremonial hunts. They used eighteen musical instruments, and a man's prestige depended to some extent on his ability to perform adequately on one or more of these, to sing and to compose poetry. The Muria brewed forty or so kinds of alcoholic liquors from the juice of sago-palm, rice, and many forest fruits, savouring and blending these with expertise. Their brass ornaments, often taking the form of elephants, horses or bulls, are now sought after as museum pieces. Elwin said that, despite a certain amount of well-regulated ritual drunkenness, 'to visit a Muria village is to receive a general impression of tidiness and cleanliness'. Mother Earth was their principal goddess, worshipped often, in the form of a pile of stones. As the Muria saying went, 'If you believe, it is a God. If not it is a stone.'

What probably stimulated the exceptional interest in this book was Elwin's account of the ghotul – the dormitory in which, beyond the reach of parental interference, adolescent Murias were schooled in the complexities of tribal conduct and ritual, as well as introduced to sex. There was nothing new in the institution, still existing in rare cases among certain African tribes, in Papua New Guinea and the Philippines, and in India, with little publicity, among the Naga, in Bihar, Orissa and Madhya Pradesh.

It was an institution, Elwin says, devoted to the

problem of infertile pre-marital promiscuity. In his day there were a large number of ghotuls. He counted a total of 347 among the Muria, and many had survived in the neighbouring states. He devotes several hundred pages to the complexity of their organisation. There was nothing left to chance in an education in which the rites were as severe as those of any monastic institution. The rules covered every aspect of social conduct between the sexes, personal attire, cleanliness, eating and sleeping habits, the polite formula to be muttered after accidental farts, and of necessity all that pertained to the sexual act. In this matter it became clear that the Muria view of what was right and proper simply turned conventional Western morality inside out. 'Here everything is arranged', Elwin writes, 'to prevent long-drawn-out intense attachments, to eliminate jealousy and possessiveness, to deepen the sense of communal property and involvement. No boy may regard a girl as "his". There is no ghotul marriage, there are no ghotul partners. Everyone belongs to every-one else, in the very spirit of *Brave New World*. A boy and girl may sleep together for three nights, after that they are warned, if they persist they are punished.' Again: 'Sexual romance is not the best preparation for a life-long union' (although) 'strong and lasting attachment to a girl in this pre-nuptial period may lead to elopement and irregular marriage'. At Kotwal, a populous village to which the Muria looked for example, only the leaders of the ghotul, who might be described as the head-boy and head-girl, enjoyed the privilege of remaining faithful to their partners. The rest were committed to a sternly conformist promiscuity. Out of 2,000 cases he examined Elwin found that only 116 ghotul couples had broken the rules by eloping. Despite such weakness and immorality by Muria standard they could eventually expect to be forgiven, and after self-criticism and atonement could apply for readmission into village society.

How much of this libertarian arcadia, I asked when in India, had survived the miners, the logging companies, the dam builders, the labour recruiters and the missionaries? Very little, was the general opinion of my Indian friends, although none had been to see for themselves. Even the experts in such matters like Dr. S.S. Shashti, the author of several books on tribal India, to whom I spoke in Delhi, held out little hope. Yet even in 1982 when Christoph von Furer-Haimendorf published his book *Tribes of India: The Struggle for Survival*, it seemed that all was not lost. Two years before the book's publication he had paid a final visit to the area he had covered before. 'The change has been mainly for the worse, few of the tribes I studied in the 1940's have been able to preserve their economic and social independence. The strong emotional ties which linked me with such communities made it hard to observe the turn in their fortunes in a spirit of detachment. Indeed I often wished that I had preserved the memory of the far happier tribal life which I had known in earlier years.'

There was an exception to this sombre picture. 'I had the unexpected opportunity in 1980 of revisiting a tribal area not far from Andhra Pradesh which had been saved from the ills afflicting the tribes of that state. It convinced me that there are still regions – rapidly shrinking unfortunately – where tribal people live a life in accordance with their own traditions and inclinations ... In the Muria villages I visited there was a relaxed atmosphere indicative of well-being and prosperity, and in my conversation with the villagers no cases of harassment by officials or moneylenders were ever mentioned. There is still enough cultivable land to go round . . . '

Perhaps to von Furer-Haimendorf's surprise he was also able to announce the survival of the Muria ghotul. 'The cohesion of the village communities also finds expression in the persistent vitality of the institution of the ghotul. In Nayanar the ghotul was not only well maintained but had been enlarged by annexes, which had not been there in 1948 . . . In Malignar village I was able to observe the preparation for a triennial feast in which the boys and girls entertain all the villagers . . . '

The tribal south beckoned, but the choice of destination and therefore the route to be followed remained in doubt. A question mark, too, hung over the significance of the stamp applied to all tourist visas by the Indian government: Not Valid for Protected or Restricted Areas. No one at the consulate could specify what these areas were. Informants were agreed that there were also 'sensitive areas'. All tribal areas were sensitive – and understandably so when one read of mass evictions everywhere, in the style of the infamous Highland clearances, before flooding valleys to provide more water for towns. A sensitive area might or might not be protected or restricted, besides which any area could become protected or restricted at a moment's notice in case of emergency. It was all very much a hit and miss affair and the best way of tackling it, I was advised, was simply to go and hope for the best. To seek to obtain official advice or sanction was a waste of time. Permission to visit a restricted area – even if eventually granted – might take up to five years to obtain. In the matter of obstructive bureaucracies India continued to lead the world.

Strangely enough, too, with the Cold War about to end, Indians were nervous of the possible presence of agents and spies, in particular the CIA. They had a phobia about missionaries, apart from the Lutheran and Catholic inherited from the past, suspecting the computerised and airborne evangelists from the West of possession of a stronger allegiance to the policies of their country than to the gospels of Christ.

The choice of objectives was Bastar, about three days away by road to the south-west, or Orissa, lying directly to the south, which could be reached in about half that time. As only the vaguest information was to be had of what was to be expected in Bastar and very little more could be discovered about the interior of Orissa, I decided to put off any decision until joining forces with Devi Mishra, who had been recommended to me by a friend, and was on his way up from Ranchi by car.

FOUR

DEVI ARRIVED AT the Mauriya, a handsome young man in a dark suit exuding a city aroma of entrepreneurial confidence and worldly wisdom. We settled to breakfast and waited for the weather to clear, while a small crowd gathered round the Contessa car he had come in – an inflated Japanese monster that inspired the veneration of the hotel staff and enhanced my status for the final half-hour of my stay.

Devi ruled out the journey to Bastar, of which he had little more news than I. Almost certainly restricted throughout, he thought, with the kind of roads that could only be tackled by a jeep. In Orissa the roads might be better and the restrictions less. In neither case would he be able to accompany me. There were too many imponderables and he did not want to risk his car. He thought it better to return to Ranchi, the de facto southern capital of the state, and there take further advice. I agreed. When I broke the news that I would like to return by a circuitous route through the notorious and sinister town of Bhagalpur, he showed neither reluctance nor surprise. 'This is a dangerous road,' he said, but with no more excitement than if he had been describing its pot-holed surface. I asked him why, and he said, 'There are some Naxalite armed bands. It is not permitted to use this road by night.'

This piece of information came as a surprise. According to the official history, the Naxalite uprising which had broken out in May 1966 at Naxalbari, a suburb of Calcutta, had been instantly drowned in blood. It had started as a peasant-style revolt, supported by the communists, against what was generally admitted as the intolerable oppressions of the feudal landlords of that area. A few landlords had been lynched and a large but never disclosed number of Naxalites either shot on the spot or taken to police stations and killed. Nevertheless, despite this instant and crushing blow directed against the original stronghold of the movement it seemed from later reports that a few small guerrilla groups had managed to elude retribution and pursuit to carry out action of a desultory and sporadic sort in the backwoods of Bihar and Andhra Pradesh. After vigorous government action against them it was announced in 1972 that all Naxalite resistance had been crushed; when I made mention of this Devi laughed. 'There are many armed bands,' he said. 'They are kidnapping landlords. Sometimes they are killing them by cutting off their heads.'

'Are we likely to have problems? That car of yours seems rather conspicuous.'

'It does not matter. We are not policemen or landlords. Naxalites recognise their enemies. They will give us no trouble.'

Devi was easy in his confidences, and had no objection to talking about himself. He was a junior partner in a thriving family business which sold – and proposed to manufacture – computers. There was evidence of a personal conflict here. His family belonged to an upper-crust sub-division of the merchant caste traditionally attracted to the professions, or government service as administrators or civil servants. Now they were no more than successful merchants and he seemed a little sad about the decline. He was exceedingly frank in his admission that business exercised a fascination over him, too. My feeling was that to come away on a trip like this in which there was no money for anybody was an act of resistance, a spiritual last-ditch stand undertaken against the guilty pleasures of mercantilism.

After an hour or so it was clear enough to make a start. The enormous and taciturn driver, who had been away filling up with petrol and checking the tyres, was back with the car, and we drove out following the road along the south bank of the Ganges in the direction of Bhagalpur and Bengal.

Ten miles of suburban muddle and mess separated us from the countryside, and then suddenly at Fatwah we were in a country town streaming with cows and cattle being taken to graze, and here I observed a novel aspect of the Indian pastoral scene. It would have been improper to employ an unclean and aggressive animal such as the dog to discipline the movements of the sacred cow, instead goats had been educated to undertake this duty, their task being to control the cows, who were seemingly indifferent to traffic, and gently nudge them out of harm's way in a maelstrom of bicycles, rickshaws, bullock carts, and thundering lorries. When I commented upon the phenomenon, Devi said, 'Yes, there is positive co-operation. Both these animals are thinking what is best to be done, and are finding a solution.' At about this time the sun broke through with surprise outbursts of colour everywhere. Ramshackle rickshaws were seen to be bespangled with medallions and flying multi-coloured flags. Burnished lions' heads jutted from each side of a temple entrance through which a man in a yellow robe made an appearance carrying a large green parrot in a cage. Twenty or thirty excess passengers fastened themselves to the sides of a departing bus painted with clownish faces and emblems of good luck, and the driver of the lorry was fixing a fringing of tinsel – a ritual repeated daily in the Patna area – to the top of his windscreen before taking to the road.

Many of us carry an image of the Indian landscape tinctured with a certain austerity, and now, even after three previous visits to that country, the beauty of the Ganges valley at this season came as a surprise. Vivacity and grace formed a background to indelible poverty, yet the eye was lured constantly away from immediate dearth and its consequences to the enchantments beyond. The river was out of sight, but the shapes of its great valley, its hollows and hillocks and its scattered groves of palms were caught in brief brush-strokes of saffron, lavender and grey. Occasionally a brick yard drifted into sight, with its millions of bricks arranged like a child's game in innocent, symmetrical piles. A village we approached was raised in a scintillation of mist. We drove into it past the landowner's great house covered with stone figures of demons and gods. The house overlooked the tank in which the villagers doused their bodies among the water lilies. At the back of the tank a tree was so full of white herons that at first glance I took them to be blossoms. Along the near bank wigwams of bamboo and reeds had been crammed into every yard of available space, and here it was that the untouchables lived.

So these were the traditional outcasts of the village,

portrayed in so many books describing the Indian scene. In this case they were neat and trim enough, and if anything a little more cheerful in appearance than their touchable neighbours. It was hard to believe that they would be debarred from drawing water from the village well lest pollution leak like a baleful electric current from their fingers down the well-rope into the water. Gandhi had done what he could for them, insisting on renaming them *Harijans* – 'Children of God' – and the government with its infallible bureaucratic touch had turned them into 'members of the scheduled castes'. Untouchables, nevertheless, they remained, perpetual victims of the Aryan invader's trick at the beginning of Indian history which divided Hindu humanity into four castes: the priestly Brahmins, the warriors, the merchants, and the peasant cultivators. There remained a faceless, voiceless, powerless multitude, the untouchables, to perform the menial and degrading tasks, the sweeping and cleansing, the disposal of excrement, the slaughtering of animals, the washing of soiled garments, by which activities they were rendered unclean.

In the anonymous city crowds the untouchable may escape notice, but in the country he stands out. Even now in a few ultra-conservative rural areas untouchables are prohibited by custom from wearing clean clothing. They may still be required to keep a certain measurable distance from their superiors: 100 feet in the case of a Brahmin, 24 feet from a lesser caste dignitary. For the untouchable there is nothing to be done about such humiliations in this life. The Hindu scriptures preach that he is no more than reaping the reward of misdeeds in a past experience. Salvation lies in the uncomplaining acceptance of his lot, and the respect and service rendered to his superiors, in the hope of moving up a caste in his next reincarnation. It is a system that has been uniquely successful in keeping the underdog in his place for over 2,000 years, and only now faces challenge. In the beginning, with only the four castes, it was simplicity itself. Now, with all the divisions and accrescences that the centuries have added, a staggering total of 520 sub-castes has been reached. Thus, in modern times, the system has become unmanageable.

From this beautiful, misted village, with its spruce untouchables the road passed over the crest of a low hill from which the view was of the marvellous geometry of new paddy fields in spring. So brilliant – almost unnaturally green – were the paddies it seemed as though lamps had been lit beneath them. The scene was full of graceful, archaic, laborious human activity; men transplanting rice seedlings, ploughing with bullocks in the shining mud, ladling water with wonderful old wooden contraptions from one ditch to another. Minute quantities of water were transferred in this way after every dip of the big spoon. The operation was so apparently inefficient and so slow, Devi said, because in this way it was easier for a hidden onlooker to keep tally on the amounts used, which would be noted down and paid for in cash.

This was the traditional heartland of bonded labour, in brickfields and on the farms. It is an aspect of the Indian rural scene with which the Anti-Slavery Society for the Protection of Human Rights and a United Nations convention on the abolition of slavery have occupied themselves for some years with little result. The convention defined bonded labour – a speciality in labour relations which Indians share with Peru – as a system operating where loans in cash or kind advanced by a creditor are cancelled by the debtor in person – or members of his family – by labour service. Some of the facts presented to the United Nations seem hardly credible. For example: '14 moneylenders in Rakshi Village, Bihar, held about 90 people in surrounding villages in debt bondage. For a loan of Rs 175 [currently about $5·50] one man has been working for 12 years; for Rs 105 another for 10 years and for a loan of 22½ lbs of barley another has been bonded for 35 years.' 'Bonded labourers commonly work for 16 hours a day,' the report continued. 'In many areas [in Bihar] children are given into bondage by their parents at a very early age. In some instances [to keep up with their debt payment] bonded labourers are forced to sell their wives and daughters into prostitution.' When a man died his bondage was inherited by his heir.

Mrs Gandhi, who campaigned against bonded labour, succeeded in putting through an act to outlaw it in 1976. Those convicted of keeping bonded labourers were to be punished by heavy fines and imprisonment. In the fourteen years that have followed, only a single case has been brought to trial and the offender was sentenced to three months. Mrs Gandhi believed there were tens of millions of bonded labourers throughout India, and it is unlikely that there are less than a million in Bihar at this moment. Sometimes we read of one trying to escape and of what was likely to happen to him if recaptured. 'Fadali will never be able to work again,' reports *India Today*, 31 May 1990. 'Last month the 30-year-old tribal had his left hand chopped off (he is left-handed) by the man whose farm he has worked for the past five years. Fadali's crime was that although he was a bonded labourer, he had refused to work for his master and had run away from his farm. According to the terror-stricken youth the master told him: "If you work, you work for me, or you don't work at all." Fadali's master, Narenda Singh Kauran, was described as general secretary of the local Congress Party. He was arrested, but released "on bail".'

On arrival in Bahr, first of the Naxalite towns, we pulled up outside a bedraggled teashop called the City Chic, to give way to a number of small boys riding on enormous buffaloes that slouched by, swinging their heads from side to side and testing the air with sensitive nostrils. Music wailed and banged from loudspeakers over the front of a cinema which Devi said was the largest in the district. This place of entertainment gave Bahr a totally misleading whiff of prosperity, and Devi took me behind the scenes.

There were many brickfields in the vicinity, he said, exploiting rich deposits of exceptionally suitable clay along the river banks. Although these enterprises received frequent press castigation for the conditions in which their labourers worked, for those who could stand the terrific pace there were always jobs to be had. Moreover, the brickfields paid 15 rupees a day – 9 or 10 rupees in the case of an energetic child – whereas the going wage on a zamindar's estate was 12. Thus in Bahr there was money in circulation.

To benefit from this financial surplus motor rickshaws dawdled along the road passing through the brickfields. They were licensed to carry three passengers, but by miracles of compression and rearrangements of human torsos and limbs twelve persons as a maximum could be taken on board. The fare was one rupee each way to the cinema and back, and the rickshaw driver could expect to pay a bribe of two rupees to the policeman waiting at the door. The cinema put on no regular programme; the continuous show instead consisted of a miscellany of old trailers and lengths of film discarded in cutting rooms, for which the patron was charged a half rupee for an hour's entertainment. At the expiry of this period the cinema time-keeper would be waiting to drag him from his seat, if necessary, and throw him into the street. The news of the Naxalites was that they had ordered a surviving handful of tenant farmers round Bahr to cease to pay rent. Thus, said Devi, they were between devil and very deep sea; threatened with beatings by the landlords' thugs, and warned against betrayal of the class struggle by Naxalites armed with M14 rifles. At Bahr, Devi said, there were girls in the Naxalite band.

Suddenly we were in cow-country, of the kind I had never seen before. Cities like Patna were full of cows which had to fend for themselves. They fed exclusively on rubbish and were in consequence stunted and skeletal versions of the species. In the country, however spartan the conditions, things were quite different. The country-side conferred a certain dignity upon its inhabitants, whether human or animal. This became very apparent in an unnamed village past Bahr where we overtook a stately perambulation of thin, upright men escorting a magnificent and immaculate cow – on its way possibly to preside at some festival – which was being most carefully groomed as it plodded along by two attendant boys, one on each side. Children went running ahead flying blue kites. It was clear that this episode set the scene for what was to come.

Despite the penury, the police harassment and the real fear of the zamindars' private armies of thugs, the villagers were friendly and kind. We stopped at a house to ask for road directions and were immediately invited in. We found a resplendent white cow occupying a stall just inside the door, which took up about one third of the total space, while the family of five were left to do their best with what was left. Surprisingly, the normally ammoniacal smell of a byre was absent, the impression I received being that more time was spent by the family in smartening up the cow than their own living quarters. When asked what they fed this animal upon the answer was, 'All the things it likes. When there's any rice left over, it gets that too. Just the same as us.'

In this village we noticed for the first time that the country folk were an inch or two taller than the natives of Patna, and that the countrywomen were more to be seen in the open, more independent and statuesque in bearing than their sisters of the town. In each village the women wore saris of a typical local colour. Here on their way to early morning temple, they were all swathed in kingfisher blue, a shining procession against a background of stained grey walls and ragged thatch. Every woman, however poor, wore a smart sari for temple-going, along with an armful of plastic bangles and, if by village standards she were rich, a little gold stud through the nose.

As we headed eastwards the ratio of cows to men increased. For peasants who had lost their land, threatened on one hand by the landlords and on the other by floods, they offered a final safeguard against starvation, and I began to understand why they should have been regarded as sacred. In the rainy season the separate beds of the Ganges united, then overflowed and the flood water poured through the streets of these villages, leaving the black tide marks still visible on the walls of the stone houses. For four months in the year all land to the north of the villages was under water, and the zamindars claimed the land above the flood level to the south. In this period of dearth the villages fell back upon their cows, and it was by grace of their cows that they survived.

In these narrow villages of a single street squeezed between feudal estates and the no man's land of the floods the cows lived in scrupulously kept courtyards, in which the human presence concentrated in sty-like out-houses was clearly of secondary importance. Once a week or so the herdsmen passed through the villages to collect the cows and goats, sometimes numbering 1,000 of each animal, then drove them to one of the landlords' fields requiring fertilisation. Watched over by the herdsmen they passed the night in the fields, grazed on the residue of the harvest crop, deposited their dung, and in the morning were returned to their owners, who regarded the outing as beneficial to the animals' health, in addition to which they could usually expect a small payment for services rendered.

The cows provided those supremely valuable products in the economy of such villages, milk and dung. The dung not only stoked cooking fires and was used in making walls and floors, but combined with earth formed the lining of baskets in which grain was stored. It was an ingredient of ointment and salves for the treatment of skin conditions, piles and sore eyes, and went into paint. A family with cows producing more dung than required for their own needs might offer the excess to a wholesaler with a pyramid of it in his backyard, where the untouchables – most useful members of any village community – earned six rupees a day, plus free dung, moulding the basic product into flat circular cakes, about 1½ inches thick and 10 inches in diameter. These were to be seen everywhere, stuck on the walls to dry, sometimes in neat rows, sometimes in attractive patterns. There were varying qualities of dung, and experts, assayers and connoisseurs existed to test it and fix a price. A hundred cakes of inferior quality might fetch ten rupees, but the finer grades employed for medicinal or cosmetic purposes could fetch ten times the amount. An enquiry as to whether buffalo dung had any place in this market was countered with an emphatic no. Attempts at adulteration, Devi said, which sometimes happened, were regarded as a social crime.

Devi was observant and informative, drawing my attention to the fact that at intervals of roughly thirty miles we passed out of one cultural zone and entered another different from it in almost every respect. These differences, he said, reflected their occupation in ancient times by invaders or settlers of different races. In one area villagers were different in their physical appearance and in their clothing from the next. To this he added that they spoke different dialects, ate different food when given the choice, and whenever it was possible to escape from basic labouring tasks on the zamindars' land, busied themselves with traditional skills and handicrafts.

We passed through a village where irrigational methods were the speciality. At some time in their half-forgotten history these people had found themselves settled on land subject to drought. In bringing water down from a mountain lake they had acquired skills in the management of water for which the zamindars could be persuaded to pay a few rupees above the rate for ordinary labour. In one village they wove enormous baskets, using a technique elsewhere unknown. In another a clan of hereditary physicians made an infusion from the extravagant beaks of the Great Indian Hornbill to cure all afflictions from tuberculosis to broken hearts. Each of these areas stood apart from the rest, above all in its style of temple architecture. In and around Patna temples were hardly more than a private house or even a cinema. In an attempt to inspire awe an often grotesque entrance had been built, somewhat in the manner of the old fair-ground tunnel of love. A few miles down the road temples became red brick pyramids with or without the addition of fantastic gods, demons and animals. Later they were pure white cones without decoration of any kind.

Outside the towns, apart from the lorries thundering down the country roads, there was no traffic to be seen. The lorries, laden with bricks and building materials for the steel towns of West Bengal, and for Calcutta, kept up a steady 70 mph. They were fantastically painted with good luck symbols, stylised flowers and beasts. Images on dashboards sniffed at constantly relighted joss-sticks, and in a few cases a small shrine to Kali – the goddess of destruction, although paradoxically also the protectress of travellers – had been fixed to the outside of the vehicle above the windscreen. Legally the companies employing the drivers had to ensure they got a ten-minute break every three hours to rest and drink tea, but, as Devi admitted, such legal provisos had little meaning in India.

Once in a while there were spaces where the lorry drivers could pull off the road. Here, inevitably, *dhabas* had opened for business. They were long, thatched cabins where tea cost one rupee a glass, and a ladleful of boiled rice with a puddle of dhal was served on a leaf plate for three rupees. A row of string beds was provided on which drivers could lounge after a meal, and of necessity sleep at the end of the day, without extra payment. Following the drivers' example we stopped at a dhaba from time to time, but only to drink tea. Possibly for caste reasons Devi refused to eat in such places, and we subsisted on biscuits.

It seemed extraordinary to me that the drivers of these exceedingly cheerful-looking lorries should be unsmiling and taciturn, as was our own driver, who always seated himself on such occasions at some distance from us, showing only a strong but somewhat melancholy profile, notably devoid of expression. When I commented to Devi on what seemed his excessive seriousness, the reply was, 'He is happy, but like all these people he is unable to express his happiness. This man is a Munda and he is always appearing in this way.'

So Price was a tribal. This came as another surprise. There was an explanation, too, for the unusual name. Some time in the last century the Mundas had staged a revolt against the British, and those imprisoned after the suppression of the revolt were kept there until they agreed to be converted by Lutheran missionaries. They were then given English names as part of the deal. I asked Devi if he thought Price understood the doctrine of the Trinity, to which his reply was, 'He is not comprehending these things.'

Price was a superb driver, as were most professional Indian drivers, I was soon to decide. Many Western visitors to India form a mistaken impression that Indian traffic responds to no rules and is wholly chaotic. This is far from the case. On the whole Indian drivers are both courteous and considerate, and if they appear to the foreigner to take impossible risks, this is only because their reflexes and their ability to judge speeds and distances are developed to a degree that, however much a catastrophe seems inevitable, when vehicles hurtle towards each other with only inches to spare there will almost always be a hair's-breadth escape. But this only applies to the city. On the open road it is very different.

It was on this occasion, coincidentally, that a further mention of the Mundas came up. Among the usual assortment of poverty-stricken shacks in sight from the dhaba, I had noticed several small, poor, but unusually neat houses, set in fragments of garden, with a painted door and even tiled roof. These belonged, Devi told me, to Munda villagers. They were the aboriginals of Bihar and, although overwhelmed and dispersed by ancient invasions and early British howitzers, 800,000 of them survived tucked away in the holes and corners of this and other states, still distinguishable from the Hindu multitudes among whom they lived.

He was well-versed in the tribe's recent history, having been born and bred in Ranchi, a Munda stronghold until the 1960s. The latest Nelles Verlag map calls it a hill resort, with a spa and temples, and the latest guidebook finds it quiet, and notes its possession of an enormous mental asylum – probably the best known in India. Since publication, this once peaceful scene had suffered change due to the discovery of valuable mineral deposits in the area and the consequent building of a satellite town devoted to heavy industry. According to accounts in the Indian press, ten villages were 'acquired' for the actual town, six more for a dam, four more for an extra factory, and five for the railway complex. In this way 2,200 families, mostly composed of Munda peasants, were displaced, finding themselves without homes or land. 'People cleared from one village were installed on the arable land of another, whose inhabitants in turn became landless.' It was a situation generating a limitless supply of unskilled labour for employment in the factories – indeed such a surplus that the wages of 1.50 rupees (5p) a day must have come close to the lowest in Indian history. Devi, who readily admitted that his own family had been much benefited financially by the great change, mentioned that all the innumerable rickshaw-cyclists of Ranchi were now Munda tribals. In the face of protests, he said, the municipality had given them preferential treatment in the allocation of the licences required.

Late in the afternoon we approached Bhagalpur, most tragic of all the towns of Bihar, where the riots originating in the general election of November 1989 had continued almost without interruption for a month, with the latest published death-roll of over 2,000. In mid-January outbreaks of violence were still a matter of almost daily occurrence. Hardly one of the outwardly pacific villages through which we passed had escaped the slaughter. Voters arriving at polling stations had been forced to hand over their slips to be stamped by mafia gangs in control. This is known as 'booth capture'. Where the landlords' gangs had not been able to capture the booths, voters known to be unsympathetic were kidnapped, beaten or killed, their bodies thrown down wells or into the Ganges – or the polling station might be demolished by hand-grenades, or blown up.

On 27 February an Assembly election would be held,

and the prospect filled the underdogs of Bihar with gloom. The *Times of India* reported pessimistically on the likelihood of a criminal takeover of the democratic process:

> A matter of even greater concern is the character of some candidates. In over 60 constituencies known criminals have entered the fray under the banner of different political parties. This is causing a lot of concern to the police administration. In a violence-prone state like Bihar the presence of so many trigger-happy candidates may turn wide areas of the country into a vast battlefield . . . The state government has been frantically seeking additional companies of the BSF and CRPF [para-military forces], but the imported force may not be of much use since the local constabulary is used to obeying the orders of one or other of the local dons, all of whom are in the fray. Indeed, quite a few of them may not only win, but may also become ministers.

Beyond Monghya, with Bhagalpur now only thirty miles away, a sudden calm fell on our surroundings. It was early evening and the sun in decline spread a saffron light over a landscape in which the animals kicked up feathers of dust as they came streaming back to the villages over the fields. Behind us the Ganges, having turned away sharply to the north, had swung back in a wide, dazzling loop to the rear. At the small town of Sultanganj the river was beneath us, close by the road. A line-up of cranes in the shallows appeared in the rippling air-currents as fishermen in white smocks. Here many lorry drivers who seemed disinclined to go further that day sat hunched morosely over their tea in the dhaba. The scene was a supremely pacific one. A group of spotlessly robed old men who might have been conducting a religious ceremony stood hands clasped together nearby in the manner of an old-master adoration of the Magi. A woman passed cradling a new-born calf in her arms. As soon as we stopped a brace of chuckling crows alighted on the car. It was hard to believe that hereabouts only weeks before, in such homely, rustic scenes, men could have been beheaded, hacked to pieces, or dragged to their deaths roped to the backs of cars.

We drank tea in the dhaba and took to the road again. Here there were trees: robust mangoes with polished terracotta trunks and limbs by the roadside. Sacred groves had survived, and enormous banyans dangled their curtains of roots. A rising mist threatened to become a fog and the sun went down behind thick foliage in flashes of green jade. We were quite alone on the road, and within a half-hour night closed in on us. We drove, lights off, over the pot-holed surface at hardly more than a walking pace, picking our way by the faint glow of a misted half moon. Devi said, 'It is better we agree a story for our presence in Bhagalpur. No tourists are visiting this place. If we must go to an administrative centre they will be questioning our motives. What must we say to them? They will not believe we are visiting from curiosity.'

The outskirts of Bhagalpur, deserted and in darkness, revealed rack and ruin when Price switched on the headlights. There had been raging fires and explosions. The charred mess of a lorry lay on its side in a gutted filling station, and beyond it we saw a fog-bound scrap-yard of battered shapes. A pile of rubble sprouted the shafts and wheels of tangled rickshaws. The fronts of a row of booths had been ripped out, leaving one with the still legible sign *Moghul Throne*. Once this had been a wretched little teashop, and such grandiose titles exemplified the self-delusion (or humour) of the poor. In Bhagalpur only one in ten could read such descriptions, or the claims by Horlicks or Wills cigarettes whose exultant poster faces looked down from the hoardings on what so recently had been a sea of blood.

Here through the scarves of mist we saw only the fringe of an area of devastation in which silk mills which provided half the town's working population with employment had been destroyed. At Sultanganj a Muslim who had lost members of his family said that 10,000 people had been killed in Bhagalpur and the surrounding countryside. This we did not believe. The figure given until now had been a vague 'several hundred', but on this very day the *Times of India* quoted figures from official sources, putting the death-roll at approximately 2,500, with the partial or total destruction of 2,800 houses.

A generator provided the wan illumination of the Rajhans Hotel, a self-effacing walk-up in the town's fitfully lit centre, where no trace of the disturbances that had ravaged its outskirts was to be seen. Our arrival took the reception unawares. Much rummaging in drawers followed before the necessary forms were produced. An additional form with many questions had to be filled in by foreign visitors; it seemed likely that it had been a long time since one of these was required. Two silent, troubled men went carefully through the details supplied, comparing them in my case with those furnished in the visa and making painstaking adjustments to the entry in the register. In the background hovered a third man I took to be the manager, ready with a third opinion when uncertainties arose. He seemed full of suppressed nervous excitement, with fluttering fingers and eyelids; whenever he looked in my direction he gave a quick mechanical smile.

Devi and Price, whose formalities took less time to accomplish, had disappeared, and as soon as I was free from the paperwork I went up to my room to tidy up, then wrote down a few notes. I suspected that we were the hotel's only guests. It was very quiet. There was no sound of footsteps on the uncarpeted stairs, no distant voices or banging of doors. The view through the window was of a narrow, misted street. Opposite in a row of shuttered shops was a medical hall in typical Indian style, with a spot-lit plaster torso from which the casing on one side had been removed to display the organs beneath. A policeman went by on a Japanese motorcycle, and at the edge of the field of vision a soldier, rifle slung, stood on guard at a street intersection.

I went down to look for the restaurant, pushed through a door into a dim room containing several tables set for a meal. Having seated myself at one of these, I waited for perhaps five minutes, then got up and went to the door I took to be the entrance to the kitchen. There was no one there. I went back and sat down again. After a while the kitchen door was cautiously opened, a face came into view and was withdrawn. With that Devi appeared. There were times when he could be inscrutable, and this was one of them.

'No problem,' he began – meaning, as I had come to realise, that some hitch had occurred. 'We are all receiving food in bedroom. This food is now being cooked. Soon it is coming.'

I climbed the stairs to the bedroom again, glanced through the window where the medical hall was now in darkness and the soldier had gone. I settled again to the notes; half an hour or so passed, there was a knock at the door and the manager was there at the back of a boy carrying a tray. The boy set the tray down and went, but the man hovered, his brow creased in a troubled smile. I transferred the contents of the tray to a table: Black Label beer ready to be poured into a glass ornamented with lotus flowers, a small-boned chicken complete with long, jungle-fowl neck, and a heap of chips. My first guess was that he had taken advice in the matters of Western culinary preferences and been told chips with everything, but this proved not to be true. 'In Glossop,' the manager said, 'they are eating chicken with chips.'

'Glossop?' I asked. The piece of information seemed strange.

'Very close to Manchester,' the manager said. 'I was in business in this town.' He dropped into the nearest chair. By now having accepted a further example of Indian informality, I took a mouthful of chicken and waited for the polite questioning to begin. 'Your impression Bhagalpur?' the manager asked.

'I only got in an hour ago. It's a terrible mess. Can you tell me what went on here?'

'You are meaning the communal disorders?' he asked.

'The riots. The killings.'

'Everyone is telling you something different,' he said.

'You live here. Surely you know?'

'Partly, I know, but I have not seen with my own eyes.

Actually there was a ramshila procession for Hindu people. Those people were collecting money for holy bricks for temple of Ayodhia. When Hindu people are going in procession, they are very noisy. Always there is much beating of drums. You have seen these processions?'

'Wedding ones,' I told him. 'They are certainly noisy.'

'The Muslim people were in their mosque. They sent a message requesting to delay procession until after call to prayer. This the Hindu people are refusing to do. Then followed stone-throwing. The Muslims had guns and bombs already hidden in their houses. They rushed out and started to kill these Hindu people. Many of them they have killed.'

'And you believe that?'

'I am believing it because my brother was among these people. Still the doctor is tending his injured leg. He has paid for and given one sacred brick.'

'So the Muslims started it all?'

'That is my opinion.'

'But the papers say there were many more of them killed than Hindus despite all their bombs and guns.'

'That is because the Hindus are fighting back very strongly.'

It was a discussion I wanted to continue, but at that moment Devi came in, and the manager went off. 'The story they are telling here', Devi said, 'is that one hundred boys in the Hindu college have disappeared.'

'I read about it somewhere,' I said.

'When their parents went in search of them because they did not return to their houses, all had vanished. There were many bloodstains on walls and floors.'

'And were they ever found?'

'No one is setting eyes on them again.'

I showed him the day before's *Hindustan Times*. 'Did you see this?' I asked.

'Newspapers are saying whatever is suitable for them to say.'

'This is a report of the debate in the House. The Opposition claims the riots were organised by police-men. No schoolboys were killed. It was an excuse to burn down 150 villages where they refused to toe the line.'

'It is possible. The mouths of political men are full of lies.'

Devi wanted to discuss the plans for the next day. 'Between Bhagalpur and Ranchi the roads are bad,' he said. 'It is long driving and there is nowhere to stay. We must either be leaving at dawn or remain here another day.'

'I should like to see the famous police station and ask a few questions.'

'It will be wise to refrain from putting such questions.'

'You think so?'

'It is the custom of police officials to make all ques-tions. "Are you a spy?" they will be asking. "What for are you doing in this place?" Better it is not to display interest in the affairs of those in power. As we are saying in India – better to keep nose clean.'

'You don't suppose we could see a refugee camp?'

'They will not be happy for you to do this. Tomorrow in the morning the hotel people will be sending the forms to the police office, and maybe they will be wishing to see us. Better it would be not to be in this place. We shall be seeing many burned villages on the road to Ranchi.

Nothing is to be gained by asking questions when you will not receive a truthful reply.'

We started shortly after dawn, plunging into a fog so thick that we could hardly grope our way through and out of the wreckage of Bhagalpur. To avoid the risk of losing the way we turned back along the main road to Sultanganj, thereafter taking the southerly turn off through Kharag, past a ghostly teak forest, and into the wide and sunlit plain of Jamui, where a tributary of the Ganges curled through brilliant fields. Here the sun sparkled like hoar frost in the sprouting crops. Grey and white strands of mist were rising twisted together in the background. Quite close to the road men in conical hats like those of Vietnam peasants were ploughing with buffaloes, and huge kingfishers flashed up and down the waterways.

Devi stopped to enquire the way. Here at the limits of the rioting, violence had it seemed struck haphazardly in an unsensational and unpremeditated fashion. Half the people were Muslims and half Hindus, but they were all jumbled together and one village escaped while its neighbour suffered. This place, said our informant, had been attacked back in November, but the wounds inflicted on mud walls and reed thatch had been healed by the survivors in a few days, and no sign of calamity remained. What had been worse than the ruin of property had been the looting of food stocks and the destruction by the feudalist gangs of standing crops. 'Do the people here have any religious problems?' I asked. 'Sir, these things are beyond their comprehension. The taste of rice is sweet in their mouths.' One man's buffaloes had been killed by the invaders, so his neighbour shared the ploughing of his field.

The absence of signposts was a problem complicated by the presence of new roads not marked on the map; this made the going slow. Leaving the wide valley behind, we moved into the dry uplands where poverty increased. Possessions were reduced to a scrawny cow and a goat per family and an acre of land cluttered by immovable rocks to be scratched round by a primitive plough. Poverty, apart from its abject version in city slums, generates its own brand of virtue ('Poor people give you good regards' as Devi had put it). Here, too, it disguised itself in gracious forms, in the classic faces of the people and their dignified bearing and the splendidly archaic processes of husbandry. There was a deceptive semblance of leisure in the ancient methods of threshing, winnowing and grinding the grain, and the carrying of pots to the well. Where there were swampy areas the peasants had been able to grow rice. This was dried on the hard surface of the road, and a bottle-neck through which traffic was obliged to pass was marked out by stones.

Oases of cultivable earth and occasional water were spaced through bleak landscapes by De Chirico, of polished bedrock and dry culverts and outcrops of metallic ores, productive not even of weeds. There were strange intrusions. Outside a deserted village, once a Lutheran missionary enclave, a row of white crosses projected from the earth. Lutheran communities were scattered through the badlands of Bihar, where they had rescued their converts from the caste system, ordered them to bury their dead, and recommended the consumption of meat, which in most cases the converts were unable to afford. A cigarette advertisement stuck up at a crossroad, miles from anywhere and with no building in sight, assured the literate 10 per cent: 'Nothing comes between you and the flavour.'

Here and there were sizable patches of mixed forest, of teak, sal, mango, pipal and many valuable hardwoods, interspersed with lesser and greater explosions of blond and rufous bamboo. I had expected the Indian jungle to be a repetition of the great forest of the Amazon, but there was no resemblance at all. To a European there was something about the jungle here that was familiar and comprehensible. These trees with their massive trunks, the symmetrical out-thrust of their branches, their compact shape and unexceptional foliage, suggested no more than flamboyant versions of familiar European species. The trees of the Amazon, by contrast, were alien and mysterious. Their roots spread over an acre of the thin skin of soil to anchor slender trunks soaring to extraordinary heights: they were part of an environmental conspiracy, fertilised often by a single species of bat, moth or bird, defended by insects they rewarded with pseudo-fruit to keep such predators as leaf-cutting ants at bay, as well as engaged in other vegetable-animal alliances for mutual survival. When the Amazonian trees are cut down the environment dies with them. In the Indian jungles the ecosystem may survive. When one tree goes another can be planted in its place.

An intruder enters the Amazon forest with caution. The Indian jungle on the road to Ranchi seemed to encourage inspection. 'Any tigers or elephants hereabouts?' I asked Devi. 'Certainly they are existing. It is no more than one in a thousand chance if you are encountering one such animal.'

I went for a walk. It was not quite Surrey, but devoid of any obvious threat. In north Bihar it was early spring, with the unfolding everywhere of springtime buds, an occasional inconspicuous flower, a bird twittering on a branch. It was a very tidy wood, giving almost the impression that the trees had been clipped into shape. There were no orchids to be seen, no lianas, aerial roots or fungus of startling colour. I have only once in many such walks encountered a deadly snake, and no snakes of any kind were to be seen here. There was a disappointing absence of visible birds, although doves that had positioned themselves out of sight in the leaf canopy kept up a powerful and persistent moaning. Devi, who had followed me, was pointing down to hoof-prints in the soft earth. 'Bisons,' he said. In these calm surroundings it seemed hard to believe. 'Very large animals,' he added, 'but not interfering in any way. It is a pity we are not seeing them.' We went back to the car, and started off again for Ranchi.

A huge grey smudge across the southern horizon was the first sign of India's great industrial belt, which we should shortly be entering. At first I took it to be a distant storm, although this would have been unlikely at the time of year. From being quite alone on country roads going nowhere in particular we found ourselves among lorries in increasing numbers, and slowly the grey smudge spread across the sky towards us, and at the bottom of it the first factory chimneys pumping out smoke came into sight. They were the outposts of the industrial belt extending almost from the frontier with Bangladesh to Raipur, which comes close to the centre of the subcontinent, almost 500 miles. It contains large deposits of coal and iron, as well as every conceivable metal, and the steel towns to the west and south of Ranchi probably resemble England's black country of a half-century ago. There have been attempts to invest these melancholic surroundings with tourist appeal, evidenced by the description of Jamshedpur, first of the steel cities, in *Bihar Land of Ancient Wisdom* issued by the Department of Tourism. '*Though the skyline is dominated by enormous chimneys, fumes of copper oxide, and dunes of coal and limestone, the city is an environmentalist's dream come true.*'

By nightfall we were running the gauntlet of chimneys now feeding a false sunset with variegated smokes. The road surface, pounded and ground by monstrous wheels, had been blown away into the sky and, imprisoned in an endless procession of lorries, we burrowed into choking multi-coloured dust. The fumes were all the Tourist Office had promised.

Some hours later at the entrance to Ranchi we came upon an unusual sight. A cow damaged by a collision had been left in the road, evidently with a broken leg. Whatever the mishap befalling a cow, it is unthinkable in India to put one out of its misery.

'What will happen to it?' I asked.

'Soon the owner will come,' Devi said, 'and bring it away.'

'And after that, what?'

'If this cow can be cured he will cure it.'

'And if not?'

'Then he may sell it to a man who is buying animals that cannot be cured.'

'So he will slaughter it for the meat?'

'This we are not asking. It is possible. He will pay the owner a very small sum. After that I do not know.'

In Ranchi I checked in at the government Ashok hotel, catering largely to commercial travellers and foreign technicians from the city's industrial complex, who came there rather despairingly for a change of scene and spent most of their time speechless with boredom in the bar.

The check-in procedure at any Indian hotel can be lengthy, but at the Ashok it occupied a record-breaking half-hour while my passport was passed up through the chain of command and back, advice was taken and heads nodded in agreement. When I enquired why I was being kept waiting the reception clerk who had taken me over said that this was the first time he had seen a tourist visa in a passport, and there had been some delay in unearthing the necessary form.

The Ashok, with its polished empty spaces and its inconsequential happenings, reminded me of one of the old Marx Brothers films. A whiff of institutional austerity was diluted with outbursts of a poetic impulse by which surfaces of the lobby furniture were freshly decorated every morning with patterns of frangipani blossom. Service was well-meaning but muddled, and to attempt to put through a long-distance telephone call was to expose oneself to unpredictabilities of success or failure rivalling those of the gaming table.

At dinner a menu decorated like an illuminated manuscript promised fish under eleven guises, each described in hyperbolical terms. The Chef's Choice was grilled pomfret, 'flown to you specially from the Goan sea'.

'Today we are not serving pomfret,' the waiter said.

'In that case I'll take the snapper.'

The waiter shook his head. 'No snapper, sir.'

'What fish have you then?'

'On this day we have no fish, reason being that all fish in Indian sea severely infected by disease.'

The menu listed nine chicken dishes. I ran my finger down the list and the waiter butted in, 'Tonight the Chef is recommending fried chicken, sir.'

'With chips?'

'Oh yes, sir. Always we are serving chips.'

'Can I have some beer?' I asked.

'Beer only served in bar, sir.'

The bar was immediately behind, its open frontier a yard from where I sat. It was permanently tenanted by silent and lugubrious German technicians separated from each other by an empty stool, and seeking oblivion in Indian whisky. I went into the bar, ordered a beer and stood it on a table in the bar area within reach of my arm, hoping that the waiter would go away, but this, as he had no other customers to serve, he clearly had no intention of doing.

The following morning, I breakfasted on the balcony of my room where looking down on the flower beds and lawns of the hotel's spacious gardens I was furnished once again with an example of the Indian nervous distrust of independent action. Three gardeners were at work planting young trees. The senior man carried only a ruler with which he measured the diameter of a hole already dug and waiting to receive the tree. This achieved, the second man placed the tree in position and, after slight adjustments indicated by his chief, the third man stepped forward, dug with his hands into the earth piled beside the hole and began to scoop it handful by handful over the roots. The gardeners had been joined by a small collection of onlookers and when after what seemed a long time the first tree was satisfactorily planted the party moved on to where the next awaited them a few yards away. Here too, in the context of the industrial sweat-shop of Ranchi, was illustrated the Indian paradox of travail and inaction.

In Delhi I had been given an introduction to a man said to be one of the Ranchi mafia dons. I called on him in his office in the city's business centre where he sold cars and road-making machinery, although he was happy to tell me that he had 'irons in many other fires'. Reputedly he was head of a somewhat specialised branch of the Indian version of the Honoured Society controlling the supply of sand used to fill in the cavities left in mines, which otherwise frequently led to dangerous earth subsidences.

We sat in deep, soft, body-enfolding chairs – also made in one of this man's factories – and sipped spiced tea from bone china cups. The view through the window was a busy one. Dispossessed Mundas pedalled their rickshaws frantically; a fleet of lorries, painted in the local manner with rising suns, jockeyed for position at the crossroads; an agile beggar hopped through the traffic, a withered leg slung from his neck. The don – if such he were – was amiable and confiding. He was in his forties, bold-eyed and handsome in the style of a prince in a seventeenth-century Moghul miniature, depicting perhaps a hunting scene among peacocks and gazelles. Kicking off his shoes he revealed small, dimpled feet. He wore a number of silver rings set with pearls which showed to advantage on his dark, smooth hands. A newspaper Sunday supplement on the coffee table was devoted, it said, wholly to astrology and horoscopes.

'So you are enjoying Ranchi,' he said. 'It is very exciting. All the time we are experiencing something like a play. Like the Ramayana. So full of excitement is my brain that I cannot sleep. Did they tell you our growth is the second largest in India, with 40,000 now employed in our new town? Here we are making, in maximum security, components for the bomb. Every one of our factories carries on its front our civic motto: "The beauty consists in the purity of heart".'

FIVE

I HAD A free afternoon. 'Can we see the asylum?' I asked Devi.

'There is no problem.'

For once there was none.

'This is a very famous hospital,' Devi said. 'You will be welcome.'

I was surprised that the visit would be as easy as he suggested. None the less, so far as I could gather after a week's acquaintance, he meant what he said.

My previous experience of Indian treatment of mental disorders had been at the unpublicised Bhagavati Temple of Exorcism in Kerala where patients were put through an energetic form of psycho-therapy based upon song and dance. I had been present the year before when a dozen or so girls in their late teens or early twenties, usually kept locked up for most of the day in windowless cells, were placed in an enclosure within sight of the doll-like image of the Goddess Bhagavati, and encouraged or compelled to dance. Each girl had her own attendant with his fingers entwined in her hair, and each rotated her body and jerked her head backwards and forwards to the tune of a four-man orchestra. The hold on her hair prevented a girl from damaging her head on the enclosure walls or the ground. A doctor claimed that two-thirds of the girls subjected to this therapy were eventually cured – as testified to, he pointed out, by large numbers of nails protruding from the trunk of a neighbouring tree. Each of these nails represented a cure; the cured patient had used her own forehead to hammer it into the wood.

Such, occasionally, were the mysterious ways of the East, but when I gave Devi a description of this somewhat eerie experience he said, 'You will be finding this hospital a different kettle of fish.'

Application for the visit had to be made to the Chief Medical Officer whose office was in a pleasant, Georgian-style house located among a complex of single-storey buildings of which only the roofs were visible behind high walls. It came as a surprise that no previous request had been made for an appointment with Dr Bhati, and that it was apparently quite in order to walk into this busy and powerful man's office, and at a pleasant nod from him seat ourselves at his desk while a small queue of staff waited at his elbow for his signature on innumerable ledgers, documents and chits. The office itself gave an impression of clutter. At the moment of our entrance Dr Bhati shoved a motorcycle helmet aside on his desk to make space for untidy sheaves of papers. I found it interesting that all the pictures in this room – several of Alpine scenes – should be markedly askew and that all the staff members wore lavender pullovers. Having done with his signing the doctor greeted us with great cordiality, picked up a telephone to order tea, and then listened to Devi's explanation, given in Hindi, of the reason for our visit.

'Normally application should be made in writing,' Dr

Bhati said. He smiled broadly. 'You may have heard of, or even experienced, our national bureaucracy. In cases where written applications are made you will expect to wait weeks, even months, before receiving a reply. This visit will be strictly unofficial. I will now ring my superior, and if he is agreeable I will call somebody to show you round.'

Dr Bhati rang through to his superior and nodded his agreement with whatever was said. People came and went without ceremony and the flow of documents for signature continued. A woman with a baby slipped into the file of orderlies and male nurses and uncovered its face to display a sore. This the doctor examined with every sign of sympathy and interest, muttered words of counsel and, having found the baby a biscuit, shoved them away.

There was a pause in the queue of petitioners. 'As you can see, we are kept busy,' Dr Bhati said. 'This hospital is a legacy of the British presence, and although there are many more patients now we have been unable to expand.' He seemed happy to discuss his work. 'In our psychiatric wards we have 643 beds of which one half are suffering from minor illnesses requiring little treatment. The rest, in most cases, are suffering from schizophrenia or manic depression.'

I asked him whether wealth or status was reflected in the incidence of such mental disorders, and he replied that low-caste patients were more likely to suffer from schizophrenia and higher caste ones from manic depression. It was the same with poverty and wealth. In these days serious disorders and minor illnesses arising from hereditary factors or chemical imbalance were treated with chemicals. For the rest occupational therapy and keeping the patient interested in life was the chosen solution. He was ready with a listing of small gains, of tiny advances into the boundless terra incognita of mental illness. 'A hard slog, but we seem to be getting results,' he droned on gently. 'Life expectation increased – that's certainly a feather in our cap . . . pulse and blood pressure consistently down . . . increased resistance to infection . . . reduction in self-induced amnesia . . . Happ's Syndrome a thing of the past . . . fissularia well within bounds . . . libido – well, just ticking over, as is only to be expected. All in all not too depressing a picture.'

A social worker came to show us over the occupational therapy unit, lodged in a number of barracks in a park-like setting of lawns and flower beds. Such places are quiet, and we had arrived at the time of the midday meal. The patients, who were very orderly, had been released from their therapy to make their way to the dining rooms. They gave little indication of mental disturbance; perhaps because the suspension of the stresses of everyday life had produced an unnatural tranquillity. I was reminded of the children of my childhood on their way to church, a little bored by the knowledge of what awaited them.

'And now let us take a peep at our production of art,' the social worker said.

He led the way into a large room with a number of paintings on a row of easels. There were unfinished pictures of other pictures, the models available being portraits of Gandhi, Nehru and some insipid colour prints of episodes from the life of Christ. In addition – and these had been chosen by every copyist – there were British works of art surviving here from the beginnings of

Indian independence, when the hospital had been handed over, lock, stock and barrel, to the new incumbents. These included cricketing scenes at the Oval, 1946, and a number of photographs of the British royalty: of King George the Sixth as Admiral of the Fleet, of his wife and of the two young daughters at Balmoral, Windsor and the Palace. This is what the psychiatric patients seeking to heal their troubled minds had painted over and over again for forty-three years: thousands and thousands of these trite, smudged and hardly recognisable ikons, to be placed on display on the walls of this and other buildings, commented upon, praised, criticised, awarded major or minor prizes, certificates or compensatory recognition before – after the lapse of years – being stored away in sandalwood chests, each made to contain a quarter of a ton of important documents and inscribed according to custom with the image of the monkey god Hanuman, protector of public records.

Turning away from the pictures I was approached by a handsome, rather puffy-faced man wearing a blazer with club tie. 'Do forgive me for butting in,' he said, 'I gather you're English. It was nice of you to come. I am happy to see you.'

'Are you a doctor?' I asked.

'Unfortunately, no. I'm a patient. My name is Prabhakar. I'm a film actor. Not very well known in your country, I'm afraid. I've played in a number of films, but naturally you won't have seen them. Perhaps I should write the name. It will be unfamiliar to you.'

He took my notebook and pen and wrote down his name. Devi said, 'Mr Prabhakar is very well known. In India we are all enjoying his acting.'

'I am here because I do not sleep well, and this affects

my head. All went well until I fell in love with Mrs Hema Malini.'

'Mrs Malini is very famous,' Devi said.

'She rejected my suit. This produced intense depression, which can only have made me less attractive to the lady of my dreams. A vicious circle in fact. With each rejection my state of mind worsened. So you see how it is.' His hand went up to his chin. 'Bad shave this morning. I must get a grip on myself.'

Mr Prabhakar studied my face anxiously. I raked in my mind for a suitable comment. Lamely I said, 'I hope the problem resolves itself.'

'It will,' he said. 'In fact it has. All goes well that ends well. We plan to marry this year.'

We shook hands and the film actor made for the canteen.

'Do you really believe this man will be marrying Mrs Malini?' Devi asked our guide.

'He will never marry her. This is a delusion. Mrs Malini is a very great actress. Mr Prabhakar is in many films but he is playing bit parts. This man has been with us now ten times. He is happy to think that he will be marrying this beautiful woman, but this will never be.'

On the occasion of a single previous visit to a mental hospital in Burma I had been bewildered by what seemed to me the normality of the patients, but after my experience with Mr Prabhakar and his ingenious concealment of a disturbed mental state, I was in a cautious frame of mind as we approached the female compound of the Psychiatric Centre. This, too, seemed well ordered and supremely tranquil. Looked after by inmates who may have been enthusiastic gardeners in the outside world, the herbaceous borders were colourful and trim. Neatly dressed ladies sat chatting over their needlework among the flowers. One strummed softly on the local version of a guitar for the entertainment of an encircling group. The Centre's splendid trees provided a haven for singing birds. This was the setting of an arcadian scene from an early miniature.

A Miss Banerjee who had taken charge of us drew our attention to many facilities. There was a pleasant picnicking area where ladies inclined to do so could entertain visiting friends. The Centre encouraged sport: tennis, badminton. Although we saw no one engaged in these energetic pastimes, it was evident that they existed. We were taken to a spacious concert hall, furnished with colour television and a music system. Once in a while, she said, the patients put on a theatrical show here, and beneath the stage a magnificent grand piano awaited the next production or display of the musical talents of an inmate. I congratulated her on this impressive piece of furniture and she smiled with pleasure. A moment later she was called away, and idly lifting the lid over the keyboard I was faced with the fact that the piano possessed no keys. It was a discovery which at that moment seemed of extreme symbolical significance.

For all this intrusion of anti-climax I felt bound to admit that the Centre was an unexpectedly pleasant place, providing all too probably in the case of many patients a haven from the sad domestic case-histories so often reported upon in the Indian press. I wondered if many of the women we saw here might feel inclined to do what they could to prolong their stay. Miss Banerjee agreed that this was inevitable. A further problem for the Centre, she said, arose because there were cases where families had been able to send female relatives here with the intention of putting them out of the way while they employed legal subterfuges to strip them of their possessions.

Leaving the concert hall we found our way barred by a pretty girl with the face, dress and slightly imperious manner of a Spanish dancer. There is a strong and fairly substantial theory in India as elsewhere that the gypsies of Europe originated in tribes driven out by Indian population displacements of the remote past. Everywhere in the tribal areas of the country these dark, handsome and slightly predatory faces were to be seen, and at this moment these frilled sleeves and skirts among the saris encouraged the flicker of a theory that something like a traditional flamenco costume might survive in the recesses of the sub-continent. The girl made a grab at us, got a grip on Devi and was able to thrust a hand into his pocket before Miss Banerjee dragged her away. She ran off. 'Could she have been a gypsy?' I foolishly asked Miss Banerjee. 'Oh no, sir, this lady has been seeing the film *Carmen*, and now she is identifying with the part.' It was the only flamboyant episode of the morning, and with its conclusion the somewhat sub-normal calm of the Centre was restored.

As we started off down the path towards the gate a group of women came out of a building. They were of mixed ages, and almost certainly mixed castes, and now I was coming to realise that there was something in the atmosphere and methods of the Centre that suppressed individuals, resettled them in groups, smoothed over differences of age and caste, creating slowly a sheep-fold of displaced persons, sedated by the withdrawal of stress and the exclusion of conflicts by these walls. For once, even at a distance of twenty yards, there was one here who stood out from the crowd. We walked past and this member of the group who had remained an individual detached herself, came after us, and caught up. This time certainly a doctor, I assured myself, but with that, doubt set in. She had a fine alert face, smiling slightly and with a briskness of expression and movement that had fought off the lassitude of the place. Such encounters in India set off a barrage of questions which are accepted as polite. 'You're a doctor, aren't you?' I asked.

'No, of course not, I'm a patient. Would you like to hear about me? I'm interested that you should have taken me for a doctor. I did four years' medical school at Patna before having to give up. My name is Mubina Thapar, my father is Dr Prasar Thapar. My uncle's a doctor, too. He raped me when I was four or five. That may have been the start of my trouble. I suffer from OCD. Obsessive Compulsion Disorder. They've found a name for it now. I'm a compulsive. I do silly things.'

Set in what I would have described as a serene face, she had fine, large, rather staring eyes of the kind given to the tragic peasants of Haiti by the gifted primitives who paint them on that isle. 'They treated me for years in Bangalore, then they sent me to Bombay where they have a different specialised treatment. My father thought I ought to get married because he'd been told the love of a husband helps in such cases. It didn't work for me, and I was divorced. Do you know what an obsession's like? For me everything is dirty. Food is dirty, flowers are dirty, everything, everything. They tell me to plant white flowers in the garden but when they bloom they are dirty. I can't touch people because they are dirty. I never stop washing myself, but I stay dirty.'

The hospital was the temple – the kingdom – of purity

imposed from without. It prescribed an environment of bodies scoured from taint, of close-clipped lawns, of disciplined flower beds, of wardens who tidied away scraps, and of feeding, sleeping and therapeutic occupations in an aroma of scrubbed wood. Perhaps subjection to unspotted exteriors only made things worse for this girl. Perhaps it only emphasised an isolation that I was sure hid behind the obsession. At that moment Miss Thapar seemed one of the loneliest persons I had ever met, suffering as much, I suspected, from a sense of abandonment as from imaginary pollution, and I was deeply sorry for her. She trailed along after us at an increasing distance, waving forlornly until we turned the corner and she was lost to sight.

SIX

FACED WITH A gap of two days to be filled in while awaiting news of the feasibilities of further travel, we decided on a side-trip to the Tiger Reserve at Palamau, some three hours to the west of Ranchi by road. The reserve, one of many throughout the country, had been a product of conservatory zeal following the news back in 1970 that there were practically no tigers left in India. It was believed, too, the nature reserves could be offered as a major tourist attraction, and this proved to be true. The number of tigers and elephants was steadily on the increase, as were those of tourists ready to pay for expensive *Shikari* holidays. By this year many reserves had waiting lists for those wishing to visit them. Fortunately for us, as there were no tourists in Bihar, this did not apply. Devi assured me that no advance booking was necessary. He suspected that we would be the only visitors, and this proved to be the case.

The Tiger Reserve at Palamau, according to the booklet, comprises most of the Daltongali South Forest Division, about 400 square miles in all. However, entering its boundary it came as a surprise to see that a great deal of deforestation had gone on and was still taking place. Villagers were emerging from what was left of the wooded area carrying great bundles of firewood on their heads, and where trees had been left standing by the roadside we saw girls busily hacking away the lower branches. The ravaged landscape where the forest had been seemed to contain ancient earthworks, mounds and trenches. These, on closer inspection, proved to be no more than deep and final erosion where nothing more than subsoil and bedrock remains. Nevertheless this was the scene of the world's first tiger census, and one of the first reserves to be included in Mrs Gandhi's Tiger Project. The booklet says that it is one of the best developed parks in India, 'catering to every class of visitor, from jaded city-dwellers seeking forest recreation . . . to serious students of the plant and animal life of Bihar'.

Elsewhere in newly created reserves there have been instances of the summary eviction of the human population to make room for the animals. A point in favour of Palamau is that a number of small villages continue to exist within the reserve, although the kind of life they offered seemed miserable. Palamau is cruelly poor; the poorest district of what is accepted, outside its industrial belt, as India's most backward and poverty-stricken state. According to the Indian press and the 1988 Anti-Slavery Society report to the United Nations, it is the hunting ground of slavers kidnapping children between the ages of five and twelve for supply to the carpet-making industry. 'India today', according to the Anti-Slavery report, has 'at least 100,000 juvenile carpet-making slaves', mostly taken from the Palamau region.

The central village of the reserve is Belta, where there is no reason why a tourist should not be able to spend a few days in forest recreation withdrawn from the nastiness of the world. Since the attraction in any case lies in the animals to be seen, isolation is not only acceptable but offered as a feature, and the tourist lodge is sited on a low hill a few hundred yards from the village, where it commands in fulfilment of the brochure's promises a splendid view of the wild life of the area. We were warned that we should see little but spotted deer in this particular area. They were there by the hundred, forming large, static but gently inquisitive groups.

Taking into consideration that the lodge was empty, without electricity, and that there was no food to be had, we opted for the life of the village, to be seen from the newly built, and also empty, Hotel Debjon. This proved to be a collector's piece of its kind. On arrival on 18 January we were presented with a Christmas card apiece by the manager. The staff were all stony-faced tribals – 'They are smiling in their hearts but their pleasure does not appear on their faces,' Devi said. In their determination to be of service they frequently burst into the rooms, which were unprovided with locks, and wherever we went in the vicinity of the hotel they followed us closely in the hope of being commanded to do something. The hotel's prize possession (and wonder of Palamau) was a model in polystyrene, salvaged from packaging material, of the Victoria Memorial in Calcutta. Despite the great difficulty in working with the soft and friable medium, the creator, over a period of five months, had carved out, sculpted and glued together 924 components. A book contained the names and admiring comments of the visitors who had flocked to see it. An MP had written, 'I am at a loss for words. This is art.'

The hotel garden was quilted with marigolds through which strutted and scuffled the most marvellous cockerels, raised from eggs collected in the jungle, with combs like red sealing wax, scintillating plumage and enormously long legs. There was very little to do in Palamau and a kind of Mexican lethargy had fallen upon the men, who squatted for hours on end in the angles of walls, wide-brimmed hats pulled down over their narrow eyes. The tribal boy who did all the odd jobs about the place took my attention. 'How old is he?' I asked Devi, who spoke to him in Hindi.

'He does not know.'

'Tell him to have a guess.'

'He thinks maybe eight.'

'What do you suppose they pay him?'

'Very little. He is not working very hard. Maybe three rupees.'

'I'm curious to see whether these people ever smile,' I said. 'I'm going to give him five rupees and watch the reaction.'

I called the boy over and gave him the note. He stared at it for a moment, and nothing moved in his face. Then he backed away.

'No effect whatever,' I said. 'Does he understand the value of money?'

'Yes, he understands it.'

'Then why doesn't he look pleased?'

'This boy is feeling great happiness at this moment. His heart is singing. It is something he cannot show.'

The villagers were listless in appearance and sluggish in their movements. Even young men walked very slowly, a few yards at a time, and it was hard not to suspect that they might be suffering from malnutrition, and under the necessity of conserving whatever energy they possessed. The feudal lord of Belta heard I was there and came to see me followed by three of his bodyguards. He was a head taller than the rest, a man with fine patrician hands and an overshadowed expression who had spent some time in Coventry and hoped that I knew that city. He despatched flies unerringly with the fly-swat he carried and spoke of his friendship with Gandhi's successor, Vinoba Bhavi, who had passed this way accompanied by his disciples in an immensely prolonged symbolical walk round the country. His object had been to induce landlords to give away a tiny proportion of their land to landless labourers, many of whom were dying of starvation at the time. 'Not an acre was donated,' he smiled sadly. 'I was wholly in favour of his movement, and if there had been a proper response I would most willingly have chipped in.'

He got up to go, extended his hand, then remembered. 'Should you be needing an elephant at any time while you're here,' he said, 'don't hesitate to take mine.'

Missionary campaigns had been very welcome to the dispossessed of Palamau. There were three groups in the field, all in strenuous competition with each other in the battle for souls, all offering inducements to conversion. The Jesuits and the Lutherans bid against each other, rewarding converts with food and medicine equal in value to the exceedingly low wages paid by the zamin-dars. It was normal for the beneficiaries to sell these medicines for cash. A year or two before our visit the Muslims entered what now became a three-sided contest. Not only medicines were on offer in this case, but the Muslim paradise with lavishly described pleasures compared to which the Christian version might have seemed intangible to some. To outwit the local practice of inflating income by belonging to three religions at a time the Muslims insisted that converts grow tufts of beard 'of a religious kind'. This left the locals, apart from attending prayer-meetings and readings of the Koran, with very little to do. 'They are bored,' Devi said. 'Now they must not gamble or drink, and these religious people are not permitting them to play noisy games.'

Despite the missionaries' precautions he reported that a few of the villagers had managed to benefit from all three religions, satisfying the mullah that they were unable to grow the regulation beard, while kidding both Christian contestants along, and even secretly visiting the Hindu temple to keep on the right side of the prominent goddess Durga, where the priest, although comparatively poor, was accustomed to bribe them with sweets. For all that, the stress-free life had become a little dull, a matter of a long linger in the dhaba over a glass of tea, mosquitoes, ritual ablutions, prostrations and prayers.

But, as Devi put it, the zamindars of the whole region were batting on a sticky wicket, for the redoubtable and mysteriously all-knowing Naxalites – avengers of ancient peasant wrongs – were drawing nearer and nearer, killing and being killed in and around Daltonganj, only nineteen miles away. Here the peasantry had supported them in a pitched battle with the gangs employed by the zamindars, who had been driven off. Now the Naxalites were more or less in control of the sixty-mile stretch of road to Auranagar, along which landlords had ceased to be able to collect their rents. It was clear from the absence of tourists at the reserve that the news had got round.

Evening approached, and it was time to go in search of the animals: since the most interesting of these are nocturnal in their habits there is very little opportunity to see them after the hour following dawn or before that immediately preceding sunset. In its booklet the reserve laid claim to a wide range of beasts and birds, most of them described in spirited terms. There were 54 tigers, 46 leopards ('most effectively cryptic in bush or grass'), herds of 'significantly robust bison', 83 elephants ('it is wiser to retreat than to show courage'), 'quite exclusive wolves', India's only hyenas, the Indian wild dog, the sloth bear, two species of monkey and four of deer.

The suggested car-tour of the Reserve was an expedition I embarked upon with no great expectations. A mild pessimism as to the outcome of all such ventures has been based upon a long experience of anti-climax. I am probably the only person having had the good fortune to have known Laos – Land of a Million Elephants, as it called itself before the carpet-bombings – without seeing an elephant. Despite travels in countries where tigers once abounded, I had never seen a tiger, either, or for that matter any wild animal of a spectacular kind. Since the great forests of South-east Asia had failed to provide such excitements, I found it hard to believe that the tiny patch of woodland representing the Palamau Tiger Reserve would do so.

Nor was the central area of the Reserve, described in the booklet as 'carved out of virgin forest', as impressive as I would have hoped. Although reprieved from the final catastrophe of commercial felling, I could not help feeling that in the denuded and impoverished surrounding area the local people would have helped themselves to a tree here and there whenever they could. The fact that such reservations could exist at all was probably only due to the British mania for killing large animals, adopted as a matter of prestige by the rich Indians who followed them. So closely aligned was shooting to status and power that as late as 1955 a 'privileged hunter' was allowed to wipe out half the tiger population in the Kanha National Park.

Using Devi's pride and joy, the Contessa, we were accompanied by a ranger on a short but uneventful tour of the roads. The ranger then suggested we should visit the prime viewing area, leave the car and go for a walk. Despite the three villagers who had been killed by a 'mad' elephant, the Reserve's attitude to such 'regrettable incidents' was nonchalant. The best place, the ranger said, to see animals – once in a while even to run into a tiger – was on a high bank overlooking the Kamaldah Lake, and there we went, parked the Contessa and set out on our walk. Reasonably enough the ranger was extremely anxious that our time should not be wasted, and he was delighted to be able to point out a slide in the mud where a group of elephants had come down the bank. This was the moment for a word of caution. Should an elephant suddenly appear, you either took cover behind a dense bush – relying on the animal's poor eyesight – or you ran for it. In the latter case you had to run downhill – something an elephant could not do, although on the level a male in top form could reach a speed of up to 25 miles per hour. Should the danger have presented itself here, the only way of escape would have been down the bank into the lake.

We waited for the elephants but nothing in the forest moved. Kamaldah Lake spread its green, shimmering waters, a mile across, fringed with peach-coloured reeds and small bright explosions of bamboo. Black, stream-lined trogons criss-crossed its surface, chasing after flies, and above fishing eagles circled contemplatively, stacked at varying heights. All round, the trees resounded with the ventriloquial squawking of birds – then came the moment that redeemed the day. A clump of bamboo parted its fronds for two peacocks in flight. They balanced delicately in the air currents immediately below before dropping to earth at the water's edge. They were both males and indulged in a brief posturing display, followed by a competitive spreading of plumes. They advanced strutting upon each other, sidled away and returned, at once both stately and skittish. Suddenly, as if a button had been pressed, they both took off at the same moment, winging away at great speed within inches of the water.

At this moment the ranger made an excited return. He had discovered bisons' hoof-prints in the mud nearby, an evidence of the small herd's recent passage within yards of where we were standing. Splendid animals, he assured us, and likely to be close by. The Indian bison (*Bos gaurus*), said the booklet, was the 'tallest, handsomest and most peaceful perhaps, of the world's wild oxen'. The ranger thought they would return, meanwhile he guided us to a clump of randia trees bearing small fruit which, although when crushed were used to poison fish in shallow pools, were irresistible to deer. If we concealed ourselves within sight of these he was sure the deer would eventually come.

A half-hour passed. The sun was on the point of setting, with no sign of bison or deer, and we started back. As we did so a small tree went down with a crash nearby. It was wiser to retreat, as the booklet advised, and this we did. The car was close and we ran for it. Both Devi and the ranger claimed to have seen a patch of grey elephant skin in a stirring of leaves. I did not, but I was quite prepared to take their word for it that the elephant was there.

There was an attempt on my part that evening to experiment with minor social adjustments, which met with little success. I have always found it uncomfortable to travel in a group in which a member, whether a driver or otherwise, is excluded at mealtimes. In India with its complex caste separations the situation was more tricky than in England, for people who seemed to mix easily enough when working together sometimes appeared to withdraw into a strange dietetic purdah when mealtimes arrived. I had already noticed that when we stopped for tea at one of the dhabas, Devi refused to eat and our driver immediately disappeared from sight. This reminded me of the scene in Burma when the Indian railway-repair staff, normally united in the stresses of the Burmese Civil War raging round them, formed three separate and exclusive circles at midday to consume their rations.

Dinner at the Debjon was to be served at 7 pm. I found a table with a spotless cloth, a bowlful of zinnias, and a little printed notice that said 'Good Morning. To salute joyfully the day.' The table was laid for one. 'Won't you be eating?' I asked Devi.

'On this day I am fasting,' Devi said. 'I will take a little rice before retiring to bed.'

'Where's the driver?'

'He is busy with the car. He will be coming later.'

I ate alone, went up to my room, read for an hour or two, then went down for some bottled water and saw Devi and the driver seated together just in sight at a table round a corner. Their backs were turned to me and I quietly withdrew.

There was a mystery here, and behind it what appeared as an unusually complicated situation. The Indian railway staff in the threatened town of Pyinmana in Burma had been playing the caste game properly, according to the rules to avoid pollution of their food. The pollution they feared was entirely spiritual. If one of the railwaymen squatting round the food had not been entirely successful in scouring the oil-stains from his fingers before plunging them into the common rice, this would not have mattered. The contaminating presence of a non caste-member would.

It was a feature of Hindu society that has never ceased to amaze the foreigner. Friar Navarrete who chose to travel in India on his way back to Spain in 1670 did so because the religious community of Canton had assured him that it was a pleasure not to be missed. And so it turned out to be but for a single incident when his servant accidentally brushed against a pot in which a fellow traveller was carrying his food. This, although it was wrapped in protective cloths and carried in a sack, was held by its owner to have been defiled and instantly taken out and smashed to the ground. So intricately complicated is this matter of spiritual cleanliness that a successful and affluent restaurant owner who happens to be of low-caste origin may frequently seek to boost his turnover by employing an impoverished and sometimes physically dirty Brahmin to do the cooking. In such cases stresses may arise when the Brahmin seeks to defend the ritual purity of his food by debarring the immaculate although ritually unclean employer from his kitchen.

The sub-divisions of caste are endless, and Devi,

although bracketed with merchants in general, had fore-bears who were in government administration; a circumstance that had edged him towards the top of that division. He prided himself on his liberal attitude in such matters, and I believed that he was justified in doing so. In an earlier conversation that day he had described city life as the great demolisher of caste. How, for example, he had asked, could a big city office be expected to run a half-dozen separate canteens? The thing became absurd.

Devi was prepared to sit down at table with a tribal, who had no caste at all. Would he have shared a meal with an untouchable? Giving some thought to it, I felt sure that he would. So where did I come in? I can only assume that he knew his Englishmen, and believed that my class prejudice might be stronger than any inhibitions imposed upon him by caste. It was a saddening thought.

Next day's programme was for a morning trip to another part of the reserve where the presence of a sloth bear had been reported with what I would have put at an infinitesimally small chance of seeing it. It was arranged that this would be followed by the investigation of some Moghul ruins of importance recently uncovered in the jungle. Just as we were about to set out, the plan was thrown into disarray by the surprise arrival of a bus full of factory workers with their families on a three-day holiday break from Calcutta. No one at Belta claimed to have heard anything of this although a paper was produced by the party's guide confirming that a visit to the reserve was included in the deal. So far, said the guide, the holiday had been a disaster. At the end of the first day's long journey from Calcutta they had been promised unspecified urban excitements, which had turned out to be a tour of a Ranchi steelworks, and tea and stale cake in a factory canteen. On this day they were hoping to see the full range of animals advertised in the reserve booklet, and the mad elephant whose fame had even reached Calcutta.

The ranger said that there was no alternative but to take them round in their aged, battered bus. It would be a short run because the bus could only be driven over a mile or two of the wider tracks, but this ruled out any possibility of our seeing the sloth bears. He was upset because the children were very noisy, and the animals would take days to get over it. The bus, which had lost its silencer, sounded like a plane about to take off. A trip would take an hour or so, he thought, after which he hoped they would go. The bus was parked some hundreds of yards from where we stood, and from it arose the hootings, the whistlings and the jubilance of children released from the grey prison of the Calcutta streets. A firework exploded with a loud crack overhead, and the ranger shook his head miserably.

We found another driver to take us to the ruins, which included a sixteenth-century fort of the Choro kings. It once must have been an imposing Moghul building, but was now a tropical ruin wrenched apart by ingrowing trees and parasitic vines. Of the profusion of decorative tiles that must have covered its walls nothing remained but a fragment under the battlements about thirty-five feet from the ground. There is something claustrophobic and oppressive about Moghul ruins, which with their small, secretive windows in vast areas of blank wall depended at the best of times upon an abundant source of artificial lighting in brilliantly decorated interiors.

The fort offered another example of the sexual mania of the rulers of those days. On a visit in the previous year to the Mattancherry Palace I had been impressed by the cruel absurdity of the roughly contemporary Cochin rajah who had arranged for the numerous members of his harem to spend their lives in one low-roofed room, from which the view through a lattice was of three or four yards of pavement crossed only by female servants. Here at Palamau a well about twelve feet in diameter and thirty feet deep had been constructed outside the walls of the fort. This was reached by an underground passage from the women's quarters, opening at a point just above the water level about twenty-five feet below the surface of the ground. The purpose of the underground passage was to ensure that no one apart from the king could ever set eyes upon the ladies of his household on the way to, or coming from, their ablutions. What a sad fate awaited a pretty girl who caught the eye of a Cochin rajah or a Choro king – and how much better off were village women, safe in the homeliness of their features, exposed only to hard labour, deprivation and hunger.

SEVEN

ON THE RETURN journey we made a side-trip to the
Dasam Falls, twenty-eight miles from Ranchi. This
was believed originally to have been a sacred spot and
place of pilgrimage of the Munda people. Now fewer
Mundas were to be seen; for it had been discovered by
Indian tourists. Suddenly, at so short a distance from
Ranchi with its web of roads, its cuprous fumes, its
vigour and squalor, this was another world, peopled by
natives who dressed as Indians but were not. Here there
were narrow and winding lanes, patches of ancient
woodland and Munda peasants going to their fields
carrying wooden ploughs on their shoulders. Here for
the first time I saw a wild animal of any standing, an
emaciated jackal that came through a hedge, loped across
the road and disappeared into a thicket. I was surprised
that it should be so long-legged and lanky. Devi, cheered
that we should have shared this small-scale experience,
claimed that jackals were more aggressive than I believed
them to be, and exceptionally dangerous to children.

Tourist buses on the way to the falls tore through these
lanes. The tourists, full of the holiday spirit, shouted and
waved to the Mundas, who returned the usual Munda
blank looks. Munda tribals were bigger men and women

86

than those on the buses, benefiting, so long as they remained in the mountains, from a better and more varied diet than that of the towns, and perhaps from their less complex religion. The Hindu women, in particular, in contrast with the free-striding Munda girls, appeared like passive wraiths.

When Devi had first driven through here the people were still naked, armed with bows and arrows, and likely to shoot at anyone who laughed at them. These Mundas still kept to their villages at the tops of the mountains and little was known of their customs. Every twelve years the women of the tribe dressed as men for a single day and went hunting. Now *that*, said Devi, would be something to photograph, although as far as he knew no one had done so. Nearing the falls we saw a stranger riding a horse. This, said Devi, was an Imli, a member of a tribe of hereditary moneylenders, tolerated by the government although seen as the worst scourge, after the feudal landlords, of rural India. The Imlis battened on tribal people without understanding of commerce and finance, and tricked them into accepting loans – usually to buy useless consumer goods. Rates of interest up to 10 per cent per month were levied.

Arriving at the waterfalls we were astounded to find that the same Calcutta trippers who had gone rattling away from Palamau the previous evening were in up-roarious possession, their children leaping about like goats on the surrounding crags, lighting fires on the hillside and slashing ineffectively at the branches of hardwood trees, while the adults played their transistors and gurgled down beer from the bottle. The best view was to be had from a flat top over a gorge. Immediately below ran a small, calm river, bordered by silver sand. A quarter of a mile upstream this river had plunged 1,000 feet over a cliff's edge into a wide pool enclosed by cyclopean rocks. It emerged from this area of compression as a great spouting of water some 200 yards above the point over which we were poised. In the rainy season the view must have been of a great aquatic tumult and even now, although in sedate fashion, it was impressive. The great attraction for the adventurous was the pool at the bottom of the cliff. Many people felt under compulsion to swim in it. A notice, in English, said, 'Bathing in these falls is very dangerous and many precious lives have been lost.' It was no exaggeration. There had been an endless catalogue of drownings. On the occasion of Devi's last visit he had taken part in a failed attempt to rescue a swimmer sucked in the outfall of water through the rocks. What was it, he wondered, that had drawn so many men, here, to their deaths? Could there be any substance in the Munda belief in a tribal god who demanded sacrifice?

A few yards away some Munda girls squatted with the alcohol made from the flowers of their sacred sarhul trees which they had brought for sale. Of all kinds of country spirits, this was the most highly esteemed. The men from Calcutta bargained in sign language for the alcohol, transferring their purchase from the elegant clay pots of the Mundas to empty oil cans they had brought in readiness. Their womenfolk watched from a distance. They were neat in their factory-made, over-bright saris; the Munda girls were unkempt although they had style. Back at the end of the century the Mundas had made fine jewellery and copper amulets now sought after by collectors, but contact with civilisation had artistically neutered them, and nothing remained of the accomplishments of those days but the finely shaped pots. Now they sold alcohol to the Hindus, and the cash thus obtained bought tawdry bangles and rings.

On the natural platform overlooking the gorge a tea-house had been built where Hindus sold special tea and millet cakes deep-fried in oil. We settled there after a laborious climb down the steps cut in the rock face part way to the river, to a point where the steps ended. Here we found ourselves chatting to a Munda, indistinguishable to me from an Indian, up for the weekend from Ranchi.

This man's history, in Devi's translation, was an extraordinary one. Like most tribal people he was hazy about dates, but some fifteen years earlier when he seemed to have been in his late teens, his family had been involved in one of the early Ranchi evictions, in which they had been reduced to outright beggars by the loss of house and land. Money allocated for relief had been embezzled, as so frequently happens, by government officials. His parents died, and he – the only child – had migrated to the slums of Patna. The change in his fortunes had happened a year or two later after his rescue of an old moneylender attacked by robbers. The old man died shortly afterwards; he inherited his house and in the course of clearing it out the Munda had uncovered a box containing a considerable collection of jewellery taken as pledges. Munda superstition did not permit him even to touch this. Instead he called in an agent who valued the articles, wrapped them in a cloth used to wipe a temple image – thus proof against the evil eye – and took them away to negotiate an exchange deal for land. The Munda received about five acres, on which he planted rice and lentils.

For three years all went well. He bought more land and took on Hindu labourers, then the Naxalites moved in and sent him the usual warning.

'Why did they do that?' I asked.

'They accused him of exploiting his workers.'

'And did he?'

There was an exchange of questions and answers in Hindi.

'He does not understand this question. I cannot make him understand what is exploitation. With tribal people he would have shared this land. These were not tribal people.'

'So he thought it wiser to come back?'

'Yes, it was wiser for him to do this.'

That, in brief, was the story, and now the Munda was safe back in his own country, where so far, at least, the Naxalites were under control.

Through the window of the tea-house I saw that a woman had just arrived carrying on her head a large jar of alcohol from which the small pots of the liquor-saleswomen were about to be replenished. The Munda smiled approvingly. 'He is saying that here women are the real bosses,' Devi said.

'And do you agree?'

'For the tribals, yes. This is true.'

Among the Hindus, the Munda went on, women were nothing. Their fathers bought husbands for them, and a man with many daughters was ruined. I would have expected Devi to come to the defence of his own culture at this point, but he stuck to translating without comment, nodding agreement to the claim that the Mundas had to buy their wives and were often obliged to pay their future fathers-in-law dearly for them. Even when the couple set up home together the wife in practice owned everything.

Our Munda friend gestured in the direction of the scene through the window where the tribal menfolk, having finished playing a game like five-stones, were now sharing a bowl of liquor pushed by one of the girls in their direction as if to keep them quiet. That, the Munda suggested, was a typical tribal setting. The men played silly games, drank, chatted and lounged about, while the women did the work. There were two things to be said in their favour. One was that they played hockey so well that there was a Munda player in most of the big teams. Other than that they had a passion for tidiness, and while the women got on with the hard work in the fields they were useful to keep the place clean.

At that moment three men staggered past us and out of the door carrying bins full of rubbish to be tipped into the ravine.

The Munda turned away his head in disgust. This was something, he told us, that could never happen in one of their own villages because it was offensive to tribal religion. We followed his eyes to a cataclysmic vision of sundered mountains and I listened in a moment of silence to the rumble of water bursting through the bottle-neck in the gorge. The Munda growled his criticism. 'He is saying the gods are angry to look down on such a mess,' Devi said.

The question of *sati*, the ancient Hindu practice of the burning of widows, came up following a discussion on the subject of dowry murders, itself prompted by a headline in a newspaper, 'Victims of Dowry Hungry In-Laws', picked up on the drive into Ranchi. The article

reported that Karmiki – a women's voluntary organisation – charged the police with often refusing to file
complaints arising out of wife-abuse or dowry deaths. In
reply the police spokesman mentioned that in Delhi
about 400 cases of dowry deaths or 'Eve-teasing' (mal-
treatment including torture) were dealt with every
month. The suggestion was that, with the number of such
offences constantly on the increase, there were not
enough policemen to go round.

What was the situation in Ranchi? I asked Devi, to
which his answer was that although he had not given
much thought to the matter, he assumed that it was much
the same as in the north. Offhand he could only think of a
couple of recent dowry deaths. He could not remember
the details of the first but thought that it was a routine
kitchen-stove killing. In the second case a young man had
ordered his wife to put pressure on her parents to
supplement the amount in cash already paid by the gift of
a new motorcycle, and on their refusal had pulled out a
pistol and shot her through the head. Both cases were
'under investigation', he said.

Sati was barred by the British over a century ago.
Although rare these days, Devi said, it was most certainly
still practised. When the 'honourable' woman's sacrifice
was occasionally performed it might receive a great deal
of publicity, or more likely be hushed up. In the case of
Mrs Rupkandar there had been no such conspiracy of
silence. Although a Ranchi girl by birth, Marwari Rupkandar's family were from Rajasthan. When the time
came to look round for a suitable husband the father
wrote to members of the Rajput merchant caste there – to
which the family belonged – to ask for their help. At that
time Marwari, aged eighteen, attended the local high

school, and Devi, who remembered her well, said that she was both exceptionally lively and pretty.

An acceptable husband, of roughly the same age, was found, the marriage arrangements went through and Marwari left for Rajasthan. In due course a wedding photograph of the radiant young Mr and Mrs Rupkandar was published in the Ranchi newspaper, soon after which silence fell. About three months later the father assembled his friends to make a simple announcement: 'My daughter has gone sati.' The facts were that Marwari's husband had died of a heart attack, and Marwari had been persuaded to join him on his funeral pyre. Pilgrims, said Devi, came in numbers to scramble for handfuls of the ashes, and the most prominent of them were given copies of Marwari's photograph taken in the last minutes of her life. The 'holy event' was whole-heartedly supported by the local population. Marwari had since become a goddess and the place where the sati had taken place a centre of pilgrimage. 'I think', Devi added, 'that the police are still busy with their investigation. Soon there may be arrests.'

A friend who had visited Rajasthan on a number of occasions and knows it well said that due to the increasing influence of the Rajputs there – the practice of sati is strongly embodied in their traditions – this form of ritual murder is on the increase in the north. In all parts of the world and throughout history women have lived longer than men. Bearing this in mind it seems evident that in the period of 2,500 years or more in which sati has been practised, Indian widows by the million must have died by fire.

The standard explanation for a public spectacle which startled so many foreigners in India in the past fails to

convince. Here is the Venetian traveller Caesar Fredericke, writing in about 1585. 'It was told me that this law
was of ancient time to make provision against the
slaughters which women made of their husbands. For in
those days before the law was made, the women for every
little displeasure that their husbands had done unto them,
would presently poison their husbands and take other
men, and now by reason of this law they are most faithful
unto their husbands, and count their lives as dear as their
own.'

Among the reading material I had brought with me
was the third volume, issued by the Hakluyt Society, of
the Travels of Ibn Battuta. It dealt largely with his
journeys through Central Asia and India in the course of
which he spent some time in the years 1334–6 at the
Court of Sultan Muhammed Ibn Tughluq at Delhi.
Leafing through the pages of volume 3 back in Ranchi, I
found, as was to be expected, his account of a sati of his
day. Such events appear to have been as commonplace as
weddings, and in the early stages of the procedure hardly
differed from the noisy and jubilant wedding processions
of our day. 'I used to see in that country', says Ibn
Battuta, 'an infidel Hindu woman [on her way to the
burning], richly dressed, riding on horseback and preceded by drums and trumpets' – going, as Caesar Fredericke puts it, 'with as great joy as brides do in Venice to
their nuptials'.

Ibn Battuta, a humane man, clearly appalled by what
he saw as barbaric practices, would have felt compelled to
include a description of them in his meticulous record of
the life of the countries through which he travelled. In
this instance three widows had agreed to burn themselves
after the death of their husbands fighting in the Sultan's

army against the guerrilla resistance of the day. It was regarded, he says, as a commendable act by which their families gained prestige, but was not compulsory. 'Each one of them had a horse brought to her and mounted it, richly dressed and perfumed. In her right hand she held a coconut, with which she played, and in her left a mirror, in which she could see her face ... Every one of the infidels would say to one of them, "Take greetings from me to my father, or brother, or mother, or friend," and she would say "yes" and smile at them. After travelling about three miles with them we came to a dark place with muddy water. They descended to the pool, plunged into it, and divested themselves of their clothes and their ornaments, which they distributed as alms. Each one was then given an unsewn garment of coarse cotton. Meanwhile a fire had been lit in a low-lying spot. There were about fifteen men there with faggots of thin wood, while the drummers and trumpeters were standing by waiting for the women's coming. The fire was screened by a blanket held by some men in their hands so that she should not be frightened by the sight of it. I saw one of them, on coming to the blanket, pull it violently out of the men's hands, saying to them with a laugh, "Is it with the fire that you frighten me? I know that it is a blazing fire." Thereupon she joined her hands above her head in salutation to the fire, and cast herself into it. At the same moment the drums, trumpets and bugles were sounded, and men threw on her the firewood they were carrying and the others put heavy balks on top of her to prevent her moving. When I saw this I had all but fallen off my horse, if my companions had not quickly brought water to me and laved my face, after which I withdrew.'

Written two and a half centuries later, Caesar Fredericke's description fits that given by Ibn Battuta almost to the detail. Even the blanket held to screen the vision of the blazing fire is still in use. 'Before the pinnacle they are used to set a mat, because they shall not see the fierceness of the fire, and still custom demands that its succour be rejected by the victim . . . yet there are many that will have it plucked away, showing therein a heat not fearful, and that they are not afraid of that sight.'

And that, until nearly 300 years on, when the British stepped in, was in all probability more or less the way it went.

The lot of Hindu women, on the whole, has been a sad one throughout the history of India: reduced so often by an arranged and loveless marriage to the status of a menial in the husband's house, to feed as a widow the fires roaring through the centuries, or in our days to contribute to the vast statistic of young women dying from usually uninvestigated causes, few being of sufficient interest to warrant press comment. ('State prosecutor Mr Lao said there was nothing peculiar about this case except the mode of burning – the bride having been doused in whisky.')

A TV programme at the Ashok that evening offered the possibility of a clue as to the reason why Hindu civilisation should have offered its womanhood so low a promise of fulfilment and happiness, so great a likelihood of the intrusion of contempt and pain. The programme was entitled 'Women's Right to Salvation', and took the form of a discussion by a panel of savants of a book by a Canadian scholar, Dr Katherine Young, whose speciality was the study of women in Hinduism. In her perusal of the Sanscrit scriptures, the author had discovered that major commentators of the past on spiritual themes had held the view that women could rightfully opt for *sanyasa*, the path of renunciation of fleshly desire, and thus attain salvation. In making this assertion it seemed that Dr Young had broken new ground. According to the members of the panel taking part in the discussion the doctor had stirred up great controversy. She had said in her book that some orthodox Hindu thinkers of these days still see women as irretrievably lost. The Bhagavad Gita contains many references to them as 'those of evil birth', at most conceding a temporary state of 'heavenly bliss'. Dr Young nevertheless had uncovered a more liberal view of Hindu femininity in the Bhagavada Gita commentaries of the 10th–11th century championing the rights of women to take the path of renunciation and thus attain salvation.

The three learned pundits of the panel in their impeccable cottons were impressive indeed, rising easily above the trivialities too often imposed by the media in such encounters. These softly purring ecclesiastical voices were armed to extinguish doubt. Listening to them I could appreciate how hypnotic suggestion by television was a proven fact. One, the gentlest in his gestures and smile, ruled out the possibility of the female soul in Paradise. The second seemed to give it a more than fifty-fifty chance. He admitted to having been swayed by recent re-interpretations of the Gita, which he accepted as being the central scriptural authority of modern Hindus. Renunciation was the theme of the third. If salvation were to be attempted in the case of a woman it seemed to him to rule out marriage, which provided as he saw it opportunities of indulgence likely to damage the Karma. His point of view seemed to reflect that of St Paul – that (at most) it was better to marry than to burn.

How does Hinduism define salvation? For the layman of any faith it is a nebulous and even arguable concept, but whatever it may signify in the Hindu religion, women's exclusion according to the orthodox stigmatises them as the inferior sex, and has served at one time or another to subject them to every form of indignity and abuse.

It became evident in Ranchi that restrictions and probable prohibitions on travel in Madhya Pradesh made an approach to the area that interested me impracticable through South Bihar. The general opinion was that the southern part of the state, and the district of Bastar, would be more conveniently reached by travelling south from Calcutta to Bhubaneswar and then heading in a westerly direction through Southern Orissa into areas of maximum tribal concentration. It was arranged with Devi that he should drive me as far as Calcutta. We decided to break the journey and spend the night at Jamshedpur, India's first planned industrial city, so warmly recommended by the Department of Tourism for its environmental attractions.

Leaving Ranchi we ran into intense industrial traffic, with an endless succession of heavily laden lorries charging in both directions. We passed the wreckage left by some of the most spectacular crashes I have ever seen, where monstrous vehicles travelling at 70 mph had sometimes been in head-on collision, literally exploding and scattering cargoes, demolished bodies, engines, axles and wheels all over the road. In one case an eight-wheel leviathan had impaled a small house and charged with it into a field. 'Often they are trying to make up time,' Devi said. 'There is a fine for lateness. They must keep to schedule.' There were deviations to avoid insecure bridges, bottle-necks, and hazards of all kinds, and often the lorries had opened up new rights of way simply by driving through the fields, creating an anonymous, churned up, dust-clogged landscape devoid of signposts, in which it was easy to lose the way.

It was on this wasteland that we encountered our first Indian motel, an establishment of the kind in which ambitious beginnings are betrayed by a shortage of funds, and perhaps a secret belief that nothing will last. This could have belonged to a Turkish beach-development scheme, with pseudo-marble cracking from concrete surfaces, naked wiring sprouting from walls, and door-handles that fell off. In the restaurant area the atmosphere was frantic with bellowing Indian film music and victims of a crash being sponged free of blood and bandaged up on the floor. Outside in the garden all was calm. Here a procession of strikingly robed tribal women, with the faces of temple carvings, brought cans of water collected at a dribbling spigot to top up a bath from which three languid gardeners filled pint-sized bottles to water the flowers.

I joined a group of German technicians from Jamshedpur, drinking beer at the edge of the kidney-shaped pool. They were here for a swim and for lunch, and had mistrustfully brought with them their own pool chemicals, but seemed to have overestimated the quantity required, as the water gave off a tremendous odour of chlorine. The meal that was to follow was of a rather special kind – beef-burgers, to which they had been introduced by an American colleague at the factory, who had come here in missionary spirit to instruct the kitchen staff in the art of cooking them. It was a secret and expensive operation, involving smuggling and bribery, as the slaughter of cows for meat is illegal in most parts of India. The unvarying curries provided by Jamshedpur's only restaurant, said the Germans, made the high cost of the black-market Indian equivalent of the Big Mac well worth it. They had been in India for periods of up to a year, and had developed a kind of protective holy indifference to deal with the boredom inevitably generated by a situation in which nothing was of interest but work. None of them had travelled more than a few miles from Jamshedpur. They received the same inflated salaries here as in Saudi, and there was slightly more to do, but the climate was worse. One had enrolled himself on an embroidery course; another had tried yoga and given it up. This, it was agreed, was like an open prison; still the money was good.

This was Ho territory, and the Hos were brilliant irrigationalists. We found ourselves in a wide plain with soft mountainous edges; there were occasional clumps of feathery trees, and neat, tiny villages of a half dozen or so huts, all of the same shape and size, rather like a conscientiously constructed scale model in an anthropological exhibit. The Hos, perhaps over the centuries, had dug out innumerable ponds, linking them with ditches, so that although we were already in the third month of the dry season water abounded. They cultivated rice and various pulses, but spent much of their time scooping up tiny fish in their nets. Where a hard, clean road surface was near at hand they had marked off segments with stones and spread out their rice to dry. It struck me as remarkable that the harassed lorry drivers should be prepared to tolerate a practice by which they were so much slowed down.

The site for the construction of the dam on the Subarnarekha River lay at the edge of the plain under the misted shape of a sugar loaf mountain. It was one of the two dams in the Jamshedpur region which are to submerge 30,000 hectares of land and 52 villages, thus displacing up to 100,000 tribals – the majority Hos – settled here since before the Aryan invasions. When served with notice to go, there were cases of villagers armed with bows and arrows raising a protest. Police 'firings' followed, and a few 'extra judicial encounter killings' – the current euphemism for the death of arrested persons while in police custody.

Many dams have been constructed in India since independence, and many more are in the making. Hydropower projects – despite many doubts as to the ultimate benefits conferred – are fashionable and make the fortunes of numerous bodies and individuals involved in the construction. A whole-hearted and fairly powerful resistance based upon pragmatic, ecological and even humanitarian grounds is a feature of Indian politics, despite which such undertakings assume ever more and more fantastic size. The Narmada Valley Project – the largest in the world so far – will include 30 major dams, 135 medium dams, and 3,000 minor dams, and since there is no previous experience of the problems involved, experts are even worried over the possibility of seismological effects. One argument raised in parliament is that it may inundate more land than it will irrigate. Dealing with the humanitarian aspects of the case, it is noted that up to 700 villages are to go with possibly 1·5 million people displaced. Never has so much land, so many homesteads, so great an area of virgin forest been planned to disappear beneath the waters of sterile lakes, and whatever the promises made, experience teaches that for the dispossessed doomsday awaits.

We stopped at a small dam near Jamshedpur which had been completed some years before and was now a place where people went for an hour or two's escape from an overwhelmingly industrial scene. It provided a recreation area where men were playing cricket, a car-park with water laid on for the washing and polishing of cars, a children's cycle merry-go-round, stalls selling assorted nuts and pictures of tigers and gods, and a portrait photographer stalking disconsolately with his polaroid.

There was an injection of something quite new to me in this otherwise normal holiday-making Indian crowd, for the recreation area was suddenly invaded by a band of local hippies calling themselves love children. Since they were involved in protest, this had to be demonstrated first by the clothing they wore, but here a problem arose. The first hippies of the West had been deeply influenced by Indian fashions, as was evident by the trailing skirts and clinging drapery. To distinguish themselves from the phlegmatic multitudes of Jamshedpur their Indian counterparts had to reverse the order of dress. Where the originators of the cult had favoured concealment, they chose physical display, with sleeveless jerkins and shorts and close-cropped hair. Where flower power had trod softly, they bustled, sprinting here and there to cover the walls with graffiti: *God is my love*.

The cows climbing the steep slopes of the dam in search of fresh grass made this otherwise a wholly Indian scene. A flight of steps led to a narrow path along the rim of the dam, and here families promenaded to enjoy as best they could the lifelessness of an artificial lake that it would take fifty years for the landscape to accept. Fish had been introduced and ingenious wicker traps were offered for hire in which several, not exceeding two inches in length, had been caught and transferred to tins full of water. These were being examined by a pretty and expensively dressed little girl, who I was to learn had never seen a live fish before. 'And what will they do with them?' she asked her father. 'They will eat them,' he told her. She seemed to turn pale with horror, and be on the verge of tears. The father explained smilingly, 'She is very gentle by nature. You see we are Brahmins. We do not eat living things.'

Jamshedpur disappointed. We arrived after dark to find the five square miles of the renowned steel city closed off like a vast prison camp, surrounded by a high wall topped with barbed wire. The skyline was indeed dominated by enormous chimneys, and the sky itself illuminated in a fitful although theatrical fashion by out-pourings of multi-coloured smoke. Perhaps the wind was in the wrong direction for the advertised copper oxide fumes, instead pollution was by noise, an infernal roaring not entirely excluded by winding up the car's windows. Tours of many of the complexes had been offered as 'a rewarding stop on a sightseeing trip', but we were warned that these might take a day or two to arrange due to industrial disputes which had had to be quietened down by the army's intervention.

The hotel was rather dark and sad. There was a huddle of worried men at the reception who had been called upon to cope with a sudden influx of guests taking part in a seminar on disaster management. At this critical moment the wind had changed and the cuprous fumes were being blown in our direction. Someone had been called to spray the lobby with a fragrance of that antiseptic kind used to squirt the cabins of planes stopping at airports in Central America. A cow that had thrust its head through the hotel door was persuaded to back out.

Next day we took the road to Ghatsila for Kharagpur and Calcutta. Now we were in Santal country, where women were in the forefront once again. Although Devi discovered that missionaries had combed the area with hand-outs of 'seemly clothing', a hundred yards or so back from the road the girls went topless, and many of them in roadside villages wore tribal-style short skirts which, upsetting as they may have been to the religious eye, were supremely suitable for work in the fields or for riding pillion on a motorbike. Some of these villages were prehistoric Venices built along canals and on the banks of omnipresent fish ponds, with water everywhere. Every Santal village was a hive of Breughelesque activity; people were ploughing with oxen in waterlogged fields, making carts, building or pulling down houses, cockfighting or just running up and down to work off energy. Often the roads had been broken to pieces by the traffic, and lorries were blundering through the ruts and tremendous potholes like a herd of elephants in flight. At the entrance to one village they – and we too – had been held up by Santal boys demanding contributions for the festival of Saraswati, goddess of knowledge and education, and there had been a long and surprisingly good-natured wait while money was counted and receipts given.

Santal villages were immaculate although status

required the headman to build a house of corrugated iron in which he lived surrounded by dwellings of beautifully woven bamboo and carved wood. The Santals had little understanding of commerce and when we stopped at a tea-house we found that the management had been handed over to a non-tribal Hindu. It was a filthy, relaxed and somnolent place. Before filling the glasses the boy smeared them with a grimy rag, then squatted in a corner to go back to sleep. Twenty yards away the lorries went raging past. Right in the middle of the village, one had suffered ultimate catastrophe, moulting a great collection of parts all over the road. Another involved in the collision had landed up in a pond where it lay on its side garnished with lilies. We took our glasses round to the back of the tea-house to escape the worst of the exhaust fumes. Here the scene was pacific indeed. Santals clothed in the white shirts and shorts they favoured squatted in a row along the edge of a brilliant square of paddy, where – although engaged in transplanting seedlings – they might have been weaving a carpet. Further out, more men were fishing with nets, an operation they seemed to turn almost into a dance. A beautiful Santal girl with skirts over her knees went past, leading her old, blind father by a stick. She laughed at something he said. Wherever there was a bush a bird warbled. A lorry driver brought his tea out to talk to us. He was grumbling about the collection for Saraswati. With a few minutes in hand he had asked to see the shrine, which he found unimpressive. It was a crudely made bamboo hut containing a Communist Party election poster, and an image of the goddess which turned out to be a fairground doll dressed in Santal style. 'What do you think they want that money for?' he asked Devi.

'Don't believe it's for education – they vote Communist. It's for dope.'

We reached Calcutta in the late afternoon, stiff and a little dazed after a drive over bad roads that had started at dawn. Smog hung like a delicately tinted gauze curtain over the city, muting, I suspected, a rawness that might otherwise have been apparent. A tremendous concentration of traffic had filled the sallow streets with smoke which billowed through the bottle-necks as if from a railway tunnel. Long-distance lorries were jammed in one behind the other – sometimes driven in an erratic manner as if the drivers had been overtaken by intense fatigue. In among them were squeezed a large variety of local vehicles, all of them fantastically overloaded, with adiposities of cargo spreading over the footpath on one side and into the road on the other in such a way as to cut off the vision of following drivers. The noise of open exhausts, horn-blowing and advertisements bellowed from loudspeakers suspended over the streets produced in the end a stunning, almost soporific effect. I had hoped to change a booking made for me at an over-luxurious hotel, but by the time we arrived I was too tired to care. We pulled into the forecourt and immediately a queue of arrivals formed behind us. Devi was anxious to be well out of the city before dark, so the leave-taking was short. It had been an excellent trip, and I was sad to see him go.

EIGHT

CALCUTTA INSPIRES THE respect and even the affection of many of those who know it well. Victorian grandeur often relieves the monotony of mean streets. Its people are intelligent, imaginative and kind, and the fact that the city has failed in my case to awake enthusiasm is probably due to an episode dating from my first visit in 1950.

I had arrived there in the company of Gautam Chautala, the Reuters man in Saigon, who had covered the French war in Vietnam and was on his way home for a month's leave. Gautam was one of the most engaging human beings I had ever met. We had shared a number of minor adventures in Vietnam, and now I was delighted that my first contact with India should be in his company.

The circumstance of our meeting had been in some way enlightening, providing as it did a first glimpse into the mysteries of caste. We met at the Continental Hotel where, through the intense demand for accommodation arising from the war, the manager felt obliged to ask us to share a room. It was a very large one, he said, and so it turned out to be, but what he did not go on to explain was that it contained five beds, three of them tenanted at the time of our arrival. In the event we shared with two French officers – one of whom raved in his sleep – and a young couple who had been bombed out of their house and were in the queue for plane seats back to Paris. Gautam led me to the capacious bathroom to define the problem that had arisen. 'I am a Brahmin,' he said, 'and I would like to ask you as a great favour not to use my towel. This is one of these religious things.' He gave a self-deprecating laugh. I told him I quite understood and would see to it that no unintentional defilement took place. Some time later there was another embarrassed request. Would I have any objection to his bringing in a prostitute? None whatever I told him, but what about the others? 'There's a war on. They'll understand,' he said. 'And the defilement?' I asked. 'I repeat a few mantras. There's no problem.'

In Calcutta we put up at the Great Eastern Hotel, which came as an experience. Five waiters of varying degrees of responsibility stood behind our chairs, although, greatly to my disappointment after the austerities of Vietnam, only English food of the most uninspiring kind was to be had. At this time I received my second insight into the workings of caste. Returning to my room for something I had left behind I disturbed the sweeper tidying up the bathroom, who covered his face with an arm as if to ward off a blow, then scuttled almost bent double from the room.

We finished our meal, ran the gauntlet of bowing and scraping, and made for the street. A row of rickshaw pullers were lined up at the doors, and Gautam got into one. 'This man is taking me to see a nurse,' he said.

I walked on, plunged in a matter of hours from the limited misery of Vietnam at war into the unlimited misery of the streets of Calcutta. The wide, stained pavement ahead stank of urine, and all over it were strewn what at first seemed bundles of rugs but which on second glance were transformed into human forms. Small stirrings from some showed signs of life, others were quite inert – dying or dead, there was no way of knowing. A man on hands and knees struggled dreadfully to draw breath; another, face down, added dribbles to a puddle of blood. A woman who had covered her face with a scarf so that none of it was visible lay legs apart, vagina exposed. I stopped, more shocked probably than ever before in my life. The war in Vietnam had imposed instant anaesthesia. There I accepted what could not be avoided. The battle scenes were part of the protocol of the circumstances: the flies on the human fat, the neat package of brains blown from the head of a tied-up prisoner. I had permitted a hardening of the tissues of sensitivity. This was different. The exposed vagina within twenty yards of a doorman dressed like a maharajah in turban and scarlet coat was no part of the protocol of peace. I was not ready for Calcutta. I had stopped, at a loss for a moment to know what to do, and thus had caused passers-by hurrying home to slow down and turn their heads in astonishment. They had long since trained themselves not to see the grim scenes such as this that surrounded them. Men and women dying on the pavement was something to be overlooked; the spectacle of a man who stops to observe these things was not.

I described the episode to Gautam.

'Of course they were surprised,' he said. 'What do you expect? They must have thought you were some sort of nut-case.'

'Was that really a nurse the rickshaw-puller took you to see?'

'We call them that,' he said. 'Often they are. It's a poorly paid profession.'

This time I found myself staying at the Oberoi, once known as the Grand. This was largely by accident since I normally avoid luxury accommodation, which notoriously isolates the traveller from the life of any country, and is unlikely to promote adventure. In this instance efforts to make a change were frustrated by the fact that Calcutta's telephones no longer worked and personal attendance was called for to settle all the details of onward travel. This, in India, can be a time-consuming affair.

Nevertheless, the Oberoi had its advantages, for it was centrally located in Chowringee, where all my business had to be done. Five-star hotels can be brash, pretentious and noisy. The Oberoi had shown respect for its inheritance from the days when it was a Victorian boarding house and was still pleasantly sedate, free from intrusive music, and provided an environment that calmed – almost in a churchy fashion – the human voice. Guests wandered stealthily through wide corridors over green marble floors. A bowl of tuberoses had been placed in every alcove and a single, perfect red rose (500 were delivered to the hotel every morning) in a vase on each table. The walls were covered by fine reproductions of late eighteenth-century aquatints of Indian scenes by Thomas and William Daniell. The restaurant offered dishes based upon meat imported from New Zealand, praised on the menu with occasional outbursts of bad poetry. Its staff were most interesting to talk to; obviously college graduates to a man. An average tip left for a waiter in the bar would probably have equalled the average Calcutta family's income for a week.

The entrance to the Oberoi is in a forecourt with a drive-in from the Chowringee Road, now renamed after Jawaharlal Nehru. A scattering of onlookers sometimes form at the junction to the private drive-in and road simply to stare at the hotel. No one waves them away. They seem like the party guests in Buñuel's strange film *The Exterminating Angel*, held back by an invisible force at a threshold over which they cannot pass. Their view is of a hundred square yards or so of inviolable territory, and here they stand, silent and motionless while the minutes pass, with their backs to the vociferous and squalid city. Of this a high percentage of the hotel guests will catch no more than a glimpse through the windows of the car that picks them up at the hotel door. A minority of the curious must venture out on foot: the macabre pageant of the handicapped taking place a half dozen paces from the frontier of this tranquil world can only have been staged for their benefit. The central figure is a man spread-eagled face downwards – a prey to constant convulsions which increase in violence at a foreign tourist's approach. From these he suffers in public for a long working day, with the assistance of a species of manager who occasionally scoops up the few coins of tiny value that have accumulated in the tin dish. The man on the ground almost exactly fits the description of a similar unfortunate to be seen in or near this spot, in Geoffrey Moorhouse's *Calcutta*, yet it is hard to believe that the same man – whose appearance gives little clue to his age – can have pursued his fearful profession for the twenty years that have passed since the book was written.

My hope had been to stay in Calcutta only long enough to clear up one or two details of travel and book the first available seat on a train either to Puri or Bhubaneswar in Orissa, these cities being separated by a relatively small distance. I had gathered that the matter of a seat on a train might not be so simple in India as elsewhere. Foreigners who tackle such arrangements unaided often discover unsuspected complexities that may take hours or even days to resolve. It is better to leave these things to be dealt with by one's hotel, and the Oberoi being what it was I foresaw no difficulties. Its impressive tourist bureau, however, had no truck with railway travel and I was referred to the porter's desk where a smiling reassurance was forthcoming that a first-class ticket on the next day's night express to Puri would be obtained. As the telephones did not work, a boy would be sent over to the station, the porter said. We chatted about Indian politics and one thing and another until a minute or two later he went off duty. The news some hours later was discouraging. All seats on the Saturday night express had been sold. Would I care for the boy to go back and try to book a seat for the Sunday night? I was handed a substantial bill for the cost of the taxi to the station.

This, from a traveller's point of view, was a cloud in the sky no larger than a man's hand, but in the light both of my own experience and that of many others it was one that could expand into its meeting with the horizon. I was sure that there were seats to be had on this train, and it was only a question of knowing who to approach.

I was given the name of an agent, went to see him and took to him at first glance. Travel on Saturday he assured me could be ruled out. Sunday was more promising. He drifted away into a back office to ask somebody's advice and left me to admire the charm of the environment: the narrow, ill-lit room cluttered with wonderful ethnic trappings, grainy, faded Alpine photographs, a dust-covered fragment of an erotic carving, an outdated calendar, a dancing Krishna with one of his six arms broken off and badly stuck on again, a cigarette advertisement showing a pretty girl, *'For the Gracious People'*.

He returned with two assistants, all of them with mild smiles and the saint-like faces of men who engaged in ascetic practices. 'We are agreed', he said, 'that there can be a seat on Monday morning 6 am Super-Fast to Bhubaneswar. The kindly smile was lost momentarily as he winced, perhaps with embarrassment. 'The price', he said, 'will be extra . . . I am sorry,' he added, and I'm sure he was.

Calcutta is the filthiest of cities, although its filthiness is largely a matter of habit and a caste system-induced attitude of mind. It is generally admitted that Indians are unequalled in their obsessive personal cleanliness. Within the city endless ablutions go on behind closed doors and the tanks and ponds of the countryside have their permanent population of washers and scrubbers in public. Yet such bodies of water where the search for cleanliness is all must be approached with caution to avoid haphazard foulings by human excrement. Poverty and overcrowding are often offered as an excuse, although many of the cities of the Far East are as poor and as overcrowded as those of India, while remaining as clean as those of the West. In Calcutta the *bhangis* (scavengers) still go about carrying baskets of human excreta on their heads, and when Gandhi sent India's first health minister to investigate them in 1947 she reported that the delegate members who accompanied her vomited and returned without completing their study. The caste system is to blame. In the case of the bhangis a lifetime of degradation is to be cheerfully endured, for if you are an efficient and uncomplaining cleaner-up of other people's messes your Karma may be so benefited as to reward you with promotion in your new incarnation. This will give you the right to leave your own messes for others to clean up. V.S. Naipaul, in *India: A Wounded Civilization*, speaks of the Shiva Sena movement in Bombay in which the dispossessed had decided to take over their own destiny, with the construction of a squatter settlement dedicated to self-help and run by idealistic committees. This largely failed because no sweepers were brought into the community. There were no untouchables to clean up the mess. 'It was unclean to clean; it was unclean even to notice.'

In Calcutta it was a dangerous exploit to turn right out of the hotel, walk a hundred yards down the city's principal thoroughfare, then cross the road to reach what appears as a wide verge close to the entrance to the underground station – for this is used as a public latrine. Yet there are areas of Calcutta that are as spruce as any other city, in particular the settings of lawns, gardens and ornamental ponds of the Victoria Memorial, face to face with which I found myself when all the trivial negotiations of the journey had been settled. This was the inspiration of so many lovingly constructed imitations in polystyrene, such as the one I saw at the Hotel Debjon – Britain's answer to the Taj Mahal. Some of those who attended its opening ceremony had been reminded of the Taj, others had found a resemblance to St Paul's and various London railway stations. Mussolini, one of its latter-day admirers, on being shown a photograph of this shining marble mountain, and believing it to have been of recent construction, is reported to have declared, 'We, too, will do this.'

It was a public holiday and families, brightly attired for the occasion, were streaming across lawns and up to the pathways dividing the trim flower beds in the direction of the entrance, where an immensely long and very slowly moving queue had formed. Something in this imperial prospect seemed to impose upon these pilgrims a truly Victorian propriety and restraint. No child plucked a flower, whistled, whined, or so much as let drop a toffee paper. In Bihar people from Calcutta were notorious for their noise. On their home ground all was modest stillness and humility.

Inside the great building the presence of so much embalmed imperial paraphernalia may have been daunting. Here were lined up the stern-visaged, confidently posturing viceroys and generals, their jutting faces, beetling brows and protruding eyes in some way exaggerated by the marble: Cornwallis and Warren Hastings in Roman togas; Clive in the attitude of a man about to carry out a physical assault. Through gallery after gallery the quiet crowd wandered, gently shoving their way, softly treading. In voices that fused in a multitudinous velvet murmur, they commented on the weapons in the armoury and Zoffany's paintings of pride and prejudice, of royal and aristocratic Victorian faces marked as indelibly by their epoch as they might have been by mental or physical ill-health. They were engrossed in the spectacle of all those things gathered here and put on show to impress or dismay.

A single episode stands out in the memory. A woman

had placed herself, holding a child of about three in her arms, under a bust on a pedestal of a particularly fierce-looking general. After waiting for a few moments to make sure she was not attracting attention, she held up the child to allow him to smooth the distinguished features with his hands, in the hope, no doubt, that he would absorb some of the power and spirit they emanated.

TEMPLES AND
GODDESSES
IN ORISSA

NINE

AT 5.30 AM on the dot my friend the agent called as arranged to take me to the Howrah Station to catch the 6 am Super-Fast for Bhubaneswar. It had seemed to me to be cutting it fine, but he replied, 'Long waiting at the station is to be avoided. There will be time.' He was a most likable man; a worrier, overburdened with responsibility, bearing the marks of strain in his face that seemed to have deepened since our last meeting. His work, he said, put him under constant pressure. With travel – especially in India – you never knew. The planes were always late and sometimes flights were cancelled, putting more strain on the railways. Booking a seat on any train was essential but it did not always mean that one would travel, besides which sometimes there were invasions by passengers who took possession of seats to which they were not entitled, and it was impossible to eject them. He was worrying now in case something of the kind happened to me, and would not be able to relax until he saw me safely in my seat.

Howrah station at 5.40 am seemed even more remarkable than its formidable reputation had promised, and it was hard to imagine how an unescorted foreigner could have found his way in the semi-darkness through these seething multitudes to the place where, with some luck, his train awaited. Apart from the travellers, the station had its own resident population of the homeless, and in it, according to the books, some of them managed to spend a fair proportion of their lives. Here they were asleep, huddled in family groups, sprawled out singly, lying on their sides, knees drawn up almost to touch the chin in the posture of pre-historic burial, or with the approach of dawn had raised themselves on their elbows, faces turned, like sarcophagus figures in Etruscan tombs. There was something in the vast claustrophobia of the station and of its earthy cavernous odour that recalled a necropolis, a sensation heightened by the presence of a circle of men who sat facing each other absolutely motionless and, as far as it was possible to see, eyes closed, in chairs with no legs, which, said the agent, were seats wrenched from wrecked buses.

The train, suddenly bursting into this scene, came as a surprise, for it was encrusted with grime – as though it had come straight from a siding in which it had lain, exposed to the weather, for several years. From long experience the agent had chosen a position on the platform exactly facing the first-class entrance when the train stopped. There was a wait for the conductor to arrive with the key, followed by a rush for the door, composed to my surprise largely of beggars who placed themselves in strategic positions to await boarding passengers. The operation had been a successful one. The agent exchanged secret greetings with the conductor, who found my name on his list and showed me to my seat, knocking its back into an upright position with a blow of the fist. I thanked the agent, and shaking hands with him I noticed that the lines anxiety had carved at the corners of his mouth had lost depth. Settling in my seat I found myself confronted with a beggar incessantly banging on his bowl with the stump of a fingerless hand. Behind him waited a man who was clearly quite blind and could only have been attracted to me by a foreigner's unfamiliar odour. The faces of both men were contorted with anger. In a street situation I could have escaped, but this was a prison, and however much small change is accumulated in readiness for such occasions, it is soon exhausted. After that the only remedy in the face of whatever fury it may provoke, is to strive after the holy indifference of Calcutta. In this case the problem was rapidly settled, for in five minutes, and exactly on time, the train began to pull out.

This was a dirty train, and it was a relief to remember that the journey was unlikely to last more than seven hours. The moquette upholstery was grimed with filth, and innumerable hours of bodily contact had left a dark polish on the seats. What had once been a white holland cover drooped in greasy folds from the back of each seat, and the conductor's first and last service so far as I was concerned was to grab at the one I was faced with, and rip it away. The windows had probably never been washed, although by luck a brushing contact with some external object had left a transparent fissure about two inches in length in the encrustation of dirt level with my head. Through this opening a smeared and narrow vision of dawning day was to be had. Thirty years before, crossing India in the clean and well-run trains of those days, I had seen a Brahmin defend himself from defiling contact by placing his hand to cover the vacant seat at his side. When, nevertheless, I took the seat it was with the obvious disapproval of other passengers who preferred in the circumstances to stand. How did Brahmins travel in these days?

The passengers were a mixed bag of families accompanied by jubilant, clambering, scampering children, young men in American peaked caps on their way to the beach at Puri, and commercial travellers in dark suits. A rich little girl with a bejewelled and elegant mother cuddled a blonde doll. A European couple, probably just released from a 4-star hotel to come on this journey, seemed out of their element in these surroundings where nothing worked, struggling with faulty light switches, jammed windows and ruptured seat-backs. The advertised air-conditioning was supplied by electric fans which either did not work or provided uncontrollable draughts.

Gloomy-faced attendants wearing football scarves came through bringing food in battered receptacles: semolina cakes, samosas, biscuits, fruit, much of it in wrappers which were to be dropped with peelings on the floor. Tea came in little earthenware bowls which, as a gesture to hygiene when emptied, went through the nearest window that could be persuaded to open. Many passengers had provided themselves with paper tissues, which after use were screwed up into small balls before letting them drop.

Lights streaked past the clear patch in the window and I pressed my eye to the glass to watch the city's grey, cardboard shapes jogging by at dawn. The wasted profiles of Calcutta shrank away. The sun's burgundy disc came bobbing up through the smog, then trees appeared among the gaunt buildings and the shacks, and the city's hold upon the countryside was broken.

The Super-Fast picked up speed, rattling in style through the flat countryside. For a while the chaos of

Calcutta was in hot pursuit: villages like excerpts from the Bara slums, the wreckage of ancient disasters, bogies and twisted iron at the bottom of an embankment. Then the countryside's victory was complete, and the transfiguration stunned. This was a vast country aquatint of utmost delicacy, at worst softened and romanticised by the thin screen of dust adhering to the glass. It was a part of India surely that had been able to free itself from the landlords and the moneylenders and the politicians who provoked civil conflict in order to increase their power. Untrained peasant art and good taste in the blood had created the clean, cool geometrical patterning of these fields, the cutting of waterways and the siting of villages and ponds. Time after time remote West Bengal presented its flawless old master compositions: flaxen hamlets set in the soft colour-washes of early spring, glossy buffaloes dragging the plough, kite-flying children, mathematical displays of bright washing laid out at the water's edge, a flight of cranes, a man repairing a thatch.

The train stopped at Baleshwar almost within sight of the sea amid the explosive excitement of a crowd for which the arrival of the Calcutta Super-Fast would have been the event of the day. Since only a handful of passengers joined the train, there could be no other explanation than this for the platform throng; people dressed as if for audience with a cabinet minister or a party with a film star, outbursts of uncontrollable laughter, the exaggerated exchange of greetings when friends bumped into one another, the unruly conduct of children who had been brought along. A great collection of food-sellers advertised what was on offer with an assortment of musical cries, blending sometimes into what might have been an intentional chorus. One man sprinted down the platform carrying a black crab and thrusting a single enormous claw into the faces of potential customers. A brace of wonderfully robed and painted holy men paced up and down; a few beggars of the more presentable kind had put in an appearance; a horoscopist sought to draw attention by ringing a bell, and a porter having delivered packages into the care of the guard stripped himself down to his underpants for a wash in the drinking fountain.

After Baleshwar came Badhrakh with more station-platform light opera, more messy titbits for the travellers, and more paper wrappings and cellophane to be trodden underfoot. By this time the farms and the glowing fields of West Bengal had slipped away taking with them the sparkle and the last of the thin mists of early spring. Now in Orissa, summer was installed. I had managed to prise open the window, and the overhead banks of electric fans were in action producing small flurries among the many crisp bags littering the floor. We rattled, one after another, across the iron bridges over the tributaries of the Brahmani River, which was then entering the great Mahanadi Delta. The view was of one of the loneliest places of India: a great blond billowing amalgam of desert and marsh, with temple ruins overwhelmed in sand, and a great refuge of birds and beasts choosing to live by the sea.

The yellow refulgence of sand here seemed to have drained colour from a sky spread with the small summer clouds that give no shade; they streamed out like soap bubbles from a child's pipe. The train rocked us away past dunes that had been licked into extraordinary shape by the wind. There were goats all over them, prospecting the hollows for edible wild marigolds. By far-off patches of sedge men burnt as black as Negroes were working on a patch of land reclaimed from the sand which they would cultivate for a few months before its obliteration by the monsoon storms. According to the guidebook there are stretches of this coastline where at low tide the sea goes out three miles. It is so dangerously shallow and full of uncharted sandbanks that commercial fishing fleets are held at bay, leaving wonderful catches for the local fishermen to make in their prehistoric boats.

Thirty or forty iron bridges separated us from the green and pleasant fields of Bhubaneswar, but despite the Super-Fast's deliberate rumbling progress across them we finally drew into the station on time almost to the minute. The train emptied here. Most of the passengers were on their way to Puri – ranking fourth in the holy cities of India – and they were committed to a 38-mile journey by road, for which normally only taxis were available. A racket was inevitable. Taxis charging extortionate rates bribed porters to capture the luggage of arriving travellers, and this inspired conflicts on the platform in which it was possible for one's property to suffer. A fellow passenger had warned me what to expect and how to cope with the situation. Before the train came to a standstill it was boarded by struggling porters who did their best to tear the luggage from passengers' hands and escape with it through the doors. 'Let us remain seated,' said my friend, 'and pretend that we are not leaving the train. Soon they will go.' They did. The tumult died away, and we followed cautiously in the rear of the scrambling multitude, only to be spotted as soon as the collector had taken our tickets. There was a concerted rush by empty-handed porters and our baggage was wrenched away. The holier the city the worse the problem for the arriving traveller.

The extortion was scrupulously organised. One man controlled his gang of three. A taxi was allowed to approach. 'Give me the money,' said the boss. 'I will distribute it.' I gave him a quarter of the large sum demanded and was amazed that he should take it so well. Probably he had asked for ten times the usual tip.

TEN

AFTER THE STRENUOUS morning the policy when it came to the choice of a hotel was, better the devil you know, and I settled unhesitatingly for the Bhubaneswar Ashok. I would not have expected the appearance of this to have attracted extra business for it contrived to resemble a picture of a strongpoint in the Maginot Line of old. Apart from the self-assertive exterior it proved saturated with the familiar Ashok atmosphere. This gave the impression that, however austere the building and fundamental the appointments, behind it all was a small, hard-working and basically pious Hindu family, liable occasionally to make mistakes.

Here, once again, were the morning arrangements of frangipani blossom, although by the time of my arrival they were strewn on the floor mixed up with screwed-up chits and telephone messages to await the coming of the sweeper. Here, too, were the three gardeners who, since there were no important operations such as tree-planting to occupy their time, picked up fallen leaves by hand, one by one, occasionally sprinting like greyhounds to catch an airborne leaf as it came floating down. As at Ranchi, the restaurant featured chicken and chips, but the waiter in his recommendation stressed a radical difference, confiding with a screwing up of the face that enjoined secrecy that this was a black-market version of the Colonel Saunders secret formula. In small matters nothing worked too well, as advertised in the behaviour of the large electric clock over the reception which was always exactly a half-hour fast or slow. This caused more amusement than confusion among the guests.

Where the hotel at Ranchi had been frequented by glum foreign technicians the Ashok was crammed with sales managers and vice-presidents, being a great place as I was told for conferences and conventions due to the proximity of Puri with its excellent beaches. At this time there was a strong contingent from the Parke-Davis pharmaceutical group on a seminar. All these Indian businessmen were exceedingly genial and friendly. It was enough to go up in a lift with one and suffer the small but regular frustration of being delivered to the wrong floor, to be given a large and handsomely engraved card and an invitation, 'If you're ever in Bangalore give me a ring.'

The amazing thing was they meant it. This was no mere engrained sales approach. The company was giving a party that evening (this was what had sent the gardeners scurrying to tidy away the leaves), and on the basis of a two-minutes' acquaintance I was invited to attend, plied with imported Scotch, and treated to the most exciting performance of the dancers of Orissa.

Inevitably, for the assembled company men this was the sugaring of the pill of duty to be swallowed, and inspiring speeches by top executives were to follow. I slipped away but listened perforce through my bedroom window to the long and resoundingly amplified eulogies of the triumph of commerce; of sales targets reached and surpassed, of increased market shares captured, of new products to be launched, of new expansion foreseen. This was received with dutiful applause. In the planning of such speeches some respite from solemnity is usually recommended, but notwithstanding an up-to-the-minute theme of scientific advancement and the triumphs of modern technology there was something strangely out of date about the light relief when it came. The speaker produced an old-style off-colour joke which had the effect of provoking a wave of obedient titters. In the calm of this transparent, perfumed, and otherwise silent night the witticism could have been overheard by a listener a half-mile away. It was sad, stale stuff, and here very much out of place.

The agent in Calcutta had given me the name of a man he thought might help in the matter of travel in the interior of Orissa. By this time I was beginning to know the ropes, and that agents are indispensable to the traveller in India. I found Subrath Bose in his office tucked away at the back of a down-town development, a small, gleeful, twinkling man, to whom, as in the case of his counterpart in Calcutta, I took an immediate liking. He was in travel in a small way, concentrating inevitably on visitors in town to do the rounds of Bhubaneswar's formidable collection of temples. Bound as he was to be a source of inexhaustible information on the subject of religious monuments, he gave the impression of yearning for involvements of a more venturesome kind.

He had been attracted into the business, he said, by the call of the far-off places, and at first there had been journeys of zestful exploration. 'In Orissa we have sixty-two tribal groups, making up one-third of the population,' he said. 'I must tell you about nomads living on the mountain tops that few people have seen. If permission can be obtained I could send you to a village where only one single European has been. Many of these people have retained their ethnic identity.'

One exploratory adventure stood out from the rest in his mind. It was in the last year before office drudgery and the onset of middle-age had dragged him back to Bhubaneswar. He had found his way into the Bonda country in the far south, drawn there by lurid accounts of the Bonda life-style and the reputation of this small tribe for casual homicide, and a detestation of interference of any kind.

The principal Bonda market was at the village of Khairput. Bose had been driven there in a jeep, incautiously pressing on up a narrow and precipitous road towards the nearest hill village when he and his driver found they had reached a point where they could neither go forward nor turn back. It was here that a swarm of tribals, bows in hand, had come out of hiding and hustled them away. They were placed on a platform and held there all night, guarded by Bondas aiming their bows at them. At one moment, believing that they were about to be sacrificed, Bose fainted away. In the morning they were given roots to chew and alcohol to drink, after which he vomited. At that point, inexplicably, their captors underwent a change of heart – possibly, Bose thought, due to some oracular pronouncement by the village god. After demonstrations by the Bondas of something approaching affection, the jeep had been manhandled into position facing down the hill, and they had been released. 'Those people are still there,' Bose said. 'You can see them. They are much the same as ever.'

There were a dozen more tribes in southern Orissa, he

said, who had managed to hold themselves aloof from our times. Police permission to travel in restricted areas was required but he believed that this could be obtained. A question mark hung over some areas infiltrated by Naxalite extremists of the People's War Group who had acquired sophisticated weapons and were said to be supported by subversive elements in the local population. He would make enquiries. Above all, I would require the services of a guide who could not only find his way into the hills, but who had some knowledge of tribal languages. He knew of a suitable man, and hoped that he could contact him.

'How long would all this take?' I asked.

For the police permit and finding the guide – if he was still to be found – he thought about a week.

'And meanwhile what is there to see and do?'

'Very much. Your problem is not to find things to see and do but how to compress all of them into one week. Not only is Puri a holy place, Bhubaneswar also is holy. Once there were many thousands of temples. Even now we have five hundred, although some are in ruins. Pilgrims come here with maps and are very happy to spend days and weeks hunting down the shrines. A foreigner may take a taxi and see perhaps fifty in one day, finding that enough.'

'And after the temples?'

'I would recommend a visit to our zoo. This is the largest in India. I am told that methods have been developed of reconciling animals to their captivity.'

'That should be interesting. I'll certainly take a look at it.'

'You must not fail to see the Sun Temple at Konarak with its many erotic carvings and it is impossible to stay in Bhubaneswar without a side-trip to Chilika lake which is the largest brackish-water lake in the East, and reputedly very fascinating, although I have not seen it personally. If that is not enough it will amaze your friends if you tell them you have been in Bhubaneswar without visiting the battlefield on which the Emperor Ashoka gained the great victory following which the Buddhist kingdom was established. There are very many other things to hold your interest. Believe me you will be kept busy. There will not be enough time for you.'

I made a start with the largest zoo in India. All zoos are depressing to the animal lover, but Bose had spoken of scientific methods employed here to increase the animals' general well-being, their resistance to disease and even their life expectation. Encouraged by these assurances and my own belief that Indians are more compassionate than most in their treatment of animals, I went along. I hoped to find Bhubaneswar less cruel and depressing a place than the equivalent in the west, but did not. There were certain native animals, such as the sloth bear, that I wanted to see, but these and all other such rarities had taken refuge from the crowds and skulked out of sight. The great apes, more likely than other imprisoned animals to die of broken hearts, seemed if possible to be in an even more pitiable condition than usual. What may have been the principal attraction of the whole zoo was a chimpanzee in an open pit that seemed to have gone off its head. It was shambling, head slumped between its narrow but massive shoulders, its back to a crowd – largely of youngsters – who were throwing stones intended to provoke it to what was quite frenzied action. No stone hit the chimpanzee – they were probably not intended to – but when one fell near the animal it would spin round, run a few skipping steps, strike the rock surface with great force with its huge open hand, then throw the stone back. Its aim was poor, but the performance caused great delight.

The zoo possessed a unique collection of 'white' tigers which although a great rarity looked bleached out and much less impressive than specimens of the usual colour. A notice on the enclosure furnished the astonishing information that in 1967 a wild tigress climbed the fence and jumped in to mate with a male in captivity. The union continued for a number of years until the tigress's death. Replying to my comment upon what appeared to me as these animals' listlessness, my guide explained that this was a Monday when Hindus fasted, and that the animals, too, were not fed on this day. 'Let us return tomorrow,' he said. 'We may look forward to witnessing some activity.'

A short distance from the zoo I noticed an open-air pavilion featuring an exhibition devoted to India's YEAR OF THE YOUNG GIRL of which I now heard for the first time. I went in and found that it was depressing stuff. Indians have little hesitation in displaying their communal wounds and many of the photographs on show, and the facts and figures accompanying them, would certainly have startled the first-time visitor with no previous knowledge of the country. There is a lively public in India for exhibitions of all kinds and this one was well attended, mostly by families with numerous children tailing along who received low-voiced explanations of such of the miserable scenes depicted as they might have failed to understand.

The main feature of the display was a series of large photographs of Indian girls, striking and attractive as they always seem, engaged either in the hardest of labouring work or in routine tasks of evident monotony. There were the usual lugubrious processions of young women carrying on their heads piled up baskets of ore from where it had been blasted out of the mountain-side down to the waiting trucks. There were girls pictured in Kerala seated by the roadside breaking stones. The very young ones, who might have been seven-year-olds, clutched tiny hammers weighing only a few ounces, while their older sisters wielded 4-pounders, with which they reduced granite rocks to piles of chips for use in road-surfacing, thereby earning some ten rupees a day. 'Contributing to the Family Kitty' was the general caption applied to this section of the exhibition.

The enduring scandal of child marriage was illustrated in a photograph from Rajasthan of a girl bride aged ten, on horseback, riding pillion in all her wedding finery, in which she appeared hardly more than an enormous doll behind a large husband with rouged cheeks and flowing moustache. Such marriages were illegal, insisted the caption, punishable in the case of parents arranging them by fifteen days rigorous imprisonment; nevertheless, up to 100,000 took place each year, and so far no one had gone to prison. No more, so far, than has anyone – as mentioned elsewhere in the show – illegally employing girls of eleven or twelve years of age in hard labour on the building sites or on the roads.

These were no more than the commonplace excerpts of the Indian scene, strange and disturbing at first to the visitor, but as familiarity increased almost overlooked. Having skipped through the commonplaces of Indian misery, however, the visitor moves on to graver things, and is confronted with facts which in some instances it seems hard indeed to believe.

Female infanticide is commonly practised, said the social investigator in Rajasthan, where traditional anti-feminism is more solidly entrenched than elsewhere. In other northern states including Uttar Pradesh, Haryana and the Punjab girl children were permitted to survive, although with reluctance. Dr Surander Jaitly of Banaras Hindu University, who questioned a number of village women, found a sinister predominance of women who had lost daughters through accidents ('they fell down'), but never a son. Lakshmi Lincom of the Tata Institute of Social Sciences found that if a girl avoided outright infanticide she could expect discrimination right from the cradle, being weaned before a boy and liable to suffer from malnutrition. She would be taken out of school and introduced to child labour much earlier than her brothers, and was four times likelier than them to be employed in the rural hard-slogging labour that comes so close to the definition of slavery. When in the past there have been famines, the girls have been the first to die.

The most horrific of the information published here – and presumably in innumerable similar exhibitions throughout the country – prompts the question of what is to become of an India shown as prepared to debauch its culture by the diversion of newly invented medical techniques from the aim of the preservation to that of the destruction of life? The photograph this time was of a seedy house in Bombay bearing a signboard 'The Healthy Boy–Girl Guide Centre'. This was one of numerous squalid little back-street clinics, set up to employ amniocentesis tests, used elsewhere to identify genetic disorders in the foetus but misused here, according to the text, to ascertain its sex and procure abortion should this be unacceptable. Almost incredibly, the Tata Institute ascertained from data collected from six Bombay hospitals that of 8,000 foetuses aborted following such tests all but one were female.

The Indian young girl who has managed to surmount all the obstacles placed in the path of her early life by a male-dominated society, faces at the entrance to womanhood the supreme handicap of marriage to a husband, of whom in nine cases out of ten she knows nothing, and who is hunted down for her by her parents through the agency of marriage brokers with whom the all important matter of the dowry is worked out. A system in which a girl's husband is in effect bought for her in the manner of a market transaction involving haggling of the most prolonged and resolute kind goes against the grain of many Indians, yet the young victim is likely to see to it when the time comes that the same humiliations are imposed upon the wife chosen for her son. It was hard to find an Indian among those I met with anything good to say for this routine degradation of their womenfolk. They proclaimed the intention – whatever their parents' wishes might have been – of having nothing to do with arranged marriages, choosing instead some girl with a similar background and tastes that they had happened to meet at an office get-together or some such function, in Western style. But would they, when their time came? That was the question.

Progress in India in the matter of social custom moves at the speed of a sprightly tortoise, but a study of the matrimonial pages appearing in the Sunday issues of

Indian newspapers suggests the beginnings of an infinitely slow post-ice-age change of attitude. 'Bride wanted. An irreligious or moderately religious beautiful girl for secular-minded graduate government employee. Caste no bar. No dowry.' The advertisement would have been unthinkable thirty years ago, and even now could only appear in a provincial newspaper – the *Kerala Sunday Express* – drawing its readership from the population of a notoriously eccentric state. It is doubtful whether the august *Times of India*, which has two tightly packed pages of matrimonial ads on Sundays, would agree to print it. The *Times* readers are more traditional in their aspirations. Boys whose fathers are in a good line of business, or army officers, or in the government, detail their requirements in the way of bride, who should be extremely beautiful, slim, fair, a graduate and convent-educated. With the flush of dawn somewhere on the social horizon, up to one advertiser in seven has decided that the time has come to rid himself of the incubus of caste. Thus the formula 'no bar' is included in the insert. Dowry – by consent in India the most crippling of its institutions – would appear to be a very different thing. Only three advertisers in the issue of the *Times* I studied specifically disclaimed interest in cash, property, motor-cars, etc., to be passed over with the bride, and one of these, clearly conscious of his relatively low market-ability, mentioned that he had lost his right leg. One advertisement was clearly in search of substantial financial inducement. It was by a Government officer on behalf of his only son, and worded in such a way that it was clearly money that mattered: correspondence was invited, with full bio-details and horoscope, from rich families of 'little-educated girls'.

Even after the initial haggling, the prospects for the candidate seem dreadful. There may be long and traumatic delays while 'bio-details' are checked, horoscopes submitted to the experts for scrutiny and interpretation, the girl's habits reported upon by persons specialising in the supply of such information – even a medical certificate in proof of virginity requested. If the qualifications in the matter of beauty, status and education are sufficiently high an acceptable husband may be picked up at a bargain price. But for each slim, fair, graduate convent-educated beauty there are a dozen (according to the advertisements) who are homely, sweet, serene, traditionally sober, wheatish in complexion, meritorious, and perfect in household affairs. These are the descriptions applied to the second-rate, for many of whom the conjugal future is likely to be bleak. It is sad to contemplate the eventual fate of the little-educated girl from which nothing is expected but the possession of rich parents.

ELEVEN

BOSE HAD BEEN insistent that I should on no account fail to do the round of Bhubaneswar's unique collection of temples. On taking further information on what this entailed the prospect seemed a daunting one. Bhubaneswar possessed a tank – an artificial lake – of exceptional sanctity. The Bindusagar, or Ocean Drop, was reputed to contain holy water collected from every suitable source in the sub-continent, and its power to cleanse away sin was still kept up to proof by additions of water provided by pilgrims returning from the Ganges carrying as many bottles as they could manage.

The Ocean Drop is accepted by devout historians as once having been ringed by 7,000 temples. One looks at the space available and wonders how this could possibly have been. There are still temples galore, some recognisable as such, others no more than vestigial shapes sticking up like decayed teeth from jawbones of rock. A Friends of the Temples society has pinpointed the location of a hundred or two, although some of these holy buildings seemed to be little more than ruins, and the Friends had classed three of these near-ruins, built one on top of the other among the brambles in a back garden, as three separate temples in their determination to inflate the tally.

Five major temples remained that were in good shape and current use. The Hinduism of this area of Orissa had come under the influence of fertility cults, and this was reflected in the phallic inspiration of their lofty towers, and in the frequent presence in the chambers at their base of the god's image in the form of a lingam, projecting from three to ten feet from the ground. The walls of most of these edifices were richly decorated with erotic carvings, some of which had suffered defacement at the time of the sixteenth-century invasion by the Moghuls, who failed to appreciate their purely religious significance.

Every traveller to Bhubaneswar is expected to make for the Lingaraj, accepted as one of India's most outstanding temples. In this case the deity is represented as a block of stone which, according to rumour, is bathed daily with hashish steeped in milk. Some fifty small temples are crammed into the Lingaraj enclosure alone, from which soars a tower carved with motifs of great interest. None of these nor any of the internal details of the temple can be inspected by the foreign visitor, who is invited to make use of the viewing platforms outside the walls erected for the use of Lord Curzon who, as a non-Hindu, was equally debarred from access, although granted leave to inspect the temple through his binoculars. When I climbed the tower I was accompanied by two temple servants, one of whose duties it was to ask for a donation, the other to enter the amount along with my particulars into a book he carried. All the previous donations, considering the sparseness of the visual experience offered, seemed very high.

Of all the temples in Orissa a visit to the great Sun Temple

by the sea at Konarak sounded likely to be the most
rewarding, there being no prohibition of access. It was at
the centre of an area containing many other features of
interest – above all Puri with its Car of the Juggernaut. I
had decided to put up in Puri for a day or two while
awaiting news from Bose, but before moving, a trip to
nearby Khandagiri, with its Jain cave temples and its
swarming pilgrims, seemed a pleasant diversion.

The Khandagiri caves were a few miles down the
Kuttack road. Although a Jain pilgrimage centre, they
were equally popular with Hindu pilgrims doing the
rounds of the holy sites. About the time of my arrival,
depending on certain astrological calculations, Jain
priests were expected to arrive – imposing in their total
nudity, with gauze covering their mouths to prevent the
sacrilegious inhalation of winged insects – and thereafter
take up residence in the upper caves.

The Jains had not yet appeared, but the hill and its
surroundings swarmed with religious devotees and holy
men of various categories who had arrived to attend what
might have been seen as a religious version of an insurance brokers' convention at the Ashok. Khandagiri is on
the itinerary of long-distance-travelling saddhus. Some
of those who were here would have undertaken the great
Narmada River pilgrimage – a journey of 800 miles
through the legendary forest so soon to be extinguished
beneath the waters of the great hydropower scheme.
Two years were normally devoted to this karma-
strengthening exercise, but some never returned. Where
almost every tree provided fruit of a kind, and caves by
the hundred offered shelter all along the banks of the
sacred river, there was no better place to practise the
holy idleness enjoined by a complete surrender to relig-

ion, and in the end almost to overlook the reality of the world.

It was hard to know what saddhus lived on when in town. At Khandagiri there were no begging bowls in sight, unlike elsewhere in the East. I was never approached by a request from one for money or food, nor were obvious offerings made by members of the Indian public. Affluence and success here are generally indicated by bodily size. A successful businessman is large, doomed to eventual coronary failure or other organic collapse. The holy men of Khandagiri, with their dazed smiles and aroma of mild religious dementia were, by contrast, as thin as rakes, yet they scampered like mountain goats up and down the hillside paths. To be just on the right side of malnutrition seemed not a bad thing.

On a natural platform halfway up the hill a party of Jain ascetics had gathered to chant mantras. They were led by a precentor with a tremendous voice, wearing twenty or thirty shell necklaces and his abundant hair dressed in exuberant style. He held a volume almost as large as a chained bible, from which he read the text, nodding occasionally in the direction of the accompanists on single-stringed fiddles and drums when their participation was required. A scout had been placed to warn women pilgrims to keep their distance to avoid spreading potential defilement. Overlooking this scene at the entrance to a rock temple was a rare sight indeed – a woman priest in a red robe, with the heavy, powerful features of a male politician. At her back a group of acolytes similarly dressed, one wearing tinted spectacles, had taken up deferential attitudes. Presently they turned to join forces and melted into a narrow pathway to become a thin flame licking up the hillside.

Khandagiri is a picnicking site of the religious kind, much suited to this purpose by its high therapeutic reputation and the innumerable caves with which it is furnished, available for childish exploration. To eat well and in a relaxed fashion in the presence of the gods is seen as a form of piety, and a number of well-disposed divinities are thought to frequent the area in order to partake of the spiritual essences of the food. Nevertheless in this devout environment a greater than usual preparational effort is called for. Ideally, new cooking pots will be bought for the occasion, failing which existing ones are burnished to a high level of brilliance. Woods of the better kind, producing a fragrant smoke, are brought along to make the fire, and women with a little money to spare may lash out for a new sari. Some thought in such cases is given to the choice of a colour to go with the surroundings – at Khandagiri terracotta earth, and the dark foliage of pines. The culinary processes at such a time can assume a certain theatricality – this is no more or less than an open-air performance, abetted by the exhibitionist antics of the holy men in the background. The women encircle their cooking pots like the players in a Greek drama: all the gestures of fire-stoking, food-tasting and the adding of condiments are ceremonial. Actions are premeditated and hieratic. At Khandagiri the onlooker should take up a position in which such family groups are back-lit by the streaming morning sunshine, muted and diffused by wood smoke in such a way that the frontiers of colour of the saris, the purples, pinks and blues, spread to merge a little.

Everyone buys something from a souvenir stall which offers carved wooden pheasants in all sizes with arrogant, matriarchal expressions, crests like Spanish combs and feet equipped with the talons of falcons. In addition there are gaudy little cabinets housing the effigy of the Lord Jagannath, seen – despite his notably liberal temperament – in dehumanised form with black face, a narrow beak of a nose, and huge, staring owl's eyes. The cabinet in which he is supplied fulfils a purpose, for at night the doors are closed cutting off the all-seeing divine scrutiny which otherwise might trouble human sleep. In another climate of faith folk art of this kind may be seen as whimsical and Disneyish. Here, a residue of belief in such objects saves them from this fate. They are good fun, but they are also invested with secret power, and to be treated with respect.

Pilgrims to the hilltop Jain shrine are accustomed, having completed their devotions, to seat themselves out in the open on stone benches under the trees. Here they are joined in orderly fashion by monkeys who accept their presence as a matter of course, seeming not only to have adopted human postures but also human attitudes in such matters as their apparent appreciation of the view. The Jains provide themselves with packets of nuts upon which, together with rice, they largely exist, and these they share freely with the monkeys. When a monkey's allocation runs out he will frequently nudge the donor gently in the hope of a further contribution.

The oldest caves on neighbouring Sunrise Hill are of Jain origin. Preceding by a thousand years the routine eroticisms of Konarak and Khajuraho, these carvings are devoted to familiar non-religious subjects, to the scenes of wild life, elephants, tigers and recognisable birds that inspired the art of the day. Sometimes a scene will be purely anecdotal – such as the ladies of King Karavela's court showering blows on a family of elephants caught devouring the lotuses in their pool. Few of the crowds attracted to the Sun Temple at Konarak come here, but there cannot be many of the ancient sites of India where the rough and tumble of pre-history is glimpsed so well.

TWELVE

IN THE MATTER of good advice Bose failed me only once. Everyone in search of accommodation in the Puri area will naturally turn first to that nostalgia-saturated local relic of the Raj, the South Eastern Railway Hotel at Puri, spoken of with gratitude by all seasoned travellers in this part of the world. Thus, naturally, I did, only to find that it was full. This was a disappointment. After accidental and reluctant exposure to what is described in the travel guide as the 'top end' of tourist accommodation in Delhi and Calcutta, and otherwise to the perfectly straightforward and pleasant commercial atmosphere of the Ashoks, the South Eastern was clearly what I had always been looking for. All the faces had changed, but these were the settings of a book with a faded Victorian cover; silent, spacious, embalmed in time.

The ambience was also faintly enigmatic. A reception clerk appeared only to say that there were no vacant rooms, then vanished. Otherwise there was nobody to be seen. The South Eastern was devoid of intrusive music, there were no footfalls, no doors slammed distantly. It was hard to imagine the Oberoi being the scene of unusual experiences, less so here. I went out and seated myself at a table on a wide, empty verandah overlooking a lawn, with a line-up of bedrooms behind me having tall blue doors closing over French windows. The interiors of several bedrooms were visible, featuring large chandeliers and beds draped in the snowy folds of enormous mosquito nets.

A waiter had come up from the rear, a silent, immaculate and almost spectral presence, bringing, as if an order had been communicated by thought-transference, tea, toast and jam. He added sugar as directed to the tea, then went on to stir it. A tiny green bird flashed out of a flowering shrub and hovered with obvious intent until he cuffed it gently away.

Afterwards I wandered into the reception area, then into a sitting room to examine some of the cupboards full of vintage English books: Pearl S. Buck, Mrs Henry Wood, Harrison Ainsworth, Frances Parkinson Keyes. Hidden clocks chimed softly from ambush; a polished gecko slid into sight from behind a Victorian landscape after Constable. I would have liked to settle down in the South Eastern for some days, but since it was not possible, Bose's choice of the Marina Gardens, six or seven miles away down by the sea, seemed the next best thing.

The change was extreme. I was confronted at the reception by a notice announcing checking out time at 8 am. On querying this I was told that arrangement could be made for guests to leave somewhat later than this if prepared to accept the charge for a half-day. I spoke to the charming and sympathetic Mrs Panda, the manageress, and learned with some alarm that she had just returned after completing a course at a London business school. Mrs Panda assured me that she would make an exception if necessary in my case, but it became evident in later transactions that traditional Indian hospitality at the Marina Gardens had been vanquished by the philosophy and methods of the Western hard-sell. Mrs Panda's mantle of enchantment was stripped away in the end by the knowledge that at the Marina Gardens you paid a little more but got a little less, and what would otherwise have been a pleasurable experience was soured by smiling extortion.

A bad mistake, but not so bad as had first appeared, for the hotel bus advertised as available to take guests to the beach was not in evidence: the alternative was a fairly expensive taxi on hire through the Marina which most guests seemed reluctant to afford, and those electing to walk found that although the beach was described as being within easy walking distance it was some three miles away. All in all this, from my point of view, was no bad thing, for in one way or another the beach had been left as it always was. When I went there the fishing fleet had just come in: big, extravagantly painted boats with the staring eyes of idols, and a few smaller ones made of planks slotted together, which could be taken apart as soon as beached and the planks carried away.

To me the catch was a phenomenal one. The sand in the vicinity of the boats was littered with splendid fish for sale, some of which still leaped into the air, twisted and shuddered. With their arched backs, snapping jaws, bulging eyes, and sail-like spread of fins they reminded me of the decorations added to old nautical maps. Puri, with its shallow waters and sandbanks and shoals, was too remote and chancy to attract the commercial fishing from the north which would so rapidly demolish this richness. A procession of statuesque girls were carrying the fish on their heads up the road to be loaded into trucks. A 20 lb monster fetched about the equivalent of 50p, and you could buy as many as could be crowded into a motor rickshaw for five pounds.

The hotel's real attraction was its garden, which had probably been laid out in a matter of weeks at a cost of so much per square yard by a firm specialising in such undertakings. There might have been three acres of it, and more was in the course of construction. A bulldozer came along, tore the original sand away and replaced this with topsoil in which seedlings were planted of showy annuals such as dahlias, calendulas and marigolds, which grow like weeds and sometimes emulate them in climates where frost is unknown and there is abundant sun. Above these great spreads of colour hovered butterflies by the hundred, and I was struck with the fact that they were almost the first butterflies I had seen in India, where every inch of the cultivable landscape is devoted to filling empty stomachs and therefore devoid of flowers. In all probability they were a local, permanent population, attracted to a reserve brimming with nectar from which no reasonable butterfly would ever be induced to depart.

Although lacking the sombre splendour of the morphos of the South American rain forest, many were large and coloured with a subdued magnificence. Above all their extraordinary tameness gave rise to speculation. They could be touched carefully without flinching. Very gently, I picked one up, released it and it flew back to the flower. Why should this have been? The possible answer was that in a country where priests were prepared to go to such pains to avoid the accidental death of insects, no one has ever collected butterflies to be pinned in rows on a board. They had nothing to fear from humans.

Nor, seemingly, had the flies. There were not many

about, but they were quite fearless, and having settled on the skin refused to move unless they were brushed off. Nobody swatted a fly. A notice by the pool said, enigmatically, 'Guests are requested to refrain from inhuman acts'. Guests came here to take their breakfast but there were no signs of inhumanity. A number of the most elegant long-tailed crows waited stealthily in the casuarinas to clear away the vestiges of the meal – including the napkins – which they did instantly and with wonderful skill as soon as a guest got up from his seat, and before he had had time to leave the table. Perhaps from reasons of caste few people used the pool. The exception was a mother and her grown-up daughters who circled endlessly and very slowly, following each other in a clockwise direction. They appeared to be well-educated and conversed in loud, clear voices in nothing but English. Workmen were doing something to the men's changing room and the mother was afraid that a man might be tempted to use one reserved for the ladies. 'It's not important Mother,' one of the daughters said. 'You will not be there.' 'Yes,' said the mother, 'but a man might see my clothes, and I should be very embarrassed.'

I was virtually under orders to visit Konarak, and as soon as I had put in an hour or two's butterfly watching, and investigated the immediate vicinity of the hotel, which turned out to be a nature reserve, I did this. The temple of the Sun God, built close to the shore, had appeared hardly more than a pile of ruins until 1904 when, after clearing away the sand and debris, most of the original building was uncovered. Because the temple had been protected from the weather since its abandonment it was found to be in almost perfect condition.

The first thing that impressed was the grandiose and imaginative concept that had inspired its building. It represented the chariot of the Sun God, drawn upon twenty-four colossal wheels by seven huge, straining and wonderfully carved horses. As was to be expected in India, hidden meanings and symbolism were attributed to all aspects of the building. 'The wheels', explains the Tourist Board's leaflet, 'represent time, unity, completeness, justice, perfection and movement, and all the measurements were found to be of astral significance.' What struck the men in the street was the nature of the many thousand carvings themselves – safely concealed from view in all probability by the sand at the time of the puritanical Moghuls coming upon the scene. The description in the government pamphlet touches on this aspect of the subject lightly, offering what sounds like an excuse. 'The temple was conceived as a total picture of the world, and without mithuna or union in love which is the fount of creation, it would not have been complete. A great part of the temple is, therefore, covered with erotic art.'

The fact is that the picture of the world presented in the carvings at Konarak is narrow and specialised. India abounds with temples belonging to roughly the same period devoted whole-heartedly to erotic statuary. It was a purely religious art form and therefore almost certainly in olden times less than exciting in its effect upon beholders in general. Christian doctrine of the day frowned upon sexual activity and decorated the cathedrals with images of elderly saints in the attitudes of prayer. In both cases the postures were largely standardised and repetitive. All the bearded saints of the medieval cathedrals look roughly the same, and so do the girls in the arms of their lovers in the innumerable carvings on the walls and the wheels of the Sun Temple at Konarak. In both so widely sundered civilisations the boredom of a sculptor, deprived of all outlet for invention and condemned to the mass production of almost identical figures, must have been extreme. Of the thirty-two amatory postures catalogued by the *Kama Sutra* only six or seven were represented here, the rest being too complicated for the carvers. No wonder that in both cases the most interesting work appears in the scenes of everyday life – of scolding fishwives, men playing cards, cheating in the market, a child playing with a dog, carved in some corner of the edifice, out of range of pious eyes.

In the old days worshippers would have been drawn to Konarak, just as they were now to Jagannath Temple in Puri, to improve their fortunes in this life and their prospects in the next. The erotic statuary is likely to have been taken for granted and passed by with hardly a glance. The most devout of the males among the crowd might have responded to the impulses of religion by coitus with a temple prostitute, the carnality of the act diluted with its devotional ingredient. Nowadays, since the temple no longer functioned as such, it was the carvings that attracted.

Pleasure may have been spiced with guilt. After long contact with the British the Indians have become a puritannical people. This was illustrated on the Marina Garden Hotel's beach, where the only visitors I saw were a mixed party of young Indians who had at least been able to free themselves of the supervision of their elders. Nudity, or anything approaching it, is banned from the productions of the Indian cinema, but some sort of breakthrough in the direction of liberation happened a few years back when public opinion was induced to tolerate shots of girls who through some accident had received a dowsing and were portrayed in wet and clinging saris. The great sport on this particular occasion was to encourage the girls to wade, fully dressed, into the sea, then emerging to exhibit forms coming close to nudity in slightly provocative postures. No wonder after all this suppression that three crowded planes fly daily from Delhi alone to Khajuraho, where the many temples display their erotic masterpieces by the acre. Inhibition is the spur.

At Khajuraho the scene must have resembled Konarak. Trippers bussed in for an hour's scramble over the terraces here, and were waylaid at the entrance by potato-crisp sellers and touts offering watches and rings they claimed to have picked up on the street. At the temple, photographers awaited to snap them against backgrounds of intertwined bodies, and postcards were proffered with pretended although quite unnecessary secrecy. Mothers and fathers brought their children along, perhaps as part of the duty of keeping up with the times. Mums speeded up a little, eyes front, to pass the danger spots. A few dads risked quick, sidelong glances, then turned away to continue conversations with young members of the family, undoubtedly on educational themes. In certain sensitive areas ropes had been stretched about a yard from the wall, possibly to prevent close-up photography of the ingenious love-making of the thirteenth century. These sections of wall were under observation by a guard, and when someone with a camera ducked under the rope and started to focus-up, the guard would blow his whistle and wave a stick.

The ladies featured in action on the walls of the Sun

Temple were known as *devadasi*, 'handmaids of the god', and although playing a lesser part perhaps in the rituals of church and state in later centuries, they were still in action at Puri in the Jagannath Temple in 1818 when R. Ward, a Baptist minister, wrote furiously in his book *A View of the History of India*: 'It is a well-authenticated fact that at this place a number of females of infamous character are employed to sing and dance before the "god".'

Although there may have been some decline in the quality of temple prostitutes by the time the Reverend Ward came on the scene, they were originally selected by state functionaries with the greatest possible care, and the 'noble maidens' occupying the highest of the seven grades were treated with great honour. They held highly paid posts at the court of King Chandragupta, taking turns to hold the royal umbrella and carry the king's golden pitcher. Punishment for rejection of the royal advances was 1,000 lashes, although it is supposed that this was rarely administered. Apart from sexual services provided for members of the court and generous contributions to temple funds, the ladies spent much of their time fanning idols. They were traditionally secret-service agents, and besides fulfilling the most exacting criteria of beauty they were expected to be well-educated and witty, with conversational standards 'much better than those of the chattering housewife'.

The stunning fact is that what is known as the Devadasi system still exists in a clandestine and wholly criminal form, acting as a vehicle with which the brothels of the great cities, in particular Bombay, are continually replenished by fresh and innocent young victims from remote country villages. It has always been there, easily foiling any attempt to repress it. The passage of the Karnataka Devadasi Act of 1981 has failed to have any effect upon a practice by which large numbers of village girls, either tribals or from the untouchable castes, are persuaded by local priests, with the connivance of parents, to allow themselves to be dedicated to the goddess Yellamma in mass ceremonies performed each February on the night of the lunar eclipse at a number of villages in Maharashtra and Karnataka. Pimps lie in wait, the police turn a blind eye, and the young girls are spirited away to Bombay or Pune, never to be seen again.

The attractions in the past for the poor, ignorant and priest-ridden families were substantial. The profession of the devadasi was, and in some cases still is, seen as an honourable one. Until recently a devadasi by law had the same inheritance rights as a son. She could perform the religious rites denied to other Hindu women, and – since in theory she was 'married' to a goddess – the family would be freed from the dowry burden. The new law has, in theory, put an end to these small inducements. Otherwise it has done nothing, for the situation has remained unchanged, and although hundreds of devadasis are known to have been dedicated in the years since the passing of the act only a single case has been brought by the police resulting in a conviction. The Indian film masterpiece *Salaam Bombay* fails to make it clear how the young girl preyed upon by a pimp in Bombay has fallen into his power, and one can only suppose that its makers may have been under some compulsion to hush up the facts. The *Times of India* reporting on the situation comments bitterly upon the irony that in the Year of the Young Girl such terrific abuses should seem unable to touch the national conscience.

What is almost incredible is there is really no mystery about these regular brothel recruitments. Everyone who reads a newspaper must know that the Temple at Saundati in Belgaum district has always held the principal shrine of the Yellamma cult, that every February a festival there attended by many thousands of religious pilgrims takes place, and that in the past numerous dedications of girls who were to become prostitutes took place; if the traffic has momentarily been halted at Saundati it carries on as before in many smaller temples in that area. The fact is that there is money in this for everybody: for the girl's parents and relatives, for the priest, for the pimp, and for the police. There is a waiting list of rich debauchees in the city ready to pay up to the equivalent of £500 for the privilege of deflowering a young girl. The police are corrupt, say Indian friends, because they are underpaid. This may be so, but in the end in matters of custom, even of criminal custom, India appears incapable of reform.

THIRTEEN

WHILE I WAS at Konarak I could not resist a little diversionary pilgrimage to the mouth of the Devi river, flowing through sandbanks to the sea some three miles away. I had been an avid reader of the travels of Sebastian Manrique, the Portuguese missionary, and one of the great travellers (and adventurers) of history. It was here in August 1640 that Manrique landed on his way back from the Far East to continue his peregrination overland, through India – the Indian section of the journey largely by bullock cart – back to his home in Portugal. His wanderings had taken nearly fifteen years.

The first point of land they identified from the ship, Manrique says, was the Jagannath temple, but they arrived at Puri a month too late for him to have witnessed in person the great car festival of that year of which he provides in his book a lively and fairly accurate description. He was never a one to miss such an occasion, and was probably delayed by bad weather. There is a routine report on the subject of sati, seen by travellers in general as the most dismal of the rites of the Hindu religion, and an extraordinary account of sacrificial rites practised in his time on Sagar Island at the mouth of the Hugli, in which devotees of a local cult, both men and women thrown into a state of ecstasy, offered themselves to the sharks. 'As soon as they have made this vow they enter the sea up to their breasts and are very soon seized and devoured . . . and since they [the sharks] are accustomed and thus encouraged constantly by tasting human flesh, they become so bloodthirsty that they rush up fiercely at a mere shadow. Yet at other times they are either so satiated . . . that they reject the offerings made by those unhappy idolators. They then look upon this escape, which they should consider as so much happiness and good fortune, as an event full of ill luck, and hence leave the sea weeping and lamenting loudly, believing that owing to their sins they were not considered worthy to have their sacrifice accepted by their false and diabolical gods, and henceforth they look upon themselves as forever damned and doomed.'

Much of the interest in Manrique's narrative lies in the fact that he travelled in areas (such as Arakan in north-western Burma) never visited by Westerners before his day and by hardly any since. His editors speak of his 'uncompromising religious zeal' but, although his writings abound in the conventional pieties of his time, he is by temperament more of a merchant – as described in his passport – than a man of God, and is not above trying to smuggle the goods he carries through customs, or in one case, in India, using silk bought in China to bribe an official when he becomes embroiled with the law.

On landing in India Manrique immediately fell in with an Englishman called John Yard, of the East India Company, who lived up river in or near Bhubaneswar, which they visited by boat. The river 'was covered over by great, pleasant, shady trees, whose thick branches here and there interlaced so as to look like an artificial avenue. This was full of most beautiful peacocks, of green screaming parrots, pure shy doves, simple wood-loving pigeons . . . ' The change since then has been a dramatic one, for with the trees long since gone the view from the low reaches of the Devi River is of sand.

Yard, with whom Manrique got on extremely well, would appear to some to have been a typical Englishman. He carried a gun wherever he went and on this occasion shot at everything in sight, so that by the time they finished the river journey he ended the day, as Manrique puts it, laden with the results of his toil. He was spellbound with admiration. After that Manrique, well supplied with funds, bought a horse, hired a number of servants and set out for the north. It was a journey to which he looked forward. India under Moghul rule was prosperous and peaceful. Rest-houses for travellers were provided at frequent intervals along the main highways, and Manrique noted that they offered all the amenities of the day, and were clean and cheap. Friar Domingo Navarrete, who followed him exactly forty years later, was enraptured by a similar experience. 'There is no such easy and restful way of travelling in the world. We always lay quiet and safe. There is no enemy here to be found.' In the seventeenth century there was no fear of dacoits or of encounters with corrupt and brutal police. Nevertheless the Moghuls kept a tight rein in their dominions and, as Manrique was to learn, their justice could be severe.

Despite fifteen years in the East Manrique could still be amazed and a little scandalised by the treatment of animals in India, which struck him as contrary to God's purpose, 'There are some', he says, 'who go to such lengths in showing this consideration that they give dogs wadded cotton coats in winter. In the Kingdom of Gujarat I saw cows and calves clothed in fine coats of this kind, buttoned and tied over their chests and round their bellies.' Even if Manrique could bring himself to tolerate such absurdities in the case of household pets he firmly drew the line with wild animals taking 'every advantage of the ample privileges accorded by that heathen sect [Hinduism] to wild animals which thus become tame and enter their houses'.

It was the season of monsoons, with roads turned to mud and much of the country under water. On one occasion the travellers took refuge with a Hindu farmer who fed them and let them sleep in his barn. Here they were found by peacocks sheltering from the weather, 'accustomed', as Manrique says, 'to being petted on other occasions', and therefore caught quite easily for their necks to be wrung. The birds were cooked and eaten, but thereafter doubt set in as Manrique and his Muslim servants remembered Hindu prejudices in such matters. As a precaution they buried the remains of their feast, but a few small feathers were overlooked. Next day, after they had left, these were discovered by the farmer, who raised a hue and cry which was followed by hot pursuit. There followed a running battle for several miles with the Indians showering them with arrows, and Manrique turning back twice to fire off his musket at them. Luckily the English marksman had been left behind for no one suffered a scratch. But the alarm had gone ahead, and at the next town they were arrested and thrown into gaol. Having to deal with the Muslim authorities, Manrique put forward the plea that according to both Christian and Muslim faiths animals were created by God for man's use and that it was lawful to eat them. With this the governor was in emphatic agreement, pointing out, nevertheless, that the Moghul Emperor had guaranteed his Hindu subjects the right to live without interference under their own laws and customs. It was a law he was bound to uphold although he proposed in this case to show leniency by punishing the perpetrator of the offence by no more than a whipping and the loss of his right hand.

This was an emergency of the kind where all Manrique's aptitude for manipulation came to the fore. Possibly as an ecclesiastic he had been freed and was in a position to make his enquiries. He undoubtedly knew his man at a glance and had been able to pick up enough of the case history of his wife to decide how the situation was best handled. 'After mollifying him [the governor] by the usual inducements on such occasions, I sent through him a piece of green flowered Chinese taffeta, worked with white, pink and yellow flowers, to this lady. It was a sufficiently rich and pleasing gift, and being such the lady gave as good a return, to show her gratitude, and did her best with her husband to get him to send me secretly to set the prisoner free on the pretence that he had escaped.'

It was to Manrique's credit that he would not settle for an alleviation of the punishment by which only the fingers of the offender's hand were to be amputated, but kept on with his bribery and cajoling until he was released. The episode not only illustrated the characters of the protagonists but that of the civilisations that formed them. Only John Yard the Englishman is missing from the tableau.

FOURTEEN

A PHONE CALL to Bose produced reassuring news.
Police clearance for the journey to the interior had come
through. The expedition he had in mind would cover up
to some 1,500 miles through most of those parts of
south-western Orissa accessible by road. He had found
someone to go with me familiar with the area, who spoke
three of the principal tribal languages, and who would be
ready to travel in three days' time. He quoted the
approximate cost involved, which seemed extremely
reasonable.

Traveller's cheques had to be changed to meet the bill
so I went to Mrs Panda. Tourists in India soon learn to
steer clear of bureaucratic institutions such as banks, in
recognition of which hotels are empowered to change
money at roughly equivalent rates, and they are under
obligation to display a notice showing what those rates
are. I found it a little ominous that the Marina Gardens
should fail to do this, and when after preliminary blandishments Mrs Panda got down to brass tacks I could
understand why. Nothing changed in the seraphic smile
when I told her that I preferred to save money by going
to the bank in Puri. This was a Saturday, she pointed out,
and the banks in Puri were closed. She wheedled: If a

large sum of money were involved she might be able to do a little better.

An Indian fellow guest who had hovered within earshot while these transactions were taking place took me aside to assure me that whatever Mrs Panda said, the State Bank of India at Puri remained open until midday. However there was some delay in obtaining a taxi, and by the time it arrived I knew that it was touch and go whether I would get there before the bank closed. The taxi was old and slow, we were held up by road-mending operations and then a procession, after which resignation took over and I adjusted to the fact that what had started as a rush to a bank about to close for the weekend would end as a leisurely tour of the sights of one of India's most fascinating cities.

Puri was five miles away down the coast. My taxi drove into its heart down the wide street built to allow the lumbering, hardly controllable passage of the Car of the Juggernaut blundering through multitudes entranced by the presence of the god. Scarlet flags flared from the icy-white pinnacle of Manrique's landmark, the Jagannath Temple tower, which thrust into the sky. Holy men overtook us and passed pedalling furiously on garlanded bicycles. Pilgrims had bought conch shells and filled the air through the tinkling of bicycle bells with their melancholy hooting. Beside the shells the stalls sold pilgrims' souvenirs saturated in the imagination of the buyer with magical force; images of the Lord of the Jagannath, bold-eyed ceramic cockerels, squares of tin-plate punched with patterns of sunflowers, mystic birds and the footprints of Lakshmi, goddess of poverty and wealth. The crooked side streets running back from the temple were full of pilgrims who washed themselves endlessly. The suds trickled down to join a mainstream from their ablutions finding its eventual way into a black gutter.

The cows of Puri were quite unlike those anywhere else. They were the best organised in India, going in single file and orderly fashion the round of the streets, pausing only for a moment to collect an offering from a regular contributor before moving on. They were calculating, nimble and sleek.

This was the Chaucer's Canterbury of eastern India. People had always come here out of the natural delight of going on pilgrimage, or to profit spiritually or physically from the proximity of holy things. Letters in the local press attested to the benefits to be derived. A stay in Puri, it was claimed, with frequent visits to the temples, promoted sublime visions, strengthened transcendental consciousness, and improved digestion and the elimination of waste products. Someone had developed a highly sensitive piece of electrical equipment which measured the strength and direction of divine influences radiated from the Jagannath shrine. A correspondent wrote that his friends had detected a current flowing from his body on his return from pilgrimage and that for the first few days physical contacts with him sometimes produced slight shocks. Many such experiences transmitted by word of mouth had added to the reputation of Puri over the centuries. Nowadays in season buses delivered and collected up to 5,000 pilgrims in a day. At the time of the Car Festival in June or July the town's population was swollen by several hundred thousand, with pilgrims bedding down in lodging houses ten or twenty to a room, covering the rooftops at night with their recumbent bodies, and lined up row after row under plastic sheeting all along the beach.

The Lord Jagannath, usually depicted in naive child-like imagery, is senior member of a family trio including a brother Balabhadra, and sister Subihadra, and replaces Durga (Kali) of neighbouring West Bengal as the most popular deity of Orissa. This partiality is derived, it is said, from his accessibility to worshippers of all castes. Nevertheless the cult is exclusive. Only Hindus are allowed to enter the temple, even Mrs Gandhi's application being turned down through what was seen as her unorthodox marriage. Foreigners wishing to see something of the temple beyond its external walls are invited to view it from the roof of a library across the road, gaining little from this although paying a charge.

The religious activities of Puri are on a grand scale. The temple itself is enormous – a city in miniature. Within the compound 6,000 men are permanently employed in temple duties, many engaged in the construction of the famous cars, always destroyed following each annual festival and taking a year to rebuild. It takes 4,000 pullers to haul the processional cars down the street. The leading car in which Lord Jagannath rides is 50 feet high, weighs over 100 tons, is carried on 16 wheels, and once started is virtually unstoppable, although the distance covered is exceedingly short. In the past instant admission to paradise was assured for those who threw themselves under the wheels. The supposed hypnotic effect produced by this pre-eminent local god featured largely in the school-book histories of old, and descriptions of mass immolations under the car of the Juggernaut were inseparable from the Indian scene. They may have been based upon such second-hand accounts as those given by Manrique: 'They voluntarily offer up their wretched lives, throwing themselves down in the centre of the road along which the procession passes with its chariots full of idols. These pass over their unhappy bodies, leaving them crushed and mutilated. Such men are looked on as martyrs.' Even now devotional frenzy may demand a lesser sacrifice. A friend, a native of Puri and witness to a number of processions, saw a man cut off his tongue and offer it to the image. Onlookers, even in these days, were some- times roused to a pitch of fervour, he said, causing them to slash their throats, although in symbolic fashion, producing spectacular, although non-fatal results.

With nearly half the day still in hand this seemed the opportunity for the excursion to the site of the battle between the Emperor Ashoka and the King of Kalinga for control of a sizeable portion of the ancient world. It is in the delta area of the Devi, the Kusha and Bhargabi rivers, up one or other of which – most likely the first named – Manrique travelled through such enchanting sylvan scenery after his arrival in India. Now whatever trees had been spared by the woodcutters must have been carried away by the annual floods consequent upon deforestation. With all that, and despite the change, this riverine landscape retained its own kind of inoffensive beauty – at least in the dry season, although it was hard to imagine the furious inundations of the monsoons. A sweep of fields down to the water's edge had been patterned like a patchwork quilt with brilliant geo- metrical shapes upon which the spring's snatch-crops were being grown. Where the receding waters had left stagnant pools a little amateurish fishing was going on and children were sailing boats knocked together by their fathers in a few inches of water rippling over white, polished stones at the river's edge. Three hundred and fifty years ago, Manrique had written of parrots and peacocks. Now there were glossy, black crows pecking over the mud at the edge of the pools. This was a calm vista – there was nothing of tropical extremism in the scene.

It was fertile soil too, enriched a little annually, in the style of the Nile valley, by silt deposited by the river in spate. There were many small villages, and in most years at monsoon time the floods poured over or through them. This being so, only a clear six months were available to till the soil, sow and harvest the crops and attend to all the other matters of production, growth and defence against annual near-catastrophe. Everything in these villages seemed to be overshadowed by the short-term passage of time, in the certain knowledge that by a set date the shallow river-bed would fill, overflow and the waters released would be lapping against the makeshift walls.

Hirapur was an enchanting place, devoted to the making of temple bells – a form of cottage industry carried out in so many hut-like buildings scattered through the village that the tinkling, musical concussion of hammers on brass came from every direction, and was never out of the ears. It began at close quarters as a peremptory black-smith's chink of hammer on anvil, but distance trans-formed it so that the hutments at the far end of the village seemed to conceal aviaries of excited birds. The work was done in hectic, fire-lit gloom; an infernal chaos of noise and heat in which order must have been concealed, round an open furnace on the floor. Bellows were pumped to flush darting sparks into the air. Men groped with tongs in the flames to pull out fiery ingots, dropping these on metal slabs by which specialists waited with their hammers. The hammers clanged down, jarring the eardrums and flattening the brass. Experts at shaping took over. The bells were dowsed in water and hammered again. Metal workers had always been the highest of the artisan castes. By local standards they made good money – fifty rupees, the equivalent of £1.60, a day – and could afford to send their daughters by rickshaw to a nearby school, a valuable precaution in a society in which female mobility comes under suspicion, and is the subject of strict control.

In Hirapur monkey gods keep an eye open for people who walk over thresholds without removing their shoes – a major solecism in this village – but their principal occupation is to keep watch on floods, and for this purpose they are placed at strategic points along the perimeter. The goddess Lakshmi also helps with flood defences and almost every house was decorated with the most elaborate symbolic designs to enlist her support in keeping out the water. This attractive custom has spread throughout the villages of Orissa, although I was never to see examples of the art-form quite to equal those of Hirapur. These designs are created by the womenfolk of the village. Originality of motif is sought after, and the very best work is said to be inspired by dreams. Otherwise the women take their inspiration from the bustle of everyday village life: its traffic of bullock carts and jeeps, worshippers at the temple, a political rally, a procession with loudspeakers and flags.

In the best specimen I found at Hirapur, all the walls including those of a large courtyard had been densely covered with stylised flowers, butterflies and musical instruments, painted in white on an ultramarine background. Most Indian village people – as all the travellers of the past have recorded – are extremely hospitable. It was only necessary to show interest in the paintings for doors immediately to be opened, with a hearty invitation to come in and look round. In the villages of the interior such Lakshmi paintings, executed under various local names, are painted and repainted with some frequency while those carried out in the street on the threshold of a house to invite the goddess to enter will be repainted every night. The Hirapur masterpieces are renewed every year, on the eve of the feast of Lakshmi . . . otherwise, as the lady of the household explained, the goddess would be bored. She added that it had taken her about five hours to carry out this major piece of creation, fitted into what time she could spare between the household tasks. When I complimented her on the unusual design she said that the goddess, famous in the locality for her musical tastes, had put the idea into her head. She felt sure that the result had met with divine approval. So far it had been a good year.

Hirapur is full of interest. The large tank permanently fringed with children splashing among the lotuses and aquatic plants is not only an indispensable convenience but saturated with beneficial influences, for a large number of images illustrating the carver's art over many centuries have been recovered from the mud. Nearby is the sixth-century open-air temple of the sixty-four yoginis, one of the four of its kind existing in India. The yoginis are lesser goddesses enabled by their not too exalted status to interest themselves in the solution of minor human problems, and consequently highly popular among ordinary working folk. All sixty-four of them are splendidly carved on the temple's circular wall, shown in the style of the period in vigorous action of the kind associated with their special powers. A few arms and legs were broken off at the time of a Muslim incursion, but as the stone employed is exceptionally hard, religious vandalism was no more than symbolic. Few people seem to know of the temple's existence.

Dhauli hill overlooks the river a mile or two upstream, and on both banks immediately below took place one of the decisive battles of the ancient world – the encounter between the Emperor Ashoka, who by 250 BC had conquered almost the whole of the sub-continent, and the King of Kalinga. The forces of Kalinga were annihilated, and an imperial inscription speaks of several hundred thousand battle casualties, followed by the deportation en masse of the survivors. At this point the Emperor is supposed to have been overcome by remorse, and to have embraced the Buddhist philosophy of non-violence, thereafter succeeding in the tricky task of conducting the affairs of the empire while turning to ascetic practices and becoming himself a monk. There were family precedents for adoption in later life of extreme forms of belief, for Ashoka's grandfather Chandragupta, who campaigned successfully against the Hellenic Greeks in north-west India, followed his victory by becoming a Jain and entering a monastery. Here he deliberately starved himself to death in orthodox Jain fashion. The turn around in Ashoka's case was almost equally dramatic, for the Mauryan Empire was based on a successful espionage system with spies working in the guise of recluses, householders, merchants, ascetics, mendicant women and prostitutes. From this unpromising ethical start, and with the final battle behind him, the Emperor moved on to his formulation of *Dhamma*, the universal Law of Righteousness, of which much is made in the Ashoka rock edicts carved at many sites throughout the length and breadth of the country.

It is assumed by many Buddhists that it was following the great victory that what had up to this time been no more than the credences of an Indian sect were carried forward on the impetus of imperial backing to become the religion of much of the eastern world. This was the belief motivating the Japanese who arrived on the spot in 1972 to erect a Buddhist Peace Pagoda on the summit of Dhauli hill. This stark white building, shaped in a way that recalls a medieval samurai's war helmet, is highly unsympathetic to the environment.

At the foot of the hill India's earliest rock-carving, taking the form of an elephant, surmounts one of the Ashokan inscriptions – in this case a collection of edicts which, although for the most part perfectly legible, were not deciphered until 1837. They are accompanied by an atrocious translation into English.

There is no way of knowing whether the edicts ramble on in the original Brahmi in this muddled and sometimes incoherent fashion. Here we are presented with a mixed assortment of imperial pronouncements – copied in style it is supposed by some from those of Darius – random moralising, and philosophical asides interspersed with detailed instructions to the Emperor's morality police, created some twelve years after his reign began. The Emperor apologised for a course of actions that departs from the principles of non-violence, but explains with extraordinary frankness, 'It is difficult to perform virtuous deeds.' At this juncture Ashoka's Dhamma was beginning to take shape, some aspects of it being revolutionary indeed.

In the earliest of the edicts – which in their entirety cover a time-spread of fifteen years – Ashoka concentrates, remarkably enough, on the welfare of animals. It suggests a rapid and compulsory conversion of his subjects to vegetarianism, and the emperor refers with distaste to the previous gluttony of the court. 'Formerly in the royal kitchen many hundreds of thousands of animals were killed daily for the sake of curry. But now only three animals are being killed, namely two peacocks and a deer, and even this deer not regularly. Even these three animals shall not be killed in future.' The sacred cow was well established in the third century BC, for the second edict is concerned largely with its welfare. Medical treatment was established by the King for his subjects, but also for cattle. 'Wherever there were no herbs that are beneficial to men and cattle, they were imported and planted. Roots and fruit were also planted. On the roads, wells were dug and trees planted for the use of cattle and men.'

Twelve years followed the Emperor's anointing before the Mahamatras of the morality force received their orders, which were repeatedly emphasised in subsequent edicts. They were to ensure proper courtesy to slaves and servants, reverence to elders, abstention from the killing of animals, moderation in spending and possessions, and liberality to the religious poor. 'All men are my children,' said the Emperor. 'I desire that they may be provided with happiness in this world and the next.' The morality officers were to furnish prisoners with money, and in the case of those with 'bewitched children' or aged parents to support, to free them from their fetters.

The Dhamma of Ashoka had something about it of the New Man political philosophy of the South American revolutionaries of the sixties. Both failed to some extent through the impossibility of defining and setting bounds upon the idealism motivating the struggle. It was hard to conceive of the principles of Dhamma enshrined in a state institution, and non-violence and imperial administration were badly matched. A sort of priesthood evolved to defend the Emperor's growing obsession with virtue, becoming in the nature of things a self-protective orthodoxy resistant to change. For a few more years slaves were treated kindly and prisoners with aged parents or bewitched children freed from their shackles, but with Ashoka's death India returned to the cast-iron rule of certainty and submission.

FIFTEEN

BOSE'S RECOMMENDATION OF a visit to Chilika Lake was one of his suggested side-trips that interested me most. Over the years I had done a fair amount of sporadic and disorganised bird-watching, and never missed on any journey an opportunity to look at birds. It was an outing, nevertheless, that I approached with certain reservations. I had actually heard of Chilika before coming to India, remembering that it had been spoken of by ornithologists as one of the most interesting bird sanctuaries in the world. For all that I had reason to consider myself as hardly more fortunate in the business of sighting rare birds than impressive animals. I went on such forays armed with hope but armoured by the unexciting experiences of the past against disappointment.

Chilika Lake is enormous, having an area of 425 square miles. The first view of it from a hilltop was remarkable, for there was no way of knowing that I was not looking down on the open sea, although the unruffled shallow water over a bottom of white sand appeared as a sea of milk, and its great luminosity imparted a sullen purplish tinge to the sky. Island shapes were sketched in here and there on the surface, and a number of fishermen's boats in thin black silhouette seemed to intensify the whiteness of the water.

The foreshore under Barkul village had been left to its own devices. It was edged with mud, and contained a number of boulders and unidentifiable masonry half-sunk in rock pools. In this setting a great assortment of small sea-shore birds, black-winged stilts, avocets, ruffs and coursers of the kind now rare in Europe scuttled from pool to pool. A hundred yards out on the lagoon a raft of pelicans drifted by, and beyond them ducks of all kinds bobbed about. This promised well, but someone to do with the hotel was quick to dispel illusions as to the possibility of any really exciting avian encounter.

'I am afraid you have arrived just a week or two too late,' he said. 'Now the nesting season is at an end and the birds are about to depart. At the beginning of the month you would have seen black storks from the position in which we are now standing. On the far side of the lagoon you will still be seeing rare cranes. Also I am told up to 1,000 flamingos including some of the lesser variety. To view them you would require to take a boat, one hour and a half in each direction.'

'I would be very happy to do that,' I said.

'Alas today that would not be possible. All the boats have been booked by parties wishing to visit the shrine of the goddess Kali Jai on one of the islands. There will be many people, but as you may imagine, no birds.'

If I wished to take lunch at the hotel, the man warned me, it might be a good thing to do so forthwith, otherwise with the press of business there might be a long delay. Several buses had in fact just arrived and were disgorging numerous passengers, largely fraught and excited parents accompanied by their many phlegmatic, self-possessed children. This was clearly to be another Indian family occasion. Charming as it was the hotel was singularly ill-equipped to deal with multitudes on pilgrimage. By way of a lavatory it offered a large single room containing several brooms, cans of paint, rope, an outboard engine, a pedestal in a corner and a cistern that could be induced to release a brief drizzle of water. With the arrival of the buses a long and, in parts, agitated queue formed at the door, and it was some hours before this entirely dispersed.

The boats mustered to carry the pilgrims to the island awaited at the water's edge, long, low in the water, rather frail-looking, painted with all-seeing eyes and naive representations of lake birds, and possessing a single square sail. They were perfectly adapted to the fishing requirements of a calm, shallow lagoon, and I suspected that apart from the recent addition in each case of a small outboard engine they had remained as they were now for thousands of years. I joined a boatful of visitors which puttered slowly towards Kali Jai island where the goddess had been installed in her cave. An Indian sitting next to me told me what it was all about. At some time in the far past a local girl was to be taken by boat to her marriage in the village of her husband on the other side of the lagoon. Last-minute difficulties arose through the non-availability of any male member of the family except the girl's father to escort her to the wedding, and for the father to do so was a serious breach of custom. Nevertheless the family, father included, boarded the boat and set out, but halfway across the lake, at the moment of passing the small island for which we were bound, a sudden retributory squall blew up, the boat was overturned, and the girl seen no more. The search for her was continued by the father until sunset, when his daughter's voice spoke to him from the water. 'I have left this world to become a goddess. Now I am Kali Jai. Make a shrine for me on this island.' The village girl is now accepted as having been an incarnation of Kali, and although hardly known in other parts of the country, her reputation in Orissa and West Bengal – including Calcutta – where she is worshipped as goddess of family troubles, is enormous. 'People do not come here to see the lake, nor are they interested in the birds,' said my informant. 'It is this goddess who interests them, who is very close to their hearts.'

The story of the girl drowned on her wedding day who becomes a goddess is typical of the East, and one of the genre based upon hope turned through breach of custom to despair that crops up in various forms in the countries of eastern Asia, and to a lesser extent halfway across the world. Can it be a matter of spontaneous generation, or is there some mysterious breeding ground from which such legends spread? Take for example the principal item of a Welsh myth, located in an actual village, Myddfai, in Dyfed. The story is that in the eleventh century, a fairy emerging from the waters of a nearby lake was persuaded to marry a village boy, providing him with an ample dowry of cattle summoned by her from the lake. Stipulations were imposed. Should he in the course of the marriage strike her three times she would leave him. This, inevitably although largely by accident, he did, and the lady, taking her cows with her, vanished again under the waters. By tradition there were offspring of the marriage. A local doctor of half-fairy origin is commemorated in a stone set at the entrance to the village church, being one of a clan of medical men of mixed human and fairy

antecedents known as the physicians of Myddfai, the last
of whom, having abandoned medicine, kept a shop in a
nearby town and died about thirty years ago.

It is a legend repeated almost to the last detail
throughout the world. In 1944, engaged in the lugubrious
duty of escorting Asiatic prisoners back to Russia, I was
entertained, almost nightly, by recitations of Uzbek folk
tales. Among them was the story of the girl drowned on
her wedding day who becomes a demon. Among them,
also, was the supposedly Celtic Lady of the Lake with
hardly a detail changed from the Welsh version. The
Myddfai story, too, features in Indian mythology except
that she abandons her human lover, vanishing with her
flocks beneath the waters as soon as she is pregnant, and
there is no talk of a subsequent birth. Thus, perhaps, in
shadowy folk-memory are recorded the sorrows of pre-
history.

While on shore the pilgrims had seemed to keep their
distance from one another, to remain isolated in self-
contained families and groups, and there was a certain
formality in the air. From the moment of setting out on
the water, wedged often precariously in position on the
swaying, overloaded boats – sometimes even obliged to
clutch at a stranger for support – they were suddenly
infused with holiday jollity and high spirits. The grown-
ups chatted happily with whoever they found themselves
squeezed up against, laughing at whatever was said, and
sometimes even did their best to clown a little, while their
previously sedate children were as jubilant and
obstreperous as they were expected to be.

So sudden, unexpected and complete was the transformation that I suspected it was part of the protocol of

the pilgrimage. Those who consume the ritual meal they prepare for the god are supposed to exhibit a satisfaction to be transmitted in essence to the deity, and it was reasonable to hope that Kali Jai would enter into the spirit of a joyous occasion. Whatever the ancient tragedy the festival may commemorate, the custom of the East is to dress in new clothing, to be effusively companionable, to eat the best food that can be produced, to play inspiring music, and let off noisy fireworks if this is permissible. Kali Jai is a scaled-down version of the Kali of Calcutta who, despite her fearsome reputation, was created by the gods as destroyer of demons. The original Kali is a valuable ally in the battle against major catastrophe, against cholera, the floods or even the Naxalites. Kali Jai, who inspires no fear, helps out with the lesser predicaments such as stomach ulcers, bad examination results, or the loss of a job.

Incense floating in clouds from the island reached us when we were still fifty yards from the shore. The island was dense with smoke from the charcoal fires lit by picnicking families who had arrived in such numbers that it was difficult to chart the way over the rocks round them. Feeding operations, as usual, were conducted with immense ceremony, and the use of a great variety and size of pots. Some families had brought along elaborate barbecues, which had to be put together before the cooking began. A number of stalls selling the usual sweets, nuts and souvenirs were jammed into a minute square of tableland at the top of the island, to one side of which steps led down to the narrow entrance to the cave containing the goddess. A small statue of her as a pretty young girl had been built into the wall of the little temple, but, dehumanised by design in the cave below, she was little more than a head wearing a sexless mask, and a featureless bodily shape draped by a patchwork of brightly flowered materials that represented a dress. This rag-doll effigy was seen through a curtain of dangling votive offerings of human bodily parts, cockerels and goats, cut and hammered out of tin.

The visit was a homely procedure. For once a foreigner was accepted, seemingly even welcomed, in a queue at a shrine. I rang the bell at the entrance to announce my presence, made an offering, accepted the ritual sliver of coconut from the priest, exchanged congratulatory smiles with the women who followed me, and went out. Outside children had clustered to eat rice cakes scalding from the pan while others tried rather hopelessly to play hopscotch in the few spare feet of vacant space among the stalls. Several transistors tuned to the same station softly brayed film music.

I was found by the friend I had made on the boat, who hauled himself up through the crowd, roaring with astonished laughter. His eyes glittered with euphoria and the upswing of his luxuriant moustaches seemed to have developed a lighter curl. He had paid his respects to the goddess, and had a feeling that everything had gone well.

'But how are we to cope with all these pilgrims I am asking?' he said. Now, with the increase in people's troubles, and therefore the increased following of the goddess herself, the problem was how to pack all the visitors on to the island. At the feast of Makrar Sakranti, celebrated earlier in the month, the boats had circled for hours waiting to disembark passengers. Once ashore they had been jammed together in a static mass so that many pilgrims had had difficulty in reaching the shrine. There was some talk of increasing the size of the island by concrete blocks of the kind used in sea walls. But opinion was divided, some saying that it would be unsuitable if not actually sacrilegious. 'On this matter,' he said, 'they will never agree.' If only a decision could be left to Kali Jai herself, he thought. That would be the ideal solution.

TO THE TRIBAL
HEARTLAND

ON MONDAY THERE was a phone message at the hotel saying that Bose would like to see me as soon as possible. When I tried to ring back I was told there was a delay of uncertain length, so I decided to check out. This, since there were bills to be paid, called for a second trip over to the State Bank of India at Puri.

Up to this point I knew Indian banks only by repute, and while it could not be said that I particularly looked forward to the visit I was prepared to write it off as an episode of travel that might add a few sentences to the account of a country in which such institutions are perfectly adapted to the environment.

At first glance the bank at Puri was like any other large bank, with the air-conditioning breathing out its faintly conventual odour of stale paper, and the meek, bovine queues of customers unmanned by the terrific indifference of the staff and the uselessness of protest. The bank had established its autocracy by a large, curt notice framed with small marginal decorations like an imperial Russian Ukaze. *COMPLAINTS DAYS. Customers of the bank having complaints are invited to see the Assistant-manager on Tuesdays and Thursdays.* I noticed a long, narrow bench of the kind on which visitors to

Spanish model prisons are seated to await their turn to be admitted, and this was crowded with customers anxiously eyeing a large clock which, like those in British taverns – and presumably for the same reason – was ten minutes in advance of the correct time.

The long wait I was prepared for at the currency exchange took place while the counter clerk dealt with the huge monetary transactions and the paper-work of those ahead of me in the queue. Finally my turn came, and the clerk took my passport and traveller's cheques and, having subjected them to a long scrutiny, signalled me to countersign the cheques. This I did. He examined the result, but was clearly dissatisfied. 'Please sign once more,' he said. It was evident that the second attempt was unsatisfactory too, for he went away to discuss the matter with a superior seated at a desk, who followed him back to the counter. 'The signatures do not tally,' the superior said. 'We must go to see the assistant-manager.'

All these men including the assistant-manager wore watches of exceptional quality; the higher the position with the bank the better the watch, and the better the watch the more sympathetic its wearer. To the counter clerk I was no more than a face in an obscure multitude. His superior, who saw fewer people, was reasonably polite, and the assistant-manager, emerging from the comparative solitude of his office, went so far as to apologise for the trouble to which I was being put. Nevertheless he felt obliged to ask me to produce a few more examples of my signature, and when this had been done shook his head sadly. 'Every one is different,' he said.

'But surely, all signatures are,' I protested.

'Yes,' he said. 'If the counter-signatures appear as

identical a suspicion of forgery may even arise, but in this case the disparity is very great.' He glanced at his splendid watch and clucked exasperation. 'We are bound to refer this to the manager, but most unfortunately he is out for a short time. I am sorry. Perhaps you would not object to going to the waiting room? I am sure he will not be long.'

The waiting room was the bench along the wall and it was here that I happened to sit next to James Womack, a man with a soft voice and a slow sleepy smile who had not the slightest objection to spending the better part of a morning on a narrow bench in an Indian bank.

'Been here long?' I asked him, not realising this.

He considered the question. 'I suppose I have,' he said. 'Quite a while.' He told me he was waiting for a call to Bangalore about a bank transfer that should have come through and had not. 'It'll take an hour or two,' he said. 'What does it matter? This is India. Everything here takes three times as long as anywhere else. So what? All you do is adjust your sense of time.' His tone suggested that delays were part of the charm of the country. He was an Australian from Sydney, a member of a group-practice specialising in homeopathic medicine, and had come to this country to advance the scope of his studies, where he had based himself in Bangalore. Now he was in Bhubaneswar for a short stay and a course in herbal remedies, for which it was a centre – well known even in Australia.

Where was he staying in Bangalore? I asked, and he told me at an ashram, not far from the town.

'Boiled rice, meditation and Vedic mantras?' I suggested.

He laughed softly. 'Well not quite,' he said. 'Something like that, but you can have a lot of fun. Have you ever stayed in an ashram?'

'On one occasion, yes.'

'Which one was that?'

'The ashram of Sri Aurobindo at Pondicherry,' I told him. 'A long, long time ago. My second trip to India.'

'That must have been a great experience,' he said, but by the way he looked at me I was not sure that he was convinced that this had really happened.

Everybody on our bench had been given a ticket with a number on it and when this number lit up on a grille under the clock it meant that the holder was wanted at the counter. After ten minutes or so Womack's number was flashed. He got up, but soon came back smiling as though someone had made him a present. 'False alarm,' he said cheerfully. 'Just to say there's another hour's delay. I was wondering, when you were at the ashram, did you have any contact with Sri Aurobindo himself?'

'He was dead by then. The Mother had taken over.'

He nodded. 'Did you see something of her?'

'Most evenings at the nut-giving ceremony. I was allowed to touch her sari at the first ceremony I attended. The secretary who took charge of me told me how it was done. She might speak to me, he said. Then I could take a fold of the sari between the first and middle finger of the right hand. He told me I might experience a discharge of power passing into my body.'

'And did you?'

'No,' I said.

His disappointment was clear. 'Maybe you were not ready for it,' he said. 'Tell me how she looked.'

'She looked like a little old French woman, which she was, although she was always dressed in Indian style. Her face was covered in make-up. She wore platform shoes with silver buckles and she had very bright eyes, like a lizard.'

'I have a book about her,' Womack said. 'She drew people to her like a magnet.'

'Yes,' I said. 'She did that. There were five hundred or so in the ashram when I was there, about seventy or eighty English of the upper classes. She took their possessions into her care and set them to work in the orchards. They did it for their food. That was enough. Nobody complained.'

'Would you expect them to?' Womack asked. 'Money would have been no concern to them.'

'I'm sure it wasn't. I got to know a man called John. He used to teach at Oxford and he was there with his wife. He was keen on photography and one day he asked the Mother if he could buy a camera. "Wait my son," she told him. "The opportunity will come" – which it did. A few days later a Frenchman came in and turned over his belongings, among them a camera. She gave it to John. He saw it as a kind of miracle.'

'It wasn't, though,' Womack said. 'There was a natural causation. Happenings like that are of daily occurrence at Bangalore. You might find them strange, but they're not. What mystifies me is how you managed to get into Pondicherry. I wonder if you're quite the type,' He laughed pleasantly. 'Excuse me for putting it like that.'

'I ran into some rich Americans who were staying there. They poured money into the ashram and were put up in its rest-house which was quite luxurious. Their idea was to make a disciple out of me and they got a secretary called Mr Padu to show me the ropes.' The mere mention of his name was enough to remind me of every detail of his face and voice. 'Please to wash most carefully in preparation for the meal. One piece of bread only. You may ask for sugar. If you cannot be seated with comfort on the floor I will bring you to a table.' The hollow-eyed English disciples squatted there in the background of memory, scrabbling with their fingers in the vegetable curry. Some had been at work in the fields since dawn, and this meal had been preceded by gymnastics and meditation. They were always eager to be allowed to explain why they had exchanged the middle- or upper-class way of life for the present one, which came close to that of a coolie. 'You see there are no problems, no doubts. Mother knows what is best for us.'

There was a confusion, with lights flashing on and off over the grille. Womack, accompanied by several of our neighbours on the bench, went to see what it was all about. They returned, with Womack's cheerful exception, gesturing exasperation.

'We're into regular flower-distribution in Bangalore,' he said, 'but your nut-giving ceremony is something new to me. Was this an important aspect of the ashram routine?'

'*The* most important,' I said. 'The idea was based on an army parade. We had an ex-regimental sergeant-major from the British Army. The Mother sat on a throne with a halo painted on the wall at the back of her head, and when the sergeant-major called us to attention she climbed down from the throne for her inspection. He walked beside her with a stick under his arm. After that came one of the secretaries carrying what they called "the book". He was supposed to note down cases of slackness, like they do in the army. Behind him was the man carrying the bowl of nuts.'

'You're kidding,' Womack said. He seemed to be laughing more at me than at what I was telling him.

'That's how it happened,' I told him. 'Every evening at six on the dot.'

'I only wish I could have been there in your place. Didn't this have any effect on your outlook?'

'A slight one. I used to watch John who had taught at Oxford weeding beans, and wonder.'

'Why shouldn't he?' Womack asked. 'It was good for him.'

'I'm sure it was. The Mother never weeded beans. She looked after the investments and drove in a big limousine.'

'That was good for her.'

'Mr Padu said he had worked with me in a previous incarnation,' I told him. 'All the ashram members had worked with each other. They had come there drawn along lines of magnetic force from all over the world to link up again. The ones I talked to about it had spent what they could remember of past lives in interesting places. John thought he could remember something of the court of the Moghul Emperor.'

'He was to be envied,' Womack said. 'He may have reached a spiritual summit most of us have still to climb.'

'Yes, but I stayed where I was, down at the bottom of the hill. Padu wouldn't give up. He put me through a few yoga exercises and tried to teach me how to stop thinking for a few minutes at a time, which was a big step towards developing consciousness.'

'But it was no go?'

'Not in my case, no. I bought a set of Sri Aurobindo's works and we parted on good terms. The books came in handy as souvenirs for friends. Some seemed grateful and even impressed, but I could make very little of them. Perhaps it was impossible to express his thoughts in straightforward English. Whatever it was, they were Greek to me. I just couldn't understand.'

Womack said he expected to be back in Bangalore in a week or two's time, and would there be any chance of seeing me there? He was very keen to hear more about the Mother, whose reputation so far as he was concerned had not suffered from my account. Above all he wanted to introduce me to his ashram, where no one had to work, or even pay for their food, and there were no gurus riding in big cars, and maybe one of the near miracles regularly performed might be arranged for my benefit. It was left that we would meet again in Bangalore if that proved to be possible. Within minutes my light showed up and I was called to the counter to be told that the manager was back and agreed that the cheques might be paid. The operation had taken not quite an hour.

I took a taxi to Bose's office in Bhubaneswar, arriving just in time to delay his departure for his siesta.

'Everything is fixed up,' he said. 'The police permit has come through, and the man I told you about will be available to accompany you.'

'The one who speaks tribal languages?'

'Three of them. This is important for you. He has also spent a long time among the Saoras, who are the largest tribe in this vicinity. He will be showing you something of the Kondh, who were accustomed until recent years to perform human sacrifices. Also if there are no problems he will take you to the Parajas, the Godbas, the Mirigans and the Koyas. You will remember the story of my trouble with the Bondas. You will go there, too. By the latest news I have received they are not very much changed, and for you that is interesting.'

I asked if an itinerary had been worked out and he said that was not possible. There were security difficulties in some of the areas which could change from day to day. There was a cutting ready on his desk from a recent issue of the *Illustrated Weekly of India*. It was a very long report on the current state of Bastar with a number of passages underlined:

> officials are deeply concerned that Naxalite extremists belonging to the People's War Group whose main base is in the adjoining districts of Andhra Pradesh have now spread to Southern Bastar and who have acquired sophisticated weapons like AK-47 rifles . . . these squads have been held responsible for various violent actions like gun-snatchings, burnings of bases and trucks . . . They are suspected to have indulged in at least 7 murders . . . to have led a mass dacoity . . . released 3 under-trial prisoners from Jagdalpur jail . . . 1,400 troops are stationed in various villages . . . it is significant that most of the activists killed by the police are tribal themselves.

'I remember that on the last occasion, you were wishing to go to Jagdalpur,' Bose said. 'It is not certain that this would be permitted. Frequently the problem is with the police. Where there are such happenings they are worried by the presence of supposed spies. If there are incidents, they do not wish them to be seen. This may be declared a prohibited area.'

He brightened as a consoling possibility struck him. 'What is wrong with an excursion along the Bastar border? This is possible for you, and really there is no difference. To see the country is the same, and the Kondh tribal people are the same on either side. There is one village where an Italian went to study tribal medicine, but no other foreigner I think. You may see this village. To go to the Bondas you must pass by Koraput. This, too, is full of Naxalites. Last week they kidnapped five policemen, but so far there is no prohibition if you have a permit.'

Thus the journey into the deep south of Orissa and the north-eastern corner of Andhra Pradesh was arranged, planned as an easy run through hilly, fairly frequented countryside for the first 300 miles or so, to be followed by an exploration as far as roads existed of the labyrinthine mountain valleys of the south where, I was assured, the main interest of the expedition lay.

The young man Bose had found to accompany me, Ranjan Prasad, and the driver Dinesh presented themselves at the Ashok Hotel at 7 am the next day. Ranjan was dark, with strongly featured good looks, an extremely enthusiastic man in his late twenties, a backsliding Brahmin who both ate meat and drank alcohol, and a history graduate specialising in temple architecture. His father was a school teacher, now retired to a smallholding having sold much of his land to provide dowries for his three sisters. His interest in tribal peoples stemmed from his birth in a village on the edge of tribal territory. This had made him familiar with their many problems. He lost no opportunity, he said, to revisit the tribes. There was an underlying hint that there had been a romantic adventure.

Despite the vagueness on the part of the suggested

itinerary, Bose had provided a fairly positive schedule which Ranjan seemed to wave aside. He was also sceptical about the packed lunches suggested for the journey. In Bhubaneswar, yes, packed lunches might be considered reasonable – but after that, what? Where were the sandwiches coming from in the Orissan back of beyond? Better to be realistic, he thought, and be ready to live off the land. At this point he mentioned that the driver, Dinesh, was a strict vegetarian, and unable to tolerate even the spectacle of others eating meat, including ham sandwiches. Despite his nonchalant attitude in the matter of provisions, Ranjan agreed that bottled water was essential, and a large reserve of this was at that moment being loaded into the car. This was an Ambassador, an Indian version of the 1954 Morris Oxford with slightly more power than the original accompanied by the asperities to be expected in what was in effect vintage motoring.

At the moment of setting off there was a surprise in store. Two thousand years before, in his ninth edict, Ashoka turned to the task of cutting out unnecessary ceremonies. They were to be restricted to a maximum of four which he saw as too important to be abolished: those connected with birth, the marriage of a daughter, illness and setting out on a journey, and here was Ranjan, wholly a young man of his times, hoping that no objection would be raised to a visit to the temple of Kali to solicit the goddess's support for our enterprise.

The temple was sited among a row of shops on the outskirts of the town. We found cars lined up outside, including some of the better kind such as recent Toyotas, while their owners popped in and out as though calling at a post-office to buy stamps, to give the goddess details of their trips and solicit a blessing. The temple's exterior was half-concealed by a complex structure decorated in fair-ground grotto style, full of allegorical violence. A heavily moustached plaster demon, villainous-looking and near naked, sprawled like a defeated wrestler on the pavement, having suffered an attack by a snarling lion upon which Kali was mounted. She was sternly beautiful, one arm upraised in victory, like a Hindu Britannia. This was the triumph of good over evil.

On its inside the temple was less impressive: a trim, suburban courtyard with a small wall-opening in which a faceless image was embowered among artificial flowers and tin-foil cutouts. At this opening a small queue of obviously busy men had formed to transact whatever business they had with the goddess in the minimum possible time. Ranjan placed himself in line to wait his turn, head bowed, to rattle off a brief account of the purpose of our journey and the itinerary to be taken. The priest materialised, eyes averted, for a contribution taken like a swallow snatching up an insect in flight. With this the encounter was at an end.

The journey began with a straightforward 180 mile-stretch of the NH5 Highway down through the coastal plain to the south with the Ambassador wedged in an endless train of thundering lorries. Once in a while a village had stretched an imploring banner across the road: *'Hello driver – we like you not to put to your speed.'* Such appeals had had small effect. Lorries had plummeted down embankments, toppled over bridges and, in one case, leaped one upon the other, like a praying mantis devouring its prey. Those judged not to be recoverable were in course of dismantling by breakdown gangs swarming over the wreckage like leaf-cutter ants.

A halt was called somewhere about midday at a roadside dhaba decorated with hundreds of paper flags and a single garlanded bottle of Old Tavern whisky – which although not affordable by any customer was regarded as diffusing good luck. Apart from the dusty inferno of passing lorries this was a supremely rural scene. Down the side-turning opposite, a cow-minder was collecting a beast from each house, for a rupee's worth of exercise and grazing on a rubbish tip. A few yards further on where the fields began, three girls dressed traditionally in blue and green saris for the particular task were spreading and turning rice to dry with the rhythmic gestures and steps incorporated in an ancient dance called the *dhemsa*. Here, too, the aerial roots of a vast banyan tree were used by the village children as a swing. In this, and all other villages of the neighbourhood, reserves of rice to last two months were stored in sunken repositories by the roadside with the earth raised in mounds over them, to give the appearance of vast newly heaped-up graves. I was reminded otherwise of the scenery of the Mexican mesa: brilliant blue houses under black rocks. There was something here of Mexico, as well, in the nasal membrane-tingling odour of toasting chillies, the peons asleep with their hats pulled over their eyes, the fighting cocks, and the silent, evasive dogs.

We opened the first and last of the packed lunches. Dinesh got up and moved to the other end of the dhaba and sat with his back to us. Crows that had settled like a coverlet on the next bed but one were galvanised into readiness, unfolding their wings and hopping about in an excited fashion. The owner of the dhaba avoided disturbing them to bring sweet tea flavoured with caraway seeds. Dust-covered drivers came reeling in from the road, drank tea, scooped up a plateful of rice with their fingers, then fell back on their beds for an hour's sleep, while the crows flapped down to clean up the plates.

Pseudo-Mexico with its black rocks, its blue houses, circling buzzards and flowering trees was with us until Berhampur, where the road narrowed, turned off into the hills, and lost most of its traffic. The forests closed in. In the early evening we reached Taptapani on a steep hilltop, a local spa of some renown and famous, says the government brochure, for the wild life to be seen by overnight visitors from the tourist rest-house. Here we stayed, and no halting place could have been better chosen. The animal viewing once again disappointed. Ranjan was enchanted by the sudden flashy appearance of a roller on the boughs of a tree at the edge of the rest-house terrace. This, he assured me, augured good fortune for the trip. Apart from this there was little to report. A few deer were kept in a paddock at the bottom of a hill, and a local boy who came roaring up on a motorbike mentioned seeing elephants a few weeks before from the position in which we sat, but at this moment we might well have been in Surrey. Shortly after this an aged man wandered into sight and seated himself to admire the view. In response to my query, Ranjan asked him how old he was. 'He does not know,' he told me. 'He is a tribal man. All he can say is that the prince gave them sweets three times. Sweets were given every twenty years. That makes him maybe seventy, but he is looking older than that.'

The matter of the roller's encouraging advent came up again. Ranjan appeared to have been emboldened by the auspice and went on not only to confirm Bose's hint that he had involved himself with a tribal girl, but admitted hoping that the opportunity might arise to contact her once again during the course of our journey. To my extreme surprise, he added that an eventual marriage was not beyond the bounds of possibility, and he was reaching the point when a decision had to be made. I assured him of my approval, and co-operation if required. Indeed nothing could have been more welcome to me than participating as a spectator in such an interesting development.

Taptapani was famous for its hot spring inhabited by a mysterious god of fertility who appeared not to possess a name. The sulphurous water issuing at nearly boiling point from a crevice in the mountain-side was piped down to a pool in a clearing above the rest-house. By the time it bubbled up in this the temperature was just bearable for a quick dip by those who came here to benefit from a range of curative effects. A notice on display nearby warned bathers of the requirements of modesty and illustrated correct bathing attire for use by both sexes. At the time of our visit there were no men in sight except a priest and his assistant, but mooching about the place were several dispirited looking ladies who had come from an encampment a short way up the hill. Ranjan, who had been here before, told me these were barren women, in course of treatment, which could be arduous and prolonged. People suffering from such complaints as arthritis and bad backs simply waded into the pool, stayed there splashing about for a few seconds, and climbed out. A barren woman was required to inure herself to high temperatures by increasingly long immersions, and it might take several days to prepare her in this way for what seemed to me the ordeal that awaited her. Seed pods dangled from the branches of a tree overhanging the pool, and the pods upon opening dropped seeds into the water which sunk to the bottom. The cure for barrenness was to enter the exceedingly hot water, grope about in the mud, and recover a seed.

While we looked on a woman attempted this. The priest's assistant took a coconut from his supply, split it open, mixed basil with the milk it contained, then handed it to the priest who rang a bell to alert the god before pouring it into the water. At that point the woman waded in, and with the water reaching her waist, bent down to grope for a seed. The assistant switched on a transistor radio which tinkled an appropriate tune, lit a number of joss-sticks, and the air was full of incense, anxiety and hope.

The attempt – the woman's fourth – failed. This, Ranjan said, was normal. Eventually she would get her seed, and return home with it to face life with renewed confidence.

'And was the treatment successful?' I asked.

'Yes,' he said, 'of course.' A doctor had written about it in a medical journal, and this had led to a mention in the press. Unfortunately, only tough tribal women like those we had seen seemed to be able to stand the scalding involved, and an attempt to modify the treatment for the benefit of the average Hindu wife had not met with success.

Apart from spectacular treatments to be watched, Taptapani offered the huge inducement to the travel-weary of a species of private mini-spa adjacent to the main bedroom. This, in effect, was a colossal bath in

which a swim of a few strokes was possible. The water
that gushed from the faucet was reduced by fifty yards of
piping down from the pool to exactly the right temperature. In such arrangements the curative reek of sulphur
fumes is psychologically as important as near-scalding
water and here the fumes were concentrated enough to
catch at the throat. Only the confirmed hypochondriac
could have resisted the benefits of the experience. Com-
menting on it later to Ranjan over a dish of the inevitable
chicken and chips that had sent Dinesh racing from the
table into the night, I said I felt better than I had for years,
although accepting that it was all in the mind. 'It is all in
the mind,' he agreed, 'but if you believe, then it becomes
real. It is a pity we cannot return to this place at the end of
each day.'

Taptapani was the frontier with Saora territory,
homeland of about 400,000 members of one of India's
most populous and successful tribal peoples. They had
been spread through Orissa since before the Aryan
arrival, although continually pushed back out of the
fertile plains, first by outright invasion and conquest and
later by various forms of expropriation masked by legal
skulduggery of the kind still generally practised. They
were notable for their collection over the centuries of
innumerable gods (a principal one being the earthworm),
and for the complication and cost of their ceremonies. It
is their custom in the case of death to conduct two
funerals, the second of which, a protracted affair known
as the Guar ritual, had bankrupted many families.

The ladies we had seen in search of fruitfulness at
Taptapani were Saoras, and the unnamed fertility god,
too, was in all likelihood from their vast collection. The

local girls from nearby villages belonged to a division of the race known as Sudha Saoras – *sudha* meaning clean – in recognition by their Hindu neighbours of the fact that they no longer ate the meat of the cow. At the far end of the Saora country where the high mountains had discouraged Hindu penetration, the Lanjia Saoras clung wholeheartedly to the old ways, and Ranjan said that the opportunity would arise to see them too.

We left Taptapani at dawn, climbing among misted forests into and over a low mountain range, held up for a moment by another of India's great vistas, with yellow morning light flooding the plain streaked with the brush strokes of shadows cast by the tall palms. The first Sudha Saora village gathered shape by a stream curling through glowing fields, and we stopped, left the car and walked to it.

It was another page of an atlas turned. On the road to Taptapani India had imitated Mexico; here were laid out the softer splendours of one of the countries by the China Sea. Here were the sago palms, first sighted from above, now seen to have pots fixed to their trunks below incisions from which dripped the sweet sap in which fermentation would begin on the same day. Something of the kind was to be seen in Indo-China of old where as here no serious obligations could be undertaken, no troth plighted and no contract sealed without ceremonial imbibings. Generally among the Saora the bride-price includes twenty pots of wine, and none of their innumerable ceremonies can be completed without libations. The theft of alcohol is their most serious crime, resulting sometimes in mortal retribution.

At this hour in the morning the village was the scene of intense activity, with men, women and children at work doing odd jobs and tidying up round the houses, or out in the fields pumping up water, weeding, hoeing, grinding millet, twisting sisal fibre into rope, cleaning out irrigation ditches and bringing in bundles of long, feathery grass with which to make or repair thatches. The place swarmed with animals, with puppies, piglets and bantam chickens, kept – since the Sudha Saora were vegetarians – as pets.

The villagers showed their excitement at the sight of new faces, and were eager to show us round. One thing about their village stood out – its spruceness. Being outside the caste system had left the Saora with no alternative but to clean up for themselves. It was a cool place in a hot country. Unlike the Hindus who being basically migrants from the north, had only been on the scene for 2,000 years, the Saora, having been obliged from time immemorial to defend themselves from the sun, had learned how to do it. They built themselves windowless houses with thick walls of wooden trellis plastered with mud, and two doors in line at back and front kept open to pass the air through. The thatch came as low as three feet from the ground, and was deep enough to accommodate a spacious verandah on which the family spent much of the time. The Saora took pleasure in pointing out and explaining the merits of these architectural features. They were proud of their decorative skills, leaving their walls coloured the rich maroon of the local earth and free of ornament, but carving woodwork, doors, door-posts and lintels in lively animal shapes: rampaging elephants, peacocks in flight, strutting roosters and an occasional whimsical and inoffensive-looking tiger.

The village Gomang – the headman – now trotted into

sight, a pleasant, twinkling little man who, said Ranjan, had taken time to slip on his ceremonial gear: a hat with white plumes, tunic, tasselled loin-cloth, training shoes and a species of silver codpiece, worn in this region perhaps as a badge of office. He had a frank and ready answer for questions. Modhukamba, he said, contained twenty families, totalling 200 people. They lived on cow's milk, various pulses they grew and the income from the sale of tussore silk cocoons – all such production being equally divided in the presence of the village god. The elections at the end of last year had provided a small cash windfall, for he had been able to negotiate a fair price for the community votes. When I showed surprise that such a transaction could be openly discussed, Ranjan explained that vote-selling was the normal practice in all such backward areas, and a vote cast without receiving a cash reward would be unheard of.

Nodding his agreement the Gomang added that the settlement in this case had been unusually generous, for the candidate who had visited the village in person had even presented him with nine pots of mohua flower wine, considered much superior to the liquor of their own production. This would be utilised in a big Guar ceremony, to be held as soon as enough funds had been collected to buy a buffalo for the sacrifice. I raised the question of the Sudha Saora's vegetarian diet, and the Gomang said that this was a rare case when departure from the rule was tolerated. The village priest, a Hindu, would abstain from the ceremony, to be performed instead by a kudan, or shaman. It was by the perform-ance of such rituals, he pointed out, that the village's health and prosperity were maintained. On the topic of health he added that the Hindu priest dealt with minor ailments with considerable success. As for the rest, he capped his ears with his hands in what Ranjan said was a gesture of resignation. Most of the villagers, he said, had never seen a doctor. The nearest town was many miles away, for which reason no child went to school. The whole village was illiterate.

The Gomang was suddenly surrounded by women who made it clear by their gestures that they had a serious problem to discuss. It turned out that they were suffering from the attentions of officials operating the Intensive Tribal Development Programme and, said Ranjan, had at first assumed that we had something to do with the scheme. The programme starts off from the premise that tribal people's unsatisfactory existences can only be improved by government interference. This often takes absurd forms. V.S. Naipaul recalls a project designed to provide farmers of India, whether tribals or not, with bullock carts fitted at unimaginable cost with pneumatic tyres and ball-bearing wheels. Bastar, along with Bihar, is considered as being one of the most exploited and wretchedly backward areas in the world, yet the *Illustrated Weekly of India* reported that a start had been made to improve the situation of the region by the installation of solar lights in some villages, 'which of course do not function'.

In Modhukamba the government Micro-Project seemed even more lunatic in its inspiration. In such communities cow dung is as highly valuable as we had found it to be in Bihar, above all as an ingredient in an ointment applied to sores and for mixing with vegetable dyes. The ITDP had turned up, built a large underground concrete chamber, ordered the villagers to fill it with their precious manure, and closed and sealed the lid, through which a number of copper tubes led into the village houses. The villagers were told that this arrangement would supply gas for their cooking fires – they only had to turn on the tap. This they did, but there was no issue of gas. 'None of the projects worked,' said the magazine article. 'Every programme is ill-conceived and found to be utterly irrelevant in a particular context.' In the case of Modhukamba there was no wood to be had in the neighbourhood, the women said. No other fuel but dung. What were they to do?

SEVENTEEN

EVERY EXPERIENCE OF this journey contradicted the picture of rural India as presented by the films. India has always been shown as overbrimming with people. Here it was lonely. Having left the main coastal road with its unceasing procession of lorries, there was no traffic at all, and on this and succeeding days we drove all day without encountering, except in an occasional small town, a single private car. The fact is that there is virtually no travel in the interior of India. There is nowhere to stay, nowhere to eat, and it is not particularly safe.

We were now making for the area of Gunupur on the Vamsadhara River close to the border with Andhra Pradesh, where the main concentrations of so-called primitive Lanjia Saora are found in high mountains and thick patches of forest. Once again the scenery had undergone an almost theatrical change: a harsh Indian version of the Australian outback: red rocks tumbling through a wood, the black, bustling untidiness of horn-bills in the high branches of trees with sharp, glinting leaves and orange trunks, terracotta earth, the copper faces of Saoras cutting wood with the sound of metal striking metal in a forge.

A dhaba in this isolated spot offered no alternatives for

the midday meal: a narrow hut with crows fluttering over the scraps at the entrance, and a three-legged dog licking at something splashed on the floor. This possessed its own landscape in miniature of eroded hills and dales – even a river in the form of a black dribbling from the kitchen area. Plates made from leaves stitched together with something like toothpicks were stacked on a shelf and a man in a dirty singlet with a bad skin condition of the forearms took down three of them, and wiped away the red dust using the rag with which he had just pushed the sodden rice left by the last customer from the table top. On to each of these leaf-plates he ladled a dollop of rice, then went off to return with earthenware saucers containing fiery mixtures of vegetables cooked with chillies.

The moment had arrived once again, after so many years of lack of practice, to eat soggy rice with the fingers, an operation never at best elegant in the eyes of the onlooker and intolerably messy until the knack has been acquired. The local method was to pick up and compress the gobbet of rice with the tips of the five fingers, raise it to the lips, then propel it into the mouth with a sharp upward thrust of the thumb. Thereafter – and this was new to me – the diner would dislodge the grains of rice adhering to his fingers with a jerk of the wrist scattering them about the floor where the three-legged dog awaited.

Discreetly I studied the performance of Ranjan and our driver, watching for fine points. Both, as to be expected, were excellent. The rice I scattered went in all directions; their scatterings were contained within the circumference of a circle no more than a foot across. The meal was conducted in total silence on our part, that of the dhaba staff, and the two Saora woodcutters, with fine, aqualine, slightly predatory faces, seated in a far corner and flicking their fingers free of rice with graceful, patrician gestures. At the door the man in the dirty singlet waited to pour water over our hands. The crows were trying to get at a silver lizard that had taken refuge from them under the Ambassador.

Suddenly we were in an area of Christian missionary effort and conversion. The Indian government had consistently opposed the presence of missionaries in wholly Hindu areas, but tolerated Christian evangelism in tribal country such as this, persuaded that the integration of the tribals into the national society can best be effected by the demolition of tribal customs and religious beliefs. The Catholics and Lutherans have long shared the harvest of souls and continue, often in fierce competition, to confuse potential converts who find it hard to understand why the same God is to be reached by such widely divergent paths. To its credit the government has banned fundamentalist sects of the kind involved in recent years in Latin-American scandals in which they have been charged with forcible conversion and genocide.

The first indications of missionary presence and success were graveyards with large white crosses planted in the red earth on the outskirts of tribal villages. Cremation, said Ranjan, had always been practised except in cases of persons dying from unnatural causes, whom it had been the custom to bury. Burial was thus associated with tragedy, calling for discussion among the elders as to the extra funeral rites required to succour and appease an unhappy soul. In all parts of India, Ranjan said, it was the same. The missionaries bought conversion with food and medicine. They were the only source of

anti-malarial pills in the anopheles-ridden mountain villages of the Saora country. If the Saoras were only
required to say, 'Yes, I believe in God,' before receiving
the hand-out, he thought it would have been an excellent
thing. It turned out that much more than that was
expected in exchange to complete the deal. The Saora
had to convince the good father, or the Christian evan-
gelist, that he no longer believed in the Earth Mother, the
gods of fire and water, the gods and goddesses in charge
of the fertility of a whole assortment of crops, in the Lord
of Thunder, the Guardian of Roads, in Thakurani, the
blackened pole under its thatched roof defending the
village, in the goddesses of each individual household, the
cobra god to be placated with flute music and fed with
rice and milk, and Labusum, Divine Earth Worm and
Creator of the World. The Saoras saw no objection to
adding the Christian deity to the others, but even with
the magic tablets within their grasp were profoundly
troubled at the obligation of doing away with all the rest.

Back in the rainy season when malaria reached epidemic proportions the Gomang of another Saora village
had discussed his problem with Ranjan.

'We Saora have many gods,' he said.

'You do,' Ranjan agreed.

The Gomang, like the rest of his people, was in-
numerate. 'Could you help me to work out the number
of these?' he asked.

Ranjan and the Gomang totted up the various names,
adding two or three who were considered too powerful
or dangerous to be mentioned by name, and could only
be alluded to in a roundabout and placatory fashion. A
total of twenty-three was agreed upon.

'Most of them have always been kind and useful to us,'

the Gomang said. 'The missionary is asking us to exchange twenty-three for one, plus a month's supply of Nivaquin. It seems unreasonable.'

In Latin America the liberation theology of the Catholic Church has gone hand in hand with a new sympathy and even respect for tribal culture. In India, instead, the Church seems to have moved closer to non-conformist fundamentalism, and there was a whiff of old-fashioned crusading fervour in the air following a recent event in the small town of Mokama, through which we passed.

Despite the bloody communal riots at the time of the last election – now generally believed to have been politically instigated – Indians as a general rule are immensely tolerant of the religious practices of their neighbours, so often mixed together in communities of Hindus, Christians and Muslims. To take an example, the first Indian friend I made while in Kerala was a Christian married to a Hindu wife, and he had no objection to agreeing to the children being brought up in her faith. Indians were devoid of the urge to proselytise. Ranjan, when questioned on this point, said, 'I pay respect to all the gods, including those of the tribal people I visit. These gods do not quarrel among themselves, and what have I to lose?'

At Mokama a procession had been organised by the Catholics for the Feast of the Epiphany, in which their converts from several neighbouring villages led by a band would march in the spirit of Onward Christian Soldiers into the town. Such demonstrations in India are normally part and parcel of electoral campaigns, planned by astute politicians, frequently supported by a strong contingent of club-waving village rowdies, and sometimes under the protection of a venal police. Religious and political demonstrations are completely foreign to tribal peoples who in neither case know what is going on. In this instance the demonstrators would have been no better than a collection of simpletons from the hills, many of whom would have been at the palm-toddy before setting out. They would have straggled along behind the pipes and drums urged by the native deacons accompanying them to shout religious slogans in a language they did not understand, and doing their best to give good value for medical or other favours received.

No two newspapers can ever be found to agree as to what has happened in incidents like this, and where there are deaths the lack of precise information is frequently increased by the secret disposal of bodies to avoid the complication of inquests. Ranjan remembered a report that the procession had been met in the town by a shower of stones and the Saora were dispersed and forced to run for their lives. Shortly afterwards they were back but this time armed with their bows and arrows. In the ensuing battle lasting some hours there had been a number of casualties, and police reinforcements had been brought from a nearby town. Riot Order 144 was solemnly read, followed by a 'firing' in which one person had been killed. Such accounts were normally little better than exercises of journalistic imagination. When we drove into Mokama a bullock cart had broken down on a bridge and Ranjan stopped to question the three men doing something to a wheel. Yes, there had been a big fight at the time of the Catholic *puja*. Many people injured. Some undoubtedly killed. One of the men's friends had been struck in the armpit by an arrow. But that was as far as it got. None of the men had personally seen anything of the riot; they had been working in the fields at the time. Eye-witnesses of such events were as difficult to find in India as in a Mafia-dominated area of Sicily. 'I saw nothing. I heard nothing. I have nothing to say,' would be the response, whatever the language.

It was a sad affair, a sad example of the intrusion of religious competitiveness into a rural area where so many faiths have co-existed in harmony for so many years.

Potasing, a Lanjia Saora village built on a hillside thirty miles away, was recommended by Ranjan as one of the least afflicted in the zone by the government's efforts to uplift the tribal peoples and guide them along the paths leading to national integration. He found it – as I did – mysterious that the main targets chosen so far for these endeavours should have been remote mountain villages, most of them difficult to reach. In these areas the teams had made a start by knocking down cool, solid and practical Saora houses and replacing them with rows of concrete cabins with corrugated-iron roofs, located normally without access to water or refuge from the sun.

Incomprehensibly to Ranjan, Potasing, which would have been so easy to reach and demolish, had so far been left alone. It was a village of eighty-five families, one of a group described in a recent government report as 'in a real primitive stage, nevertheless of instant visual charm'. The low houses with their plain, immensely thick walls of red mud had been fitted into the contours of the hill in a way that recalled the harmonies of Taos. As in the case of Modhukamba, doors, door posts and lintels were richly carved and painted with flower and animal motifs, and like the lowland village it gave the impression that daily routines of house-scouring and sweeping went on. Here mountain rivulets ran down through the lanes with butterflies by the hundred at their edge, opening and closing their wings as they sucked at the moisture.

Someone had run to fetch the Post Master, who appeared in Potasing to have taken over the function of the Gomang of old. He was pleasant and eager to be of assistance, a young man in well-pressed slacks, a wrist watch with a metal band, a button lettered PM pinned to his white shirt, and a fair amount of English. His official duties, he said, occupied little of his time and left him free to pursue his spiritual studies. He announced that Potasing was now a Christian village, and that he himself in the absence of a resident Catholic priest was empowered to act as deacon in charge of the welfare of the religious community.

The mass conversion at Potasing – so close to the road and the Hindu sphere of influence – had been a major achievement carried out in five years. In other cases where Christians had allowed their guard to drop – 'Christian inspiration slackened' were the words he used – the Hindus had moved in. 'But now we are giving battle on this front,' the PM said. The battle was to be against illiteracy, which impeded access to the Scriptures. We were informed that there were twenty-four places for pupils in the new village school. And how many attended classes? I asked. 'One,' he said, in no way abashed by what would have seemed to me a melancholic truth. 'The teacher is sent by the government. He is to teach in Hindi,' he explained. 'This they are not understanding.'

The Saora were famous for their ikons, as they are generally termed, although known locally under the name *anital*. Charming and vigorous examples of folk art of the kind are to be found with local variation among most of the tribal peoples of India. There was a recognisable affinity with the vast paintings with which the housewife of Hirapur covered her walls, although ikons were limited in size to a few square feet. In Hirapur inspiration of old had been diluted by custom, and by the sheer necessity of employing space-filling patterns to be finished in a matter of hours in between odd jobs about the house. At Potasing the artist sat alone in silence, and in a darkened place, waiting for a vision to form. Only a few families – the Brahmins of art – were allowed to paint ikons, thereafter made available to the general public in exchange for a small gift or service. An ikon was painted in commemoration of a recent death, in honour of an ancestor, or to celebrate a festival when, like a magnificent Christmas card, it was often offered by the artist to a friend. It was also employed in the treatment of illness by a shaman who might prescribe the dedication of an ikon to the village deity, together with, say, a course of massage and the sacrifice of a white cockerel.

For the PM the ikons had become meaningless, and therefore slightly boring. The Church of Christ did not require such paintings, nor, he added, did the new generation of the village. 'They are looking', he said, 'another way.' And the carvings in and around the doors? I asked. Were they to come to an end, too? That was to be expected, he said. The few carvers left would find other things to do. Some were learning to carve toys for sale. People no longer wished for carvings on their new houses. They were a sign of backwardness. And were the new houses to be made with concrete and corrugated iron? When these materials could be had, he thought.

For all that – for all his distaste for those things in which Ranjan as well as I showed what must have been

such inexplicable interest – he was an impressively tolerant man, and ready to help us in any way he could. It was
at his suggestion that we set out to scour the village for
any ikons that might have survived. A small hitch arose.
Most of the villagers were out, he explained, working in
their fields, and nowadays when they left their houses
they locked up after them. Even the PM seemed surprised
to encounter this sudden intrusion of un-tribal practice.
In a land in which, by my experience so far, all doors
were open, this indeed was a break with the past. The PM
led us to several houses known to belong to notorious
conservatives who might have had an ikon about the
place, while a few villagers who had joined us, including a
young man in a Toshiba T-shirt, scampered up and down
side lanes in search of a household that might not have
moved with the times. In the end one was found and an
elderly lady festooned with bangles and beads invited us
in to inspect her ikon. It was painted in Saora style in
white upon a red background, recalling aboriginal rock
drawings, or palaeolithic hunters on the walls of caves, or
even more the figures and scenes woven into the *huipils*
of the Indians of Central America. Here Saora manikins
pranced and capered in ceremonial hats and under ceremonial umbrellas, rode elephants and horses, pedalled
bikes, and were carried by fan-waving attendants in
procession. They played the musical instruments of the
past but shouldered the guns of the present. Gourdfuls of
wine awaited their pleasure, displayed like Christmas
gifts on the branches of palms. The flaming sun illumi-
nating this scene might have been copied from an Aztec
codex, as might the Saora medicine-men too, who had
conjured it from darkness with their feathered wands.

The PM, watching us, smiled at our pleasure. He was

happy for us. 'We are lucky to find this,' he said, 'it is belonging to one old lady. I am thinking it is the last.' I tried to match his face with the faces of the Saoras who had crowded into the dark room after us, but they seemed to belong to a different race. 'Can he really be a Saora?' I had whispered to Ranjan. 'Yes, he is a Saora,' was Ranjan's reply, but centuries of evolution miraculously crammed into five years had produced an astonishing metamorphosis. The PM had leaped out of the stone-age of Saora art and belief, and the change seemed even to have paled his skin among the deep mountain complexions of the men at his back, and to have smoothed and softened the Saora aquilinity of his once Saora face. He had stripped away the credence that inspired paintings and carvings. Life, as he tried to explain, above all had become simple. 'Too many gods,' he said. 'Too many processes. Now one process only.' The concrete and corrugated iron shack was all part of the process of simplification.

The village of the Sudha Saora had swarmed with people. Potasing, with about three times its population, seemed strangely deserted; as many as four houses out of five were locked up. I asked why this should be.

'They are working in the fields,' the PM said. 'They are very active in employment.'

'But this is an in-between season with not much to do,' I suggested.

'If there is a willingness to work it is always to be found. We shall be growing new crops which now they are planting. One government inspector was here. He is sending us pineapple to try. In the old times people were lazy. They were drinking much wine. Even the young children were drinking wine. That was bad. We have cut down those palm trees which were giving the wine.'

'But what do they do to amuse themselves? Do they drink at all, dance, go to harvest festivals, stage the Ramayana, put on cockfights? Surely it is not all work? I know they've stopped painting.'

'Well, we cannot say it is all work, but we are not wishing to do these other things. I am telling you that everything is different now. On Sunday we are attending church. Practising also to sing hymns. They are telling us that soon a bus will be coming on Fridays for the cinema in Gunupur. This is something for which we are all very glad.'

The PM had turned his back on art, and art had forsaken him.

We had hoped to stay in Gunupur in the heartland of Saora territory, but could find nowhere to put up, so were obliged to press on to Rayagada in the country of the Dongria Kondh, where we found rooms at the Hotel Swagati. The façade of this, apart from old election posters, carried a large notice above the entrance: PILES WILL BE CURED IN HALF AN HOUR WITHOUT PAIN. SPECIAL TREATMENT FOR ASTHMA.

After the sluggish pace of the mountain villages Rayagada provided a small but concentrated dose of the excitements, frustrations and bustle of the city. Here was re-emphasised the familiar craving for travel – whatever the conditions – by public transport. Twelve people, arms and legs ingeniously folded, were crowded into a small Japanese version of the Jeep licensed for four, and passengers had piled up on the roofs and hung in layers from the outside of buses. Commercial activity was intense; there were medical halls and electrical shops galore mixed in with a sprinkling of astrologers' booths. Men were making chairs and beds all over the rudimentary pavements. Country medicines were handled by a nicely decorated kiosk at the far end of the town which sold things like dried bats, curative snakeskin and above all hornbill beaks, which were relatively expensive due to their reputation when administered in ground-up form as a cure for almost all the ills to which the flesh is heir. There was a permanent queue at the kiosk, largely composed of tribals – some of whom, unable to cope with cash, had brought bags of rice and vegetables with which to negotiate a deal. The centre of the display was a coloured action-photograph of Miss Datta, a gigantic weight-lifter who would shortly represent her country at the Asian Games in Peijing. 'Take our products regularly,' said the wording in translation. 'You, too, could be like this.' In Rayagada they also made excellent toys, and a kerbside vendor had lost control of a couple of lively plastic dogs which wandered into the street to be promptly kicked over by scampering goats. A wash of sheer noise flowed over this town and its car horns brayed from all quarters like the trumpets under the walls of Jericho.

Here, once again in a prosperous small town, people who could afford to do so ran to fat. It was to be supposed that they fell prey to the grosser satisfactions, over-ate and over-drank, suffering also the consequences of the townsman's conviction that it was mean-spirited, even eccentric, to walk if it was possible to ride.

We shared the hotel dining room with five enormous men slumped round a table bearing a bottle of imported Scotch. When one was obliged to haul himself to his feet it clearly involved a conscious process of calculation of the displacement of weight. Absurd notices surrounded us exhorting consumption and offering remedies for excess . . . QUALITY THAT'S FOREVER . . . CHOICE OF THE GRACIOUS PEOPLE . . . STAY AHEAD WITH A LUXE SURGICAL ORGANIC CHECKUP . . . WHAT A GREAT WAY TO START THE WEEK.

Down in the street a line-up of rickshaws awaited custom, their pullers if Hindus consoled perhaps in the belief that the uncomplaining fulfilment of their destiny in this life might help their promotion to the status of sixteen-stone whisky drinkers in the next.

After several days without access to newspapers we had picked up a collection at Rayagada, one of which, coincidentally, contained an article on the Saora. It was particularly concerned with the problem of bringing them, along with the other tribal minorities, into the mainstream of Hindu society.

'We must turn our back on this talk,' Ranjan said. 'For forty years they are talking but nothing is done. Are they wishing these people to be Hindus? For this they must have caste. A man who is born a Saora cannot have caste.'

One of the rickshaw men down in the street had found a customer. An immensely corpulent man, helped by a small friend, climbed in. The rickshaw man stood up on a pedal, bringing all his slight weight to bear, and they moved off.

'Is that a Saora?' I asked.

'That is a Hindu. When a Saora becomes a rickshaw-puller it is end of road. They speak their contempt for working for pay. "I am a farmer," they will say to you. "I am not a slave."'

I read on. 'It says here that the Saora are exceptionally primitive.'

'Primitive, yes. Backward. Most people are seeing it in that way.'

'But in their villages there is no real poverty.'

'That is my personal opinion. They have no possessions, but no one is hungry. No, they are not poor.'

'Would you say they are devoid of personal ambition, and that crime is unknown?'

'They have no ambition. It is safe to mingle with them. You will not be robbed.'

'Do they work in each other's fields, as it says they do in this paper?'

'This is automatic. They are also helping to build each other's houses. They are very democratic. Not even the Gomang may give them an order. He will say, "Let us sit down and talk." Then he will say, "This is my advice."'

'And this is backward?'

'The government says it is. The government tells us it is backward. I am very much liking these people but they are backward in all the things they do. Our national society is requiring from them the opposite of all these things.'

Beneath us another customer – this time of average size – had turned up for a rickshaw, and Ranjan called my attention to the transaction taking place. The slender, boyish rickshaw-puller at the head of the line waved the fare to a grey-haired man waiting behind him.

'This young man is passing an easy fare to the old man who is following,' Ranjan said. 'He is a Saora. I think only a Saora will do this. They have a goddess who tells them they must help, so they are eager to behave in this way.'

'Are they going to survive?'

'If they learn to use money they will survive.'

'How does that affect the situation?'

'Because if they are not understanding money they will be cheated.'

'Who by?'

'Everyone who comes who is making business with them. Always it has been their custom to barter the things they make or grow. They know how many bags of rice to a goat; they cannot handle rupees. If a tribal man cannot barter he must sell to a merchant. He cheats them with his weights and with his money. When the merchant has robbed him it is the turn of the moneylender. Maybe the Saora's crop has failed and he must buy food, but he does not understand what is meant when the money-lender speaks to him about interest. So this man cannot pay and he must give up his land and go to be a labourer and break stones or dig coal for all his life.'

'How often does this happen?'

'All the time. Who can tell you? Now we have industries more labour is wanting. Also politicians and landowners are desirous of obtaining more land. This is happening thousands of times every day.'

EIGHTEEN

WE WERE ON the road again with the first light for a
detour to the north for Badpur, Ranjan's favourite
Dongria Kondh settlement, under that part of the
Eastern Ghats known as the Niyamgiri hills. There may
be as many as a million Kondhs, who make up Orissa's
most numerous tribe. They are Proto-Australoids,
having exceedingly dark skins, and are divided into
several sections, according to their degree of development. Of these the Dongria Kondhs are about halfway up
the list, as eaters of meat who do not worship the Hindu
gods. Remarkably enough, they have retained a large
degree of their original culture, although this is under
constant and increasing threat.

Once again, as the sun lit up the landscape, we found
ourselves back in the dry, metallic, glittering scenery of
the Australian outback: red earth, silver-leafed trees –
often with scaly trunks – great boulders balanced one
upon the other. We passed under burnished, coppery
cliffs, by the edge of a scalloped gorge at the bottom of
which a river had been scorched away probably thousands of years ago. Fire storms had happened here,
leaving trees complete with a meticulous spread of
branches turned to carbon as a monstrous, sepulchral

decoration of the landscape.

Ranjan said in a reassuring and hopeful way that there were many tigers and hyenas in these forests, but for mile after mile I saw nothing but an occasional scampering squirrel. Once we stopped to examine a shed snakeskin, and then to listen to the broken-hearted hootings of the birds, and here by chance I saw my first and last Great Pied Hornbill. It was much bigger than I would have expected it to be, grotesquely magnificent – something that should have become extinct but had mysteriously survived – awkward in its movements, stabbing at nothing with the huge unmanageable beak, before suddenly appearing to lose its balance and to go crashing with a shower of black and white pinions down through the foliage, out of sight.

Badpur came into view in a great, yellow eroded patch where trees had once been. The village had been built by design on an easy slope down from the road and at right angles to it: an enormously wide, single street, perhaps 200 yards in length. It was possibly the most beautiful tribal village I had seen anywhere. At the top end of the village a pump delivered water through a conduit running down the exact centre of the street, and halfway down a small shrine contained a stone representing Jhankar, the Earth Mother. Following the principle of the Sudha Saoras at Modhukamba, the Kondhs' houses had extremely low, thatched roofs – all joined together – but in this case so low as to make it necessary almost to crawl under the overhang to reach the verandah. It was the custom of the Kondhs to build their villages so that the occupants of a house could stand at its entrance to greet their neighbours face to face across the street with the rising of the sun. This genial and impressive morning ritual must soon come to an end because the Government proposes – as soon as it can afford to do so – to rehouse villagers in barracks-pattern army huts. A dispiriting photograph in a publication by the Tribal and Harijan Research Institute shows one of these dwellings, which looks like a white cowshed at the edge of a sun-roasted building site. The photograph bears the title MARCHING TOWARDS PROGRESS. I was told that the actual house was occupied for a week or two, then abandoned.

Just as the Saoras had been, the Kondhs were clearly stimulated and delighted to have new faces about the village. In a comparable Hindu village the womenfolk only too often appear as subservient shadows flitting in the background, but here the women took over and strutted giggling at our sides while the men tailed along in the rear. It was a lively scene indeed. In one house a cigar-smoking travelling medium, face striped with white like a New Guinea tribesman, had dropped in to offer his services on the matter of laying a troublesome ghost. On the verandah of another several jungle-fowls had been induced to sit on eggs contained in ornamental baskets, and a boy crouched nearby with a flute ready to soothe them with music if they showed signs of restiveness.

The women – who alone were permitted to carry out such work – had decorated every surface to which ornamentation could be applied. No two designs, they insisted, of birds and butterflies, of peacocks, elephants and tigers linked by the swirling tendrils of convolvulus, were the same. They had carved geese along the wooden framework of beds, because the flight of geese through the recesses of the drowsy mind was conducive to sleep. The women smoked short, fat cigars, performing what seemed to us the dangerous feat of drawing on the lighted end, inserted in their mouths. Doing this they managed a half-smile, while rolling their eyes. They drank like fish, stopping frequently for a nip of alcohol offered by a neighbour in a brilliantly painted gourd. I was induced to try this, but found it both sour and sharp.

This female self-sufficiency, this pleasantly arrogant independence, reflected the fact that in Indian tribal society, as a general rule, a woman is accepted as more useful, responsible, and above all more hard-working than a man, in consequence of which her value finds expression in the matter of marriage settlements. In Hindu society one of the greatest strains most families are called on to face arises from the problem of finding tempting dowries for marriageable daughters. A husband is in effect purchased, whereas among the tribals a girl is sold – often, too, in this case, the price may be crippling. As Ranjan wryly pointed out, the dowries for his three sisters had left his family's fortunes in a shaky state. Had they been tribals they would have kept their land and probably even added to it. These women owned most of the property, carried out all the business transactions, and above all were guardians of the all-important alcohol they kept in constantly polished aluminium pots and distributed according to their own severe rules as to when it was to be drunk, and by whom.

Dongria Kondh feminism was again reflected in the fact that they were the only tribe to train and employ female shamans – the Bejuni – who after years of preparation become trance-mediums through which the gods speak their oracular utterances. The Bejunis practise healing and divination, are denied sexual contacts, but enter into life-long 'marriages' with their guardian spirits. It was the Bejunis who conducted the human sacrifices for which the tribe was notorious until their suppression by the British in the middle of the last century, and it was they who distributed the parcels of the victims' flesh about the fields in such a way as most effectively to increase their fertility.

Sacrifices of this kind were likely to have been practised in a discreet and sporadic fashion by a majority of the hill tribes, until the British took action, but it was among the Kondh that they became a systematised and increasingly important feature of tribal life. The Kondh carried out these procedures in the full blaze of publicity, informing neighbouring groups well in advance of the date fixed for what had become a major religious occasion, with subsequent distribution of highly valued parcels of flesh among favoured local communities. The inevitable military campaign to put a stop to this state of affairs was launched in 1851 under the command of Major-General John Campbell who wrote an account of his experiences and of the ritual killings he had investigated.

The Kondh had convinced themselves of the existence of a mathematical relationship between tribal prosperity and the number of victims immolated. These always remained in short supply, *meriahs* – as they were called – being obtained in three principal ways. Donations of children for what was seen as a supremely spiritual purpose were made by devout parents. Meriahs were in effect bred, using a class of women paid by the community for their services, and to make up any short-fall professional kidnappers were employed to capture adults (for which a huge price had to be paid) in other tribal areas. The meriahs received considerate, even pampered, treatment while awaiting their eventual fate.

A sacrifice was a spectacular event, attracting visitors who often travelled great distances to be present. The atmosphere was festive rather than solemn, as all participants were piously intoxicated for days in advance and, says the general, the victim was virtually unconscious from the effects of liquor before the end came, death usually from strangulation.

Major-General Campbell appears in this as a humane and tolerant man, somewhat loth, as the British often were, to be forced to interfere with other people's religious freedoms. In the British way, too, he shows evidences of a sneaking sympathy for minority peoples in the areas of conquest. One of the centres of trouble was Jeypore and – once again in imperial style – he does his best to shift responsibility for action to the local rajah. Nevertheless a few obstinate sacrificers hold out and a village here and there has to be burned down. Even then amends are made by a cash contribution towards the costs of their rebuilding. Thus, in the end, the two sides part good friends. To remove any source of temptation the general takes the precaution of rounding up meriahs. These he shares out among eagerly awaiting missionaries.

Ranjan had a surprise for me. We had discussed Verrier Elwin's work on the Muria and their Ghotul, and I was informed that the young people's dormitory system continued to flourish among the Kondh. He quoted the opinion of S. Routray, who has dedicated some years to the study of the tribe, that the exceptionally low rate of fertility in Kondh women results from what may be described as ritual promiscuity practised in early life.

Discussion of such matters is probably overshadowed by Hindu taboo. The Kondh are well aware that such sexual practices still existing among a high proportion of the tribes of Orissa and Bastar are regarded with disfavour by the national society, and whereas they were once prepared to discuss them openly – even with relish as it would appear from Elwin's accounts – they are now inclined to shamefacedness and secrecy. The Japanese anthropologist Sugiyama Kolchi, who spent the year 1963 among the Mundas in a village only a few miles from the vast industrial complex of Ranchi, was surprised to discover, for example, that all the young men and women there spent their nights together in the 'sleeping houses' before marriage. Adult villagers criticising this conduct were ashamed not for their licentiousness, but their backwardness. The opinion of the outside world was what bothered them. It was quite possible that such a youth dormitory existed in Badpur, Ranjan thought, but only the most tactful of questioning would have been likely to persuade the Kondhs to admit to its presence. The Kutia Kondhs, cousins of the Dongrias, tucked safely away from the benefits of civilisation in their mountain valleys, would still believe that they had nothing to hide, otherwise it was a subject, he thought, better avoided.

A number of young girls now appeared on the scene. Ranjan explained that as we had been spotted they had all dashed off to titivate, and here they were, each laden most attractively with junk jewellery: up to a dozen aluminium hoops worn as necklaces, earrings and nose-rings from the market, twenty or so plastic bracelets on each arm, a cheap little knife stuck into the hair, together with a comb behind the right ear. Examples are to be seen in museums of exquisite jewellery made by the Dongria Kondhs up to forty years ago, but a short step along the road to acculturation has put an end to all that. Nevertheless, whatever the quality of the materials employed and the sad artistic loss, the general effect was charming.

Before leaving the village we had noticed a few ramshackle-looking houses failing to conform to the local style, placed moreover in such a way that they were out of sight of its single street, with its water conduit and its earth goddess. These were occupied, we were to learn, by the Dombs. By the exercise of some wholly mysterious power these untouchables have established a parasitic grip on the Kondh that nothing, including the passage of an act of Parliament to curb their activities, has been able to break. Wherever there are Kondh communities the somewhat sinister Dombs are in watchful attendance. The Kondhs, who may have picked up the trace of a caste attitude from the Hindu populations of towns they occasionally visit, have no social contact with them. A Domb – despised as an inferior being – is not allowed to enter a Kondh house or even to be received on the verandah, yet the creative, energetic and intelligent tribals have allowed themselves to be trapped in a species of hypnotic dependency upon this clan of moneylenders and manipulators.

A partial explanation may lie in the fact that the Dombs first appeared as itinerant traders carrying supplies of goods such as dried fish, sugar and oil, which otherwise could only be procured at great cost in remote hill villages. From small beginnings they expanded their trade, establishing near-monopolies in the supply of sacrificial animals, alcohol and various kinds of cloth otherwise not to be found in the neighbourhood. The Kondhs remained stubbornly improvident and illiterate while the Dombs took all they needed of what the school had to offer: enough reading and writing to be able to understand and draw up contracts, and a knowledge of how to work out percentages and keep accounts. They became the barrack-room lawyers of the hills, with the police in their pockets, and ready to go to law at the drop of a hat. They isolated their Kondh victims from their contacts of old, with whom they had been accustomed to practise fair trading in barter deals. Now more and more they were compelled to buy and sell for cash through the offices of cunning, worldly-wise and unscrupulous go-betweens who fattened on the profits.

It was a strange experience to visit the Domb settlement. In the way of most Hindu villages it was messy, but there was something nomadic about the scattered odds and ends outside the houses that reminded me of a gypsy encampment with its litter left to rust or rot. It had attracted a number of crows, of which Badpur was virtually free. More extraordinary was the fact that the Domb males dressed in such a way as to be indistinguishable, apart from certain physical differences, from the Kondhs. Ranjan said that they did this to be able to come and go among market crowds without drawing attention to themselves. Their womenfolk appeared as average Hindu low-caste women wearing rather dingy saris, and in Hindu village style they spend most of their time in their houses out of sight. Unlike the Kondh women who put on their best clothes and embroidered scarves to flock to any market in the vicinity – sometimes walking all night to be able to do so – the womenfolk of the Dombs stayed at home.

It is altogether astounding that the Kondhs feel under compulsion to buy cloth from their unwelcome neighbours, which they then embroider and sometimes sell back to the Dombs, who are unable to undertake decoration of any kind.

Ranjan was determined that I should see for myself the physical force the Dombs were prepared to apply, when necessary, in order to keep the Dongria Kondhs subjected to their domination. This was best to be witnessed, he said, at any local fair, and having learned from our friends at Badpur that one was to be held that day some fifty miles away at the village of Chatikana, we turned back to Rayagada, and took the road to the west leading to Koraput and Jeypore. Immediately we plunged into another climatic region, bringing with it a stark change of scenery. The finely incised clarity and the burnished metallic colourings of Badpur were at an end. Now there were heat hazes and grey misted shapes: volcanic cones and mountain humps floating above the subdued greens of the forest. Scraps of savannah held huge, isolated cotton trees around which birds swarmed like bees. Sometimes we saw a patch of cultivation with a branch-and-leaf hut beside it, and in this a guardian would remain all night, Ranjan said, beating an enormous drum to keep the monkeys and wild pigs away from the crops.

Chatikana had justified its description as a village by a single unfinished building to be constructed of breeze-blocks and asbestos. Otherwise it was no more than a crossing of the ways most easily accessible to tribals coming down from the surrounding hills, and here, by the time we arrived, the Kutia Kondhs were present in force. These, however, were no more than close relatives of our friends the Dongrias. Living, as they did, at the tops of the mountains, they were much less affected by what is now often called the process of Sanskritisation.

The Dongrias and their other cousins, the Desia Kondhs – who have settled in the immediate vicinity of Indian towns – are quite happy to wander in and out of Hindu temples, and buy a sari for their wives to wear to visit a fair. The Kutias do none of these things. In the case of the Kutias, too, the stern laws of the survival of the fittest continue to apply. They are always on the move, wrestling with the poverty of mountain tops, a wiry athletic people, with – as their appearance here suggested – a touch of controlled ferocity about them.

Every man carried his spear or an axe on his shoulder. Some wore loin-cloths alone and some were quite naked except for a strip of cloth twisted round the waist and drawn up through the loins. The girls, by contrast, were overdressed in spectacular tribal finery, with multiple earrings, nose-rings of extreme complexity covering most of the top lip, richly embroidered scarves, and combs plus a dagger in their hair. They came skipping down the mountain paths in parties, flashing their eyes in all directions, chattering in high-pitched bird-like voices, then settling themselves in rows, arms linked together – in theory to avoid abduction although, as the Tribal and Harijan Research Institute book informs its readers, 'both marriage by consent and capture are popular'.

The Kutia Kondhs sold jungle berries and fruit, medi cinal herbs, grain and leaf-plates made of sal leaves stitched together, and they bought or obtained by barter dried fish. An interesting surgical skill was on display at the market, for a Dongria Kondh woman – almost certainly a female shaman – was removing thorns embedded in the feet of patients who had walked barefoot anything up to fifteen miles across the mountains to reach the market. In this way, the worst sufferer had picked up eleven thorns.

But there was no intrusion by Dombs in this potentially formidable assembly. To see them in action, Ranjan decided that we should make a side-trip, if necessary, to visit Kundili where the greatest tribal market in Orissa, attracting at least 10,000 visitors, would be held on the coming Sunday.

We took the road again for Koraput, pulling in to the side after a few miles to watch men at work in an extremely primitive sisal manufacturing plant, set up here because it was a convenient place for lorries to dump their loads of the great, spiny agave cactus leaves used in the process. Labourers with bleeding hands were feeding these at great speed into the jaws of a machine linked to an old Ambassador engine, which crushed and masticated them, separating in some way the tough, valuable fibre from the mass of vegetable pulp. This done, a team of dejected looking women took over, using a succession of archaic wooden contraptions to dry, comb and twist the fibre until in a remarkably short time it was transformed into rope.

All those engaged in this operation seemed close to the limits of exhaustion. As usual, labourers here worked a ten hour day, the men receiving fifteen rupees (50p), less 'small' deductions, and the women twelve rupees. The men, said the overseer, got a day off once in a while, and went to a market – 'To try to capture women,' he added as if by way of an afterthought.

It was hard to know how to take this. Was it intended to be a joke? Ranjan had translated, and a grim thought struck me. 'Do you imagine these women working here could have been abducted by them?'

'I do not think so,' Ranjan said. 'Many girls are captured at the markets for the purpose of marriage. This is the custom. After the capture an arrangement will be reached with their parents. It is not the custom here to capture the women for the purpose of labour. This man may be joking. I cannot tell. Of one thing we can be assured. No lady will take up this employment of her own wishing.'

Suddenly, within minutes of our arrival, everything had come to a standstill. It was the midday pause. The workers dropped to the ground and went instantly to sleep. The overseer sauntered across to exchange a few words with Ranjan, who told me that a Paraja wedding was being celebrated at a nearby village and that he had offered to show us the way to it. A deputy was left with instructions and we set off together.

The village was only a few hundred yards away across the fields, although obscured from the road by clumps of trees. We were guided to it by the tremendous festive hubbub. The first thing that became quite clear when we arrived was that the whole population, men, women and children, were drunk – many of them uproariously so. The narrow, shadeless main street was full of musicians traipsing up and down, playing squeaky pipe music and banging drums, and lines of dancing girls colliding with them, and the menfolk staggering about, drinking alcohol from aluminium jugs and bawling noisy choruses.

The fact that the Paraja girls danced together made it clear, Ranjan said, that no boys from other villages had been able to attend. Like the exogamous Kondh, Paraja women may only dance with males born in other villages. The atmosphere so far as we were concerned was hospitable to the point of effusiveness, and, having been subjected to close and speculative examination by a tipsy girl, Ranjan said to me, 'I do not believe there is any shortage of sex in this place. These people are normally strict in their behaviour but they are letting their hair down for this celebration.' He then told me that it was a Paraja in whom he was interested, and described the circumstances in which they had met.

The vast majority of tribal villages in Orissa are only to be reached – usually with some difficulty – on foot. However, someone had told Ranjan about Kangrapada, down near the frontier of Andhra Pradesh, which only the odd government official and itinerant trader had so far discovered, and to which a road of kinds had recently been built. He went there and was delighted to discover an unusual situation in which two tribal peoples, the Parajas and the Godbas, had decided to settle down together, forming a satisfactory mixed community in which they had probably lived for a hundred years. There was an amicable mix-up of circular Godba houses and roughly square Paraja ones, and an open area in the centre of which the goddess Hundi, represented as a pile of stones, was worshipped by both peoples. Ranjan parked his car in this space and went for a stroll round, noticing that a mixture of Paraja and Godba elders had seated themselves on benches round the shrine and were gossiping in exceptionally loud and clear voices. He was later informed that the goddess was expected to listen in to such conversations in which problems were ventilated: it was hoped she would settle these on the spot without recourse by the villagers to formal offerings and prayers.

Ranjan made a brief tour of the village, took tea with a nice old man, admired the old circular houses and the heavy silver neck rings worn by the old women which could only be removed after death, and struck up a two-minutes' friendship with a pretty Paraja girl. The village was exactly as described to him, saturated with a drowsy calm, free of the presence of moneylenders and labour agents, with its people drinking, dancing and sleeping on the threshold of an Eden from which they would shortly be driven. He went back for the car and found it ringed by the old men who had previously been seated chatting in their loud, clear voices round the shrine of the goddess. Kindly smiles received him but he sensed there was something wrong. When he made to get into the car the village elders gently restrained him. He had offended Hundi by not presenting himself to her and requesting her permission to be in the village. It would be necessary to sacrifice a buffalo to appease her before he could remove the car. The villagers were hazy on the subject of figures but thought the cost of one might be in the neighbourhood of 1,000 rupees.

It was the second time in a year Ranjan had been in trouble with local deities. On the first occasion he had wandered into a remote and nameless village of the Bhunjias, the smallest of the tribes of Orissa, isolated in the Kalahandi hills. The people received him well, offered him food and were happy to show him round. He was unable to understand a word that was said to him, and for that reason could not be warned not to enter any of the sheds built adjacent to each house which – although quite empty – constituted the sacred and inviolable shrine of the household god. The Bhunjias skipped along at his side, smiling and gesticulating, but were too polite to keep him out of a shed by force. Finally he entered one, found nothing inside and came out. Instantly the owner, according to the rule in such cases, set fire to it and burned it down. Ranjan offered money in compensation which, as the Bhunjia had no use for it, he smilingly rejected. His parting from the villagers was as friendly as his reception. From their gestures he gathered that the owner would soon build a new shed. 'These country people are making allowances,' Ranjan said.

Once more, at Kangrapada, Ranjan found himself up against a language problem. The Dravidian tribal languages in which he could get by offered no help in his efforts to argue his case with the Parajas, but villagers were forthcoming who knew a few words of Kondh and of Oriya – the official language of the State of Orissa – and with the aid of these negotiations stumbled ahead. Ranjan was able to make the Parajas understand that the car was not his property and produced a convincing mime of poverty to persuade them that he could not find 1,000 rupees to pay for a buffalo. At this point the Parajas, who were clearly very nice people, began to show signs of sympathy for his plight, and it was decided to put the suggestion to Hundi that the cost of the sacrifice should be reduced to 100 rupees. Further discussion was put off until the following day. He stayed in the village that night, and next morning the Paraja elders announced that Hundi had been kinder to him than expected and had reduced the cost of the necessary sacrifice to 10 rupees – this being the price of a large white cockerel.

At the leave-taking, the Paraja girl brought her father along to say goodbye. It was clear that he had made a good impression not only on her, but on the family, for the father made the announcement – unprecedented in tribal society – that if Ranjan wished to marry his daughter he could have her without payment of the usual bride-price. The matter had already been cleared with the headman and the council of elders, and if the offer were taken up the village would build a house for them in a matter of days.

Ranjan thanked all concerned and asked if he might be given a little time to consider the proposition. He was a man of enthusiasms which he made no attempt to conceal, and his genuine admiration both for the girl and the village in which she lived would not have been lost upon the Parajas. I had come to regard him as a bit of a romantic, as well as a rebel against the claustrophobic and caste-ridden Brahmin environment in which he had been brought up. It was a picture of which Kangrapada, overbrimming with freedoms, presented the reverse. Sri R.P. Prusty, writing of the tribal culture of Orissa, had set the scene. 'In cultivation, agricultural work and the construction of a house, group labour is required. A feast is offered to participants after completion of the work. The ultimate incentive is the maintenance of goodwill. The boys and girls of these villages visit each other on dancing expeditions, and leisure is enjoyed through feasts, dances and music.' It was a place in which any Gauguin of Orissa might have made his escape, and it seemed likely from our discussion that Ranjan had considered the possibility of taking eventual refuge here from our times.

A minor obstacle was his relatively slight knowledge of the Paraja, about whom little information had appeared in print apart from anthropological data hardly intelligible to the layman. Ranjan had grown up in the proximity of the Saora and the Kondh – the nearest of the tribal groups to his place of birth. These he could cope with. He had taken the measure of the Saora with their strange sexual taboos, knew the order of precedence in which alcohol is offered, with whom to exchange ritual jokes, how to reprove a dog in the presence of its master, and when to lose purposely at a game of hazard. With the Parajas, by comparison, he was at sea. They complicated their existences, he explained, by totemistic affinities with animals. Thus, although meat-eaters, under obligation to consume animal flesh on ceremonial occasions, the meat of the totem animal was strictly taboo, and it was therefore desirable for both husband and wife to belong to the same totemic group. He sighed. There were little pitfalls awaiting the unwary everywhere in tribal society. You were liable to commit one solecism after another until you knew the ropes, he said. The only remedy was to watch what other people did, use your head, and not be afraid to ask advice.

My impression was that Ranjan had been turning this episode over in his mind in the year that had passed and that the allurements of Kangrapada and a union with an unspoilt child of nature had strengthened against the background of the urban stresses and strains of Bhubaneswar. It may even have been that he had seen my arrival on the scene, hoping to travel in the area that interested him, as not so much a coincidence as the intervention of the hand of fate in his affairs.

The news in the previous day's paper was that the Naxalites had appeared again, in and around Koraput, where we proposed to spend the night. It seemed very much a sign of the times that in such reports Naxalite activity – while clearly played down in the press – should be mentioned in a way that suggested cautious or even open approval. The paper in this instance noted that in Bastar tribals had been cheated (the newspaper's word) by contractors who forced them to accept as little as 3 paese for a bundle of fifty tendu leaves, and that when the Naxalites came on the scene, this price was forced up to a record 30 paese – which clearly struck the newspaper as being a good thing. 'The tribals', said the newspaper with something that sounded like enthusiasm, 'are increasingly turning to the Naxalites for justice.' Government resistance to this slowly simmering rebellion might have been weakening, for Dr Channa Reddy, Andhra Pradesh Chief Minister, announced here that he 'supported the genuine demands of Naxalites and would take steps to meet them. In the crucial matter of tribal lands', he said, 'the government stood very clear, and it wanted to restore all tribal lands to tribals. However it was not possible to oust all non-tribals [from lands that had been invaded] in one go.'

Despite such wavings of olive branches, well-armed guerrillas, both male and female, specialising in kidnappings and the taking of hostages, had appeared for the second or third time in the vicinity of Koraput, where the atmosphere struck us as apprehensive. Although we had seen few vehicles on the road in a day's journey, some had passed, and here they had been stopped at a road block and lined up for what was clearly to be a lengthy examination. It was a situation to be faced in a casual manner. Fifty yards short of the line of lorries we found a dhaba and went in for tea. Having served us, the owner rummaged among his stock of cassettes for one left in error by a party of foreigners who had passed this way some months before. This was a very Indian scene. A lorry parked nearby had lost the oil in its sump and the strong odour of this mingled with that of curry was characteristic of such roadside stops. We were surrounded by ravaged red earth bestrewn with abandoned odds and ends, among which hopped a few alert and elegant crows. Once in a while the bellowings of an enraged policeman reached us faintly, then the music started. It was yodelling recorded in the Swiss Alps. The dhaba owner turned the volume up, and after a while we climbed back into the Ambassador and drove up to and past the road block in the most inconsequential fashion.

NINETEEN

JEYPORE, TWO HOURS further on, captivated us with its
charm at very first glance. We found rooms at the Hotel
Madhumati where the whole reception area was occupied
by guests being shaved by a team of barbers in readiness
for a wedding taking place that night. The hotel was
infused with homely disorder, and its barely furnished
spaces resounded with the outcry of guests and their
many friends who had suffered from its inefficiency. The
system in such places was to flatter the better-class
clientele by addressing them in English, and the staff
rushing hither and thither on abortive errands responded
with averted eyes and routine soothings to their complaints, whatever the language in which they were
expressed. 'Not to worry, sir. Now at *this* moment it is
coming. I am sorry for your patience.'

This town was the centre of the arts and entertainments
of South Orissa; full of conjurers and fire-eaters, of
strolling players, musicians, mind-readers and illu-
sionists. It seemed impossible without retreat to a
bedroom to shut out the nearby sound of someone
tuning up a stringed instrument or producing desultory
blasts on a horn. Near the entrance stood a cart drawn by
two bullocks in which, under paper chains and sprays of

artificial flowers, twenty-two musicians and a har-
monium had been crammed. A notice said *Our propo-
ganda is travelling 10 kms anywhere for your pleasure.
Say yes to life.* A man pleaded into a microphone, 'This
night we must sing and dance together. We must banish
heaviness and care.' Across the frontier of these blandishments, on the far side of the road, the scene was strangely
calm – almost reverential. Here at sunset, scrupulously
avoided by the throngs of passers-by, the housewives
were on their knees decorating the flagstones in front of
their doors with the white powder design representing
the footsteps of Lakshmi, drawn in the hope of inducing
the goddess to enter the house and there spend the night.

At this season of the year, with most of the harvests
already in and the rains awaited before sowing could
begin, there was nothing much to be done in Jeypore for
those who could afford it, but relax and enjoy themselves. People stayed up most of the night promenading
in the brightly lit main street, window-shopping, chattering with friends and drinking tea. Frequently there was a
power failure to delight the children. Cars cruised up and
down with their radios turned up to broadcast film theme
music much distorted with over-amplification. Noise
was all part of the fun.

Everyone in the theatrical business had to come to this
town for their costumes: splendid, tawdry finery, star-
spangled jackets, sherwanis, embroidered pantaloons,
masks galore, and pleasantly ridiculous multiple crowns
hung from the façades of the shops. Such was the local
obsession with the theatre that every village in the area
had a field set aside for the staging of performances of the
Ramayana and the *Mahabharata*. Of these two epic
Sanskrit poems, dating from about 500 BC, the longer,

the *Mahabharata*, contains 100,000 stanzas – about fifteen times the Bible's length, and is presented in poetic form as the Great History of Mankind. Both the *Ramayana* and the similar *Mahabharata* have been dramatised in India and the countries of South-east Asia where they have been playing to audiences for at least 1,500 years. At Jeypore a short version of the Ramayana went on all night, but a full-scale production might last a week. The show usually started at ten and lasted until six in the morning, after which people went home and slept for the rest of the day.

'What sort of an audience do they get?' I asked Ranjan.

'All kinds. Everyone is going who can.'

'Tribals, too?'

'Many of them. Most of the actors are tribal people. Their memory is very good for the long parts.'

Some people, Ranjan said, had to have medical treatment to cope with the exhaustion. In addition a mysterious epidemic had broken out – as a result, it was thought, of all-night open-air theatre-going. This took the form of a high fever and a temporary loss of balance, caused by the bite of a noxious night-flying insect attracted to its victim by a faint odour released through the pores by the stress of constant excitement.

There had been a break in the sequence of such performances at about the time of our arrival due to an unsatisfactory confluence of the stars. It was one, however, that favoured marriages, and one or more took place each night, the more stylish of them based upon our hotel. All the rooms apart from those we occupied had been taken over by the male members of a wedding party, with the bridegroom and his guests engaged in dressing themselves in archaic costumes which in most cases did not fit or were short of indispensable parts. The bedroom doors, left open as guests rushed in and out, showed half-clad men tripping over tin swords, or wrestling with enormously long turbans, and the endless buttons of *achkans* made either for fat men or dwarfs. Barbers, cut-throat razors at the ready, groped their way from customer to customer in the half-light.

At 7 pm the town's lights went on, and as if to show the citizens' exultation and relief a great, crashing reverberation of drums was to be heard in all directions. Lined up outside the hotel were the vehicles, both ancient and modern, which would convey the bridegroom's party to the bride's house, each of these being connected to a bicycle rickshaw carrying a small generator and an amplifying system. The band had arrived in something like an old-fashioned school brake, with an ear-shattering uproar of drums, fifes, flutes and horns of various descriptions, and rockets hissed up and exploded with stunning detonations immediately overhead. At this moment the hotel lights went out to an outburst of cheers. It seems to have been expected, something that had developed perhaps into a good-humoured convention for people who had acclimatised themselves to a situation in which nothing worked for long. This suspicion was strengthened by the sudden appearance of a number of beautiful girls who came scampering up the stairs with lighted candles to be placed in position all along the passages. With that, instantly, the lights came on again and the bellowing of the hotel's television, on full blast, was added to the street uproar outside.

There was no place better in which to imbibe the pure aroma of provincial India than Jeypore's main street. It was very long and quite straight, beginning with the splendid decrepitude of the once Maharajah's palace at the top of the town, and petering out among the bullock carts and banyan trees and children flying kites on the edge of the tattered vestiges of a jungle. The Maharajah's palace had fallen into decay after the last ruler's death in 1920. This sombre though magnificent building was entered through a gateway 35 feet in height to permit the passage of an extremely high processional vehicle resembling the Car of the Juggernaut, and the great width of the street at this point facilitated its manoeuvrings and those of its accompanying elephants among surging festive crowds. The gateway was flanked by lions said to have been modelled on those by Landseer in Trafalgar Square. Facing this grandiose entrance was the lesser gateway of the palace annexe, guarded by green demons and two more lions with black raging faces and crimson manes, both imbued with a ferocity that Landseer's animals comfortably *couchant* across the road quite lacked. The top half of this prospect was always obscured by ranks of sherwanis by the hundred, displayed on their hangers like a headless army marching upon the town. An enormous brass statue of the ruler of old occupied a domed building like a bandstand in the ravaged palace enclosure, gazing with satisfaction over vistas that had long since vanished. It was pointed out to me that his brass boot caps had been polished by the kisses of his faithful subjects, a few of whose descendants still attended here regularly to salute his memory in this fashion.

The peace and the apparent prosperity of Jeypore seemed remarkable when the miserable insecurity of Koraput, so short a distance away, was advertised by the presence of the Naxalite People's War Group. In Jeypore there were no policemen in the streets and queues of its citizens waited outside the principal cinema to be subjected to the anodyne of the Indian masses. The cinema was showing *Young Love Blooms* with Monisha Koirala and Salman Khan – both given fashionable mousy hair – and dealt with teenage lovers who keep their innocence.

Another sign of affluence was the presence of many pharmacies, and their blown-up versions known as medical halls. India manufactures and exports a huge range of pharmaceuticals, and these, flooding the home market and advertised with persistence and cunning, are on sale even in the smallest towns, mopping up a high proportion of any spare cash that happens to be about. I read that such is the craze for self-doctoring in search of the improvements of health promised by so many products, that clubs are formed of hypochondriacs created by advertising. These spend their spare time discussing the merits of patent remedies, and a hard core have reached the point of devising menus in which a fistful of rice will be supplemented by capsules supplying the necessary minerals, vitamins and synthetic flavours.

Jeypore appeared to be full of people well-off enough to worry about their health, and medical halls sowed the seeds of fear by window displays showing what could happen to those who tried to bypass the medicinal road to well-being. The evidence provided was startling, but since it was accepted that some citizens with spending power might be illiterate, and that most tribals were, the facts and figures were supported by photographs that spoke for themselves of the ravages of disfiguring diseases. The most popular display included a wonderfully convincing working model of a defective digestive tract, with arrows pointing to the zones of malfunction. This was garnished with large colour photographs of abscesses, tumours and cysts. The exhibit drew a constant crowd, and people stopping to inspect it on their way home from the cinema may well have found it an antidote to the sugary images of *Young Love Blooms*.

The day was passed in pleasant exploration of the oddities of Jeypore. Back at the Madhumati for dinner we found the scene hardly changed from the previous evening. The advance guards of another wedding party had arrived to invest the hotel with its daily quota of confusion, charging up and down the stairs, pressing every bell in sight, and bursting into already tenanted rooms.

Rickshaws bringing the evening contingent of wedding guests waited to discharge their fares at the moment when a sudden and probably brief splurge of urban illumination would do justice to their glittering attire. At street corners musicians carrying ancient instruments stood in silent anticipation, like a bullring band waiting for the procession of the toreros. Indifferent to the growing tension and excitement, the women across the road got on with the evening decoration of their thresholds.

The Madhumati gave the impression of being the intellectual centre of the town, frequented by young men of outstandingly liberal views, with advanced opinions on such controversial matters as arranged marriages, the dowry system, caste, and the abolition of the inequalities from which the women of India suffered. It was a setting in which it was possible to speak with qualified approval of Naxalite successes.

We were seated in the hotel's somewhat austere dining room, furnished with a sideboard piled with empty bottles, with pictures of dispiriting Alpine scenes, and plain tables spread with rumpled cloths in preparation for the evening meal. An open serving hatch afforded glimpses of the arriving wedding guests in their coruscating gear, trying one after another to make urgent calls on a phone that did not work. No one in the Madhumati dared complain at the spectacle of beer being drunk openly in one of the public rooms, as it was here by a group of young men at the table next but one – although they had screened the bottles behind a fence of the hotel's large menu cards, offering in reality little but chicken and chips.

Ranjan had been joined by an old friend he had run into here by chance. Anand Gopal, now an inspector in the Department of Works, was from a high-caste background and the possessor of an exceptionally fair skin endowed by forebears who watched over such attributes as jealously as they did their wealth. It was the sight of the public beer-drinkers that sparked off the topic. Anand, now twenty-nine, said that he had only been allowed to drink water up to twenty-five years of age. Tea was banned until then as excessively stimulating, and he had only drunk it in secret and as a guilty indulgence.

'How do you feel about such prohibitions now?' Ranjan asked.

'I am unable to acquire a taste for beer, but I move with the times.'

'Have they arranged a marriage for you yet?'

'I am not permitting it,' Anand said.

'But many years ago there were some discussions. This I remember.'

'Nothing came of them. My father sent many letters to friends and some leads were established. It all fizzled out.

I was opposed to anything that was suggested.'

'You are a difficult fellow,' Ranjan told him.

'I am not difficult. It was against my thinking. You see I am progressive.'

'So now what is happening?'

'Nothing is happening. There is an agency called Life Partners. My father was in touch with them secretly but I would not co-operate. I am as free as the air. They were proposing ten lakhs of rupees as dowry for a lady with eastern features, but I am not prepared to be sold like a calf in the market. If there is a lady with whom I can share an ideal, that is a different matter.'

'I am of your opinion. Absolutely,' Ranjan said.

We were interrupted by a group of hotel regulars who came in carrying a television set. While watching an instalment of a religious epic in the television room, they had been disturbed by the invasion of the wedding party. The set was plugged in next to the sideboard, and with a garland placed round it out of respect to the spiritual message embodied in the programme, it was switched on.

'And there is no present activity for you on that front?' Anand asked.

'For the moment there is none. I am awaiting developments. This is a problem I may discuss with you, but no decision has been reached.'

'Take your time and consider carefully,' Anand said. 'We are defending principles.'

This being the kind of discussion it was, the enmeshments of caste were bound to come up, and condemnation by these two Brahmins of the system which had favoured them was a foregone conclusion. Had there been any real improvement in this direction since Gandhi had admitted the untouchables to worship in the temples back in 1938? Ranjan thought not much. Now blandly renamed Children of God, they were still condemned by custom if not by force to dismount from their bicycles and wheel them through his native village. In rural areas he knew of they were still likely to be stoned if they attempted to draw their drinking water from the village well, and had to drink from the tank in which clothing was washed and buffaloes cooled their skin in the mud, unless a higher caste villager could be persuaded to draw their water. Anand agreed with Ranjan. In the past days a television news item from Rajasthan had reported the case of a harijan, determined to ride a horse to his wedding, being set on and lynched by a hostile crowd, along with five of his supporting friends.

Had I seen anything of the recent caste atrocities in Bihar? I was asked, and my reply was that as a foreigner I would not have expected to, but I had talked to people and read the newspapers.

I told them about Mira Kumari, daughter of a high-caste family of Loyabad, Bihar, who eloped with a low-caste suitor, Satyendra Singh, and was secretly married to him. Mira was carried off, and subjected to thrashings in an attempt to induce her to remarry. The family hired four killers to drag Satyendra away to a quiet place and cut his head off.

'And what was the outcome?' Anand asked.

'There wasn't one. The chief of police said, "I don't recognise this marriage. After all, ours is an Indian culture."'

'I am not wishing to visit this place,' Anand said. 'Did they kill the girl, too?'

'No, they just kept up the beatings for eighteen

months. In Patna Anita Pandey came off worse. She married out of caste, and her father had her abducted by a gang who broke her arm, scarred her for life, damaged an eye, and bored an inch deep hole in her back. After that she was shut up in a home for fallen women in Patna.'

'But this is impossible if she has been legally married,' Ranjan objected. 'In that case her husband may set her free.'

'Her father produced a certificate in court', I told him, 'giving her age as thirteen. This was intended to give him custody.'

'And this was true?'

'No, it was found to be false, so she was released.'

'In this case,' Ranjan said, 'justice was done.'

'With some reluctance,' I said. 'Yes. I read about the case in a magazine which quoted interviews with people who could see the father's point of view. There was some talk of caste associations which place a ban on inter-caste marriages and imposed sanctions on members breaking the rules.'

'This is so,' Anand said. 'Even now, this is the case.'

The writer of the article seemed to feel fairly sympathetic towards the father himself. 'If he'd accepted his low-caste son-in-law, he said, he stood the risk of being ostracised by his caste-fellowship and being disinherited from the large family property.'

'It is true,' Anand said. 'To give example, even in my case I must move carefully. If I am in open revolt against our custom it is certain that my father will not disinherit me, but it is not so certain that I will be keeping my job. And if I lose this job, where in these times shall I find another?'

TWENTY

WE DECIDED TO base ourselves on Jeypore and make a number of sorties from it into the surrounding countryside where it would have been otherwise hard to find anywhere to pass the night. Next morning we left early as usual, running immediately into thick mists. The only signs of life were the shrouded forms of women on their way to the field, each carrying on her head a burnished pot, which in the grey monochrome of the landscape appeared to emit soft rays of light.

Dense clumps of sugar cane had spread through the fields here and provided refuge for numerous cobras. A lot of people were bitten by them, Ranjan said, but forceful eradication was impossible for religious reasons. Instead non-violent persuasion was traditionally practised. The great event took place every year at the time of the November half-moon when a large contingent of snake-charmers appeared on the scene. The snake-charmers located the ants' nests in which the cobras had taken up residence and played music to induce them to leave their holes. They were then fed with milk, molasses and the only-recently discovered gastronomic inducement, pop-corn, which had become their favourite food. The ceremony of feeding at an end, each cobra was presented with a new *dhoti*, after which the priest would wish them a happy and successful year and beg them to cease to bite members of his community. Nevertheless some continued to bite as before, and many countryfolk in the neighbourhood died in this way. Victims were carried to the temple, the area surrounding the bite excised by glass, and a tourniquet applied, after which 100 gallons of cold water was poured over them while mantras were recited. Ranjan said there was a 60 per cent chance of survival, both for the religious who were treated in this fashion, and for the non-religious who preferred to call in a doctor, although treatment in the temple was normally cheaper.

Patches of jungle were beginning to show the effects of the dry season. Flagging blossoms and limp clumps of bamboo lay like a wilting flower arrangement among the trees. The road emptied for two hours before we overtook two men on a bicycle carrying a large image which had flowing red locks fixed to its front. Taking a left fork along the road to Jagdalpur, we shortly arrived in the village of the Mirigan tribe. This small but extra-ordinary group are believed to have been a branch of the Murias of Bastar, called suddenly to a puritanical form of salvation by the Kabirdas sect, causing them to take refuge in Orissa from the advertised wrath to come. Here, in the plain just across the border, they installed themselves to begin the practice of chastity (ideally sexual activity was restricted to seven occasions in a lifetime), abstinence from alcohol and strict vegetarianism. Un-fortunately, back in the mountains they had lived as hunter-gatherers. Now they were forbidden to hunt, there were no minor forest products such as fruit and berries to collect, and they knew nothing of the cultivation of the soil. Their predicament was crucial and they were only saved from extinction by the pronouncement of a Kabirdas elder that the ibis did not rank as an animal. Many of these congregated in local swamps and on ibises the Mirigans lived.

Apart from this they were able to gain fame locally as weavers of cloth, using vegetable dyes mixed with cow dung, varying the colours by increasing or decreasing the proportions of aloes or turmeric as required. The abstract designs employed, and low-key colours, seemed to me a little dull, and all too well to reflect the solemnity of the village and its inhabitants. Little girls would go about tittering softly all the time, but after a certain age, as Ranjan said, laughter was frowned upon. Local cultivators gave the Mirigans grain in exchange for their cloth, or sometimes bought a little for cash. The people kept a few sheep for their milk, feeding them – since no grass grew in this area – upon fallen leaves. It was a scene of which Ranjan appeared on the whole to approve. 'They have no desires,' he said. 'All they need of this life is easily obtained. They fiddle with their looms, which cannot be called work; they walk about talking of God in his heaven, they sleep.' Sometimes, he thought, they danced. This surprised me, and in the hour or two we were with them there was no such evidence of merriment.

Kotpad was another weavers' village, and once again sober abstraction was the keynote of the work, which may even have fallen under the influence of its Mirigan neighbours' puritanism and restraint. Nevertheless, there was evidence that Kotpad had been reached by Christian missionary endeavour, for the principal object in the office of the weavers' co-operative secretary was an ikon of the Crucifixion.

We skirted round Jagdalpur in Bastar by taking the road to the Dhurua district, seen by Ranjan as the Ultima Thule of Orissa. This was flat country, once thick jungle, and the wind sweeping unchecked across the plain cut silken swathes in the long grass. We used a railway bridge to cross the River Halti, and waiting at the nearer end was a crippled itinerant musician, with a wife in attendance, playing a one-string instrument some four feet in length. For a half rupee he would play a tune guaranteed to disperse the evil spirits known to lie in wait for travellers at such places.

Dhurua, the last village of any size along this road, had a mixed population. A majority of Kilvas lived side by side with Parajas and Godbas in their separate and widely different cultures, yet in what appeared to be perfect amity. A forest guard – a government official having limited police functions – attached himself to us. He was a low-caste official from Bhubaneswar with a leathery city smell about him, and a habit of calculation that constantly narrowed his eyes. The tribals who had been trying to talk to us backed away respectfully when he came up, and stood like soldiers awaiting the next order. Ranjan translated. 'We all get on fairly well together,' he said with sinister emphasis. 'Sometimes a problem arises over land because no one is really sure who owns what. When this happens I plant a white flag in the field under dispute. No one may cultivate it until the case is settled by law. This can take up to seven years, by which time nobody can pay the costs. The government then takes over the land and sells it by auction.'

Even Dhurua, so far from anywhere, was in the grip of crack-brained advancement, and the first of the beautiful old houses had been torn down to be replaced by atrocious corrugated-iron shacks. Many of the remaining houses were painted on the outside with curiously modern-looking designs inherited in all probability, Ranjan thought, from the remote past. The ikons and the wall-paintings of the Kondh and the Saora had been exuberant and complicated, with an intense feeling for pattern. In Dhurua ornamentation was sparse and restrained: here and there a stylised flower, butterfly or fish; once only a flying jeep isolated among the crows. There was an obsession with abstract mountain shapes which seemed curious as no mountains had been visible for some hours. Were these representations, I wondered, rooted in nostalgic memories of a tribal past in other surroundings, like the Alpine vistas of the Hotel Madhumati? Occasionally a musical instrument had been hung on the façade of a house to supply additional decoration. No attempt had been made to improve the appearance of the stark government shacks foisted upon the villagers. Instead the owner had sometimes ordered a new door carved with traditional designs to break the monotony.

Ranjan had bought sweets in Jeypore for such occasions. We found a central space where people were invited to line up for the hand-out. They were received with acclamation both by children and grown-ups. But sweets were a rare sight in Dhurua, and demonstrations were called for as to the way in which they were unwrapped. Hundi, the Paraja Earth Mother, accepted by all three tribes-people under different names, presided here from within her usual stone-pile, and village councils when in session placed themselves, as recorded by Ranjan in Kangrapada, in a position where she could readily overhear their deliberations. In Dhurua itself the custom was to marry for love but lack of choice of suitable partners and of the opportunity in remote hamlets for young people to meet sometimes obliged parents to apply to the councillors for their help in arranging a marriage. We watched their bland, aged faces unmoved by the urgencies of desire. A wide-eyed child contemplated the miracle of an unwrapped sweet. A musician passed through, playing a complicated tune on a bison's horn. A man in a tiger-mask peered out from cover, before slipping from sight. The forester remembered to tell us about the bride-price which had dropped to a new low. A third of local income depended upon such forest produce as honey, and the local sal forest was being cut down for its valuable timber as fast as this could be done. No one in Dhurua had any money or livestock to spare to finance a marriage. You could pick up a bride for next to nothing, he said.

Murtahandi was almost at the end of the road, a spillage of huts with little fenced-off gardens sheltering the small odds and ends of tribes who had gone to earth here, as they hoped, out of reach of human predators. Among them were a few Muria Vatra whose name unflatteringly signifies 'non-animal', and the Dumajadi, who wore blue-painted masks believing them to be an infallible defence against bounty hunters in search of bonded labour fugitives, and against the tigers with which some of their villages were said to be overrun.

Small as it was, Murtahandi was celebrated for its possession of the only school for many miles around. There was a rustic calm in this setting of neat little houses around an open space that was not quite a village green which faintly recalled a corner of the English countryside in high summer. The village school stood in a large garden with a picket fence in which innumerable asters and marigolds bloomed in beds divided by a crazy-paving path. The schoolmaster, hastily called, who was young and ebullient, came bounding into sight, rushed up the garden path, and round the back of the building to open the front door and greet us. We found ourselves in a large, clean room in which the only article of furniture was a table upon which rested three books. Squatting all round three of the walls were about thirty small boys, who at our appearance began a prolonged droning which, Ranjan whispered, was a traditional chant of welcome. This stopped when the master held up his hand.

A problem arose, for the master, as was to be expected, launched into an immediate account of the activities of the school. He spoke English very rapidly, in an excited high-pitched monotone that I found difficult to under-stand and some embarrassment arose when I was obliged to ask Ranjan to help out with what almost amounted to a translation of what he said.

The school had been opened, said the master, as part of the campaign stemming from the 5-Year-Plan for tribal advancement, the immediate target being the defeat of illiteracy, which in the case of males reached about 83 per cent. Women were totally illiterate since the ability to read and write appeared to the tribals to serve no purpose. Families were concerned in extracting the maximum bride-price for their daughter. A girl, for example, who could castrate a goat might command a couple of hundred rupees more than one who couldn't, but knowing how to write her name would not add the value of a single hen to the amount a father could reasonably ask.

It was almost as bad with the boys. They had an

obsession with manual occupation, with building and making things, and using their hands. They enjoyed rearing animals, cultivating the land and working as blacksmiths. Part of the government drive was to put an end to the universal practice of slash-and-burn cultivation, which was bad for the environment, but the only way to stop this was through education.

Ranjan asked the teacher if he knew the Kilva language generally spoken in the area, and the man winced and said, 'Not very well.' He had had a long struggle and it was still going on. Small inducements had been made to families to send exceptionally bright boys to school and a few had been made to understand that literacy could change their lives. Companies working to develop backward areas were constantly on the look out for literate tribals to act as overseers, and there were any number of minor government jobs going for promising young men who could cope with some paper work. He had to admit that it was still hard to make his pupils see the point of it all.

'What are they being taught at the moment?' I asked.

'Some Oriya,' he said. 'Also we are making a start with English.'

He called a boy up from a row squatting along the wall, who came forward in a hesitant and reluctant manner. The master beckoned to him impatiently to come closer, and the boy placed himself in front of us, swallowing nervously and for an instant showing only the whites of his eyes. 'This boy is very good,' the schoolmaster said. 'His father is an illiterate basket-maker, but he is wishing to become assistant to the supervisor of markets. For this he will be recording the numbers of all animals in a book.' He picked up a ruler from the table and raised it as if about to conduct an orchestra. 'Now he is to speak English to us,' he said.

The boy squeezed his eyelids together and opened them again. 'My name is John,' he said.

'Hello John,' I said. 'How are you? Can you say anything else?'

'Well come. What iss your name? Where are you going in? My name iss John.'

An effort to prolong the conversation led to blank looks and a little string of gibberish. I congratulated the master on the boy's accent and he led me smilingly to the door and out into the sunshine where someone thrust a marigold into my hand.

Ranjan, an amateur of remote places, had found a dot on a large-scale map denoting a village some ten miles away in what was shown as jungle. He suggested we go there. There was no road but the forester offered to guide us through the tracks made by loggers to take out the timber. The village's real name was Gulmi but it was familiarly known by an expression meaning the end of the world. And what, asked Ranjan, did people do for a living in a place like that? The forester told him that they made the best arrow poison to be found anywhere as well as hand-rearing baby parakeets, taken from the nest, for which there was a strong demand among what he called normal people, i.e. non-tribals.

Both pieces of information fascinated me. 'So they use arrow poison here?'

Not all the time, the forester told Ranjan, but every year just before the rains the people from all the neighbouring tribes got together for a great annual hunt whatever their differences of language and custom and the disputes over one thing or another that might have arisen throughout the year. They would come together to stake out the areas in which as many as a thousand hunters might take part, burn off the underbrush, and move in for the kill. In preparation for this the Gulmi people who were possessors of a secret formula sold all the arrow poison they were able to concoct. A small animal like a rabbit, said the forester, would die of the merest scratch and so great was the bag of rabbits and edible forest rats that the only problem was to keep the meat fresh. Some hunters who went without meat for eleven months in the year would gorge themselves on so much that they would blow up like balloons. 'What about the larger animals?' Here they ran into religious prejudice. They were all sacred to one god or another. They killed a few deer, but these had to be prayed to first. A shaman would rub the sap of a certain tree all over his skin to cover up the human smell, then wrap himself in the skin of a hind to attract the stags. The trick always worked but most of the villagers refused to eat the meat.

We bumped on slowly over the branch-strewn tracks. A lacing of dark shadows hung from the trees, and I waited in hope for the metamorphosis of obscure foliage into the shape of an elephant twitching its ears. This part of the jungle, said the forester, remained as it had always been, for no one was allowed to cut timber, not even to remove the dead trees that had clutched each other before falling among the grey castellations of ant-hills. Then, with the hutments of Gulmi in sight we drove out of the wood into a yellow plain, with the spring grass already razed away by the sun and parakeets glinting like smithereens of glass in the sky.

Things on these travels were never as expected. Gulmi,

nestling in the cloak of invisibility at the back of beyond, now appeared as a trim hamlet of four houses, protected (ineffectually) by a tiger fence but otherwise, like Murta-handi, remarkably European in appearance. It possessed twelve adults and seven children. The population of all such places was on the decline, said the forester. It was a decline Ranjan explained through the difficulties in getting the children married off – none of whom by custom could marry within the village. The solution would have been to move to Dhurua, but this would have confronted people with the intolerable predicament of abandoning the megaliths implanted in the village soil linking its people with the souls of their ancestors. It might have been the worst of the traumas, he thought, that the tribal peoples had ever faced, for thousands of families had been driven from their villages to build the dams, provoking innumerable suicides among hopeless oustees.

The pace of life in Gulmi was leisurely in the extreme. The tiny harvests of millet and dry rice had been gathered in and consumed by the time we arrived, and now people tightened their belts and made sporadic excursions, when they felt the need to do so, into patches of jungle where at this season there were trees to be found producing a variety of minuscule and not particularly tasty fruits. Some of these they ate but most went into the making of alcohol – an activity pursued here with the usual tribal enthusiasm. Ranjan said that if pushed to it the villagers would eat almost anything in the way of animal flesh, but their limited meat diet was based largely on small animals – edible rats and an occasional bird. These were shot with bows and arrows.

I asked to see a bow and the man who up to this point had been describing village life here with considerable vivacity showed signs of nervousness at the prospect of having to produce this weapon in the presence of an official. This seemed strange as it was to be assumed that every forest dweller in the state possessed one. However, he went off, rummaged in an outbuilding and returned with the bow, which could hardly have exceeded a yard in length, and looked like a superbly made child's toy. The arrow, too, was short and light. Through Ranjan I asked the man to give us a demonstration of his skill, and having balanced a small jack fruit on a rock some twenty yards away he took aim and scored a bull. Was that the maximum effective range? I asked, and he said it was. It seemed extraordinary that while Amazonian Indians had developed a bow up to six feet in length, with which once in a while they managed to kill a jaguar, these tribals whose proficiencies had evolved in roughly similar surroundings were unable, except on an organised communal basis, to hunt any large animal.

Creativity, that mysterious compulsion, assisted here by a natural desire to fill in the vacant hours between essential chores, kept these people occupied. At the moment of our arrival two or three men gathered socially round the Earth Mother shrine were carving lumps of wood into animal shapes in an abstracted, almost automatic fashion. They might have been knitters of sweaters who manage to fashion a garment while watching the television, yet every crouching tiger or rampaging elephant was individual and unique. Gourds were used as drinking vessels, and each one, scraped clean of its vegetable content, had been carved with flowers and birds.

From these occupations the womenfolk were debarred. Instead, at this hour they were promenading with their fledgling parakeets on their shoulders. The birds received considerate, almost ceremonious treatment, being fed tit bits taken from their lips. In the matter of their sale a stipulation was imposed. The purchaser was obliged to take the bird away before it could fly, otherwise it could not be parted from its human foster mother. One often saw unsold birds fluttering round the women's heads, the forester said. These in the end were taken back and released in the jungle.

In Dhurua, tribal people of the same stock painted butterflies, stylised mountains, and the occasional jeep – Pegasus of the tribal imagination. Why then in Gulmi this mass production of carved tigers and elephants? This is our way of showing our admiration and respect, was the reply. In recent years the tigers had not taken a villager, but a single bound carried a hungry one over the useless fence, and off he went with a goat. The elephants were a worse problem. Here as in most of the tribal liquor-producing areas they raided alcohol supplies and in the end turned into alcoholics. They sniffed the liquor from afar and came charging out of the forest in a plundering herd. An intake of liquor enraged and incited them to vandalism, and they laid about in all directions tearing off thatches and butting down walls. The only sure remedy against such an invasion was to bury the liquor stores underground. But the workings of the tribal mind would also have suggested an act of propitiation, a token obeisance to irresistible force, the soft answer that turned away wrath. Hence all the carvings.

TWENTY-ONE

IT IS INEVITABLE that those who have studied the tribals of India should have devoted ample space to their lovelife – so often in contrast not only with Western mores but those of the Hindu majority still a little encumbered with the legacy of Victorian England. Even the Puritan Fathers with their fear of the human body could hardly have matched the ibis-eating Mirigans in the field of sexual abstinence. The large and flourishing tribes of the Saora regard copulation as offensive to the gods – particularly in woodlands and open fields directly under the divine eye. Engaged couples are thus required by the community to keep their physical distance, to be virgins at the moment of marital consummation and thereafter remain faithful to each other for life. Intercourse is discontinued after childbirth for a period up to three years.

There are a few other tribals with attenuated sexual activities, but on the whole the tribal is liberal – sometimes outstandingly so. Sugiyama Kolchi, the Japanese anthropologist investigating the Munda in 1968, noted the existence of 'love markets', and that the young men and women of Maranghada, where he carried out his field studies, spent the night together in local 'sleeping houses'. According to Dr. N. Patnaik, the Kondh, of whom we had been able to see a little, possess dormitories where unmarried boys and girls pass the night. A brief glimpse of Paraja girls in action at a wedding party had suggested that they were easygoing in their attitude to sex, while Verrier Elwin finds conventional Western morality turned upside down among the Murias, who fine a young man who attempts to confine his passionate advances to one girl.

To the list of emphatic non-adherents to our standards must be added the Koya, numbering some 55,000 and inhabiting the Malakangiri Hills on the border between South-west Orissa and Madhya Pradesh, who have attracted some renown for their own peculiarity in the matter of marital customs, insisting that a wife should be substantially older than her husband at marriage. The writer P.K. Mohapatra says that marriages are frequently conducted between a boy of thirteen and a woman of about thirty. When we went to their principal village, Bhejaguda – which means 'The House of God' – a happy couple of such a kind were pointed out to us. The Koyas are said to attach little or no importance to a girl's physical beauty when it comes to marriage, the criteria for a coveted wife being her sound health and capacity for hard work. Despite this reported indifference to good looks we found the Koya a most handsome people. In his account Mohapatra goes on to say that the wife has to wait for her husband to be fully grown before sexual intercourse takes place. 'She sleeps with her husband and is expected to remain chaste,' he says, adding wryly, 'but actually it does not happen so.' To this, after a short conversation with our Koya hosts, who spoke quite frankly about themselves, Ranjan added the rider – 'If a woman shows some impatience her father-in-law may be called upon to do the necessary.'

The Koyas had grand manners, and were at pains to put all visitors at ease. The village was a street of yellow houses built on and among the rocks of a hillside and as we came into sight a number of splendid matriarchs in crimson togas appeared at their doors to receive us with expressions of interest and enthusiasm. Next a bed was carried out into the street and covered with a clean mat and we were invited to be seated upon this. It was a signal for what might have been the lesser families to drag out their beds. Upon these more impressive-looking ladies settled in imperial fashion. They smiled and nodded and their gold ornaments clinked. A strapping late-comer arrived with her husband, who might have been fourteen, at her heels. He was left with all the other men, standing meekly in line at the back of the assembly. 'We are waiting for the headman,' Ranjan said. In a moment this dignitary arrived, accompanied by an assistant of sorts who was outrageously drunk. The drunkard was got rid of, and the headman went into his speech. Like the other men he was dressed in a white loin-cloth, was bare-foot and naked from the waist up, and despite his office there was something subordinate about his manner in this context of praetorian women. One eye was half-closed and I detected eccentricity in his movements. Two women who had arrived for whom seats could not be found seemed to be swaying slightly. Could they all be drunk? I asked myself. Ranjan explained what it was all about. They had put on a theatrical show and been up all the previous night. 'They've been hitting the bottle,' he said.

The time for sweet distribution had come and once again there was the minor problem of how to set about unwrapping a factory-wrapped product. Perfectly behaved children were led forward to be exposed for the first time to the joy and excitement of synthetic raspberry flavour after the varied mediocrity of those the jungle could offer. One, who must have been about five, had to be deprived of the nipple before he could join the queue. Were some of the children tipsy too? I wondered. It seemed a possibility. Most of the adults also tasted Western-style sweets for the first time, and there were wild guesses as to their provenance, the most conservative and religiously minded taking the view that, like the universe, they had always existed, but only recently been discovered.

We were shown over a house, but there was little to be seen. The Koya take refuge from the great heat of summer by doing without windows and putting up with the total darkness – and airlessness – of their sleeping quarters, while spending the daylight hours on shady verandahs surrounding the house. At this season – as elsewhere – nothing much happened apart from the search for pleasure. Most nights, said the headman, reeling and hiccuping occasionally, there was a show on somewhere. Work was strictly taboo, and anyone found engaged in surreptitious labour was subjected to reprimand. Only the making of liquor was permissible, and this used up half the time. There was hardly a tree in the vicinity from the leaves, sap or fruit of which the Koya had not learned to distil liquor. As Mohapatra says, 'Without alcohol the Koya cannot survive. A Koya can carry on without food for a few days, but not without liquor.'

Now was the time among the Koya when their un-
equally matched marriages took place. Strapping women,
valued after much chaffering in terms of cattle, would be
handed over to diminutive grooms. Much as they strut
and preen in their togas and gold jewellery, with their
self-effacing menfolk in the background, there is no
economic basis for this swagger: in reality these impressive girls are no more than their fathers' chattels. Nothing
makes this clearer than the fact that whereas love marriages are favoured by two-thirds of the tribes of Orissa,
here they are out. Instead the father sets out to negotiate
the best possible deal for a valuable piece of property,
looking forward to being ten to twenty head of cattle
richer if a successful bargain is struck. Love cuts across
bargaining, and marriages where an infatuated couple
elope in the night and in consequence no bullocks change
hands are considered self-indulgent and disgraceful.

At a push the Koya settle for marriage by capture, a
down-market procedure not without its farcical aspects
as the bridegroom is invariably smaller and weaker than
the bride, and the violence largely symbolical. In such
cases tribal mechanisms exist by which fairly standardised sums are paid out by the family of the abductor
by way of compensation. Finally, in the case of poor
families unable to pay a bride-price a service arrangement
may be agreed by which, in the traditional Old Testament
fashion of Jacob and Laban, the son-in-law pays for his
wife by working for his father-in-law for a number of
months or years.

The Koyas rationalise marriages between mature
women and adolescent boys by explaining that their
women in early life work harder than men, employed not
only in field work and their household tasks, but in

bringing up children, and when the time comes to take it easy they need a husband in full possession of his physical powers to come to their support. This is a myth. The Koyas may at times work hard but only over short periods, and their life-style offers an instance of the relative idleness of so-called primitive people. Indian tribals work when there is forest clearing, sowing, weeding and harvesting to be done, enjoying the long work-free pauses in between in a way that Westerners with their noses to the grindstone might find it difficult to understand, just as a set working day of so many hours is inconceivable to the tribal mentality. Almost certainly someone like Mr Mohapatra will have calculated the average of daily working hours put in by the Koyas at their various forms of husbandry: among Amazonian tribes (equally expert in the pleasurable exploitation of what we call waste time) engaged in the cultivation of market gardens in a similar environment to this, the average can be as low as 1½ hours.

Religious ceremonies and observance are bracketed in the esteem of the Koya with public entertainments of every sort. In addition to the large assortment of their own gods they are quite happy to add those of their neighbours to their pantheon, as these, including a half dozen Hindu divinities, serve to increase the number of feast days and the opportunities for the villager to have a good time. We noted that the Koyas even had a version of the Car of the Juggernaut, which being too large to accommodate in the village street had been shoved off the road at the bottom of the hill and left until the August festival.

We happened to be at Bhejaguda at the moment of the

arrival of the peripatetic team of a priest and two acolytes touring the countryside with an image of Mongola, an up-country version of Kali Jai who watches over depressives and is hugely popular among the tribal peoples. Mongola was represented only by her head and up-flung arms. Her face was that of a startled child, with wide staring eyes and bright cheeks. Beneath the head was nothing but a bunched-up floral dress, and concealed in it was a pad which supported the image when carried on the priest's head. The priest's eyes were wide too, perhaps with the strain and exhaustion of so many miles covered in the burning sun. In token of his standing he wore a white vest in addition to his dark blue pantaloons. His assistants, each of whom carried two tambourines, were clad in loin-cloths only. All three were bare-foot.

Their presence, immediately following our arrival, set off a new explosion of excitement. All country people living in isolation welcome a new face, and since, as they will often admit, boredom is the enemy, excitement can be distilled from almost any variation of the day's routine. In this case the newcomers offered a dramatic performance of an unusual kind and, throwing off the torpor induced by hangovers and an all-night staging of the Ramayana, the villagers braced themselves to enjoy what was on offer.

According to the tribal philosophy, sickness is largely the product of an unsatisfactory life-style. The patient has succeeded in annoying one or more of the gods who punishes him accordingly. All villages had a shaman, going by different names, whose principal task it was to decide which god had been offended, and why, and decide upon the appropriate offerings to be made.

Although in theory the sacrifice of a cockerel, or the painting of a ritual picture, should have been enough, it was normal to assist the processes of recovery by the administration of herbal remedies based upon a rich tribal pharmacology which has yet to be fully investigated. A dogged empiricism assisted by faith had produced a fairly successful result. The life expectation at birth of non-tribal Indian is fifty-seven years. A tribal in an optimum situation, comparable to that of the Koya, and free from outside interference, can add five or six years to this figure. The tribal benefits from a diet of fresh and more varied food and an outdoor life, and probably from a more amusing and relaxed existence as well. Perhaps, too, the practice of an extreme form of democracy, unknown in industrialised society, may be of help. Among the Koyas the headman is chosen from candidates presenting themselves against whom there has never been a complaint. His job is to settle disputes with absolute impartiality, to make sure that the village is well supplied with liquor, and to stand up to brow-beating government officials. At the end of a year's tenure of office, the whole village gathers to discuss his performance, and if this is found to be below standard he is replaced on the spot.

It seemed that once in a while people suffered from disorders resistant both to medicines and offerings to the gods. Women whose affairs of the heart had gone wrong – whom nobody had ever wanted to capture, suggested Ranjan – were nearly always the sufferers, and in such cases Mongola could be effective.

The treatment was novel. A party of the sufferer's relatives and friends would be gathered together to accompany the three Mongola men and the image to the patient's house. A dance followed. The priest's assistants beat their tambourines, capered about, and sang a lively song, while the priest danced with the image, in which most of those present would have assumed the goddess herself to have taken up temporary abode. Inevitably, at a certain moment, caught up by the general excitement, the patient would join in the dance. This was the moment to thrust the image into her arms and compel her to dance with the goddess who, according to the headman, was a lively partner despite the absence of legs. The climax came when the goddess, speaking through the image's mouth, counselled the patient as to how she could best be cured. The headman mentioned that she had a strange, squeaking voice. 'A case of ventriloquism?' I suggested to Ranjan. He translated, and the headman said, 'Perhaps, but stones are Gods, if you believe. That is all that matters' . . . A wry evaluation, it might have been thought, of so many doctrines.

Had there been any prospect of witnessing treatment by Mongola we would have happily delayed departure from Bhejaguda, but as no suitable patient could be found we left, making for the Malakangiri Hills. This small mountainous area on the Madhya Pradesh border in Southwestern Orissa is of exceptional interest. As late as the seventies the hills were covered in dense forests of sal and teak and possibly – despite the ravages of the timber extraction industry – much of this remains. Conservation, as ever, as been favoured by the absence of good motorable roads. Inland there are a few *kachas*, as they are locally called, with terrible surfaces and no bridges, and thus only usable for the six months of the year when it does not rain.

When last reported upon, the animals included almost every species currently recorded in India, together with a spectacular array of birds. These, in particular the birds, are increasingly under siege by collectors employed by dealers, who succeed in exporting them with or without licence, all over the world. Once their principal customers were zoos, but with the increased demand for exotic pets in the affluent West, pet shops are now the worst offenders. It is a trade which shows no sign of abatement, and one is likely only to be reminded of its existence by an occasional report of an illicit cargo discovered at Heathrow of once live animals which have died before reaching their ultimate destination.

The animals are hunted with great skill by the Koyas and other small groups in the vicinity. They use trap-cages with call birds, or occasionally the sticky substance once known as bird-lime, to capture the birds, having been shown photographs of what is in demand by the sinister Dombs, who act as agents of the trade. Normally the tribals hunt only for food. To catch a sizable animal, a pit is dug, covered with branches and leaves, suitably baited, and armed with iron spikes upon which the trapped animal impales itself. To deal with the commercial demand for live animals a modified system is called for, and this is based upon a complicated system of trenches and pits always employed in the capture of the sloth bear.

This bear, sometimes spoken of as India's most dangerous animal, and once existing in great numbers in the jungles, is now rapidly disappearing. As in the case of the unfortunate rhinoceros, part of its body is valued as an aphrodisiac in the Far East, to which sloth bear gall bladders have been exported in numbers. More unpleasantly, it can be easily taught to perform. Once captured an iron ring is fixed in its nose, and attached to a rope with which it is dragged about. Despite its natural ferocity the animal is soon disciplined by a hot iron applied to the tender parts of its body. The training begins by chaining it on a metal platform beneath which a fire is lit. When in agony the bear is compelled to raise one foot after another while a simple tune is played on a pipe. After a week or two of this, a Pavlovian reflex is established and the bear is ready to go into its dancing routine whenever the tune is played, without encouragement by fire. Dancing bears are still to be seen all over India, but in South Orissa the Dombs have practically cornered the diminishing supply.

We were making for Bonda country to the east of the Malakangiri Hills, but since the local verdict was that our Ambassador could never tackle kacha roads our only recourse was to turn back through Matil, thereafter branching right for Khairput, administrative centre of the Bonda area. At Matil we stopped for tea in the centre of another idyllic rural scene. The building opposite had once been a temple and was now a ruin in almost classic style. In what remained of an archway a woman in a blue sari was taking bananas – held as if they were precious objects – from a basket having a wide, amphora-shaped neck. These she polished scrupulously with sal leaves before arranging them in a design at her feet. In the background doves and crows, mixed in together, wove slow, elegant patterns of flight. An old, nearly nude man whose bones under the tightly stretched skin recalled an anatomical chart, was couched supported on one elbow, a few feet from the woman, playing a jew's harp. The faint wheezing of this was obliterated momentarily by the rumble of a bullock cart, and at the moment of passing its driver, walking by the head of the offside animal, leaned down to whisper something in its ear.

After Matil the road was dead straight, an ochre slash that might have been cut by an axe through a grey wasteland of stubble and weeds, with no houses in view, and the green hump of the Malakangiri afloat distantly in the haze. It was now that for a brief moment we were in contact with the drama of sloth bears. Suddenly a group of women were hurrying towards us down this deserted road. The driver pulled up, and they came clamouring round the car. Their story came out in a Dravidian outpouring mixed with the Oriya that helped piece it together. Three of their menfolk out hunting with their bows had been killed by a single gigantic bear. It had held one in its forepaws and ripped him apart with its claws, while the others held their fire for fear of hitting their friend, after which the bear turned on them and killed them too. Those who die unnatural deaths cannot by local custom be cremated, but must be buried as near as possible to the spot where the death occurred, and these women were on their way to join friends in another village with whom the burial party would be formed.

The Bonda, whose territory we entered shortly after this, have attracted great and continuous publicity due to their capacity for sudden and deadly wrath. This has occasioned numerous homicides within the tribe itself, and also the death of sundry strangers who have wandered incautiously into these hills and given unwitting cause for offence. Isolation in a single, relatively small area has deprived the Bondas of the study devoted to larger and more accessible tribal peoples. They are Australoids surrounded by peoples of Dravidian origin, their language is difficult and their origins obscure. A dozen or so anthropological works have been devoted to them, but the outsider consulting them is likely to find himself lost in a wilderness of social anthropology, struggling with hardly comprehensible jargon and expected to derive excitement from such topics as territorial exogamy on two levels, fictive siblings, marital taboos, moieties, and joking and avoiding relationships. This may seem as dry as dust when what is likely most to concern the average layman is why the Bondas are ready to kill at the drop of a hat when they are surrounded on all sides by tribal people of exemplary tolerance and pacific behaviour.

In the anthropologist's world political action can play little part. His job is to assemble facts for scientific study. It is possible to find one, for example, gathering such data as the names of the parts of a fish in a language which, because a tribe is about to disappear, will cease to be spoken in a matter of a few years at most. *The Bonda*, published in 1989 by the Tribal and Harijan Research Institute, is the latest book about the tribe. In the main it concentrates as it is expected to on anthropological information, but makes occasional ill-conceived forays into an alien world of opinion in which the authors flounder without direction. Some confusion, too, may be due to the existence of two or more contributors having different, or even conflicting, views.

The first departure from verifiable fact deals with assessment of tribal character. 'The Bondas exhibit', says the contributor, 'a kind of personality which is characterized by aggression and criminal propensity. The village officials do not have any control over such cases of murder, and the tribal political system does not seem to have any responsibilities in the matter of bringing about any reform in the homicidal activities of the people. The general social control works only to the extent that the murderer is ex-communicated and handed over to the police for trial.'

This reads like unscientific stuff, but a few lines later the writer is back on course with a discussion of magico-religious rites as an aid to conception, only to fall into difficulties further on with a news item dealing with a government micro-project. As a result of this 'the Bondas have become change-prone and adopted many schemes for their development . . . Thus a transformation from the stage of stagnation has come about. Visitors to the Bonda villages can now move about and mix with the Bondas freely and without fear.' The improved security and change in atmosphere, said the book, had been due to changes in the socio-economic life. The Bondas had learned to grow several new crops like potato, wheat, pulses, ginger and vegetables, and were using improved seeds and techniques of cultivation. Even chemical ferti-lisers were now applied to the Bonda fields.

More opinions and a whisper of consumerist propa-ganda follow. The Bondas, enthuses the writer, are to become cash spenders . . . 'Now that they need this and that [consumer goods] and that they express their eager-ness to have them, frequent contacts with outsiders have influenced their religious beliefs and practices. Changes are also taking place in their dress and material posses-sions. A Bonda woman puts on a sari when she goes out. Similarly the Bonda are now very much interested in giving education to their children. In order to meet this need some schools have been set up.'

Perhaps Bonda women do wear saris in token of these

advanced times, but we never saw any that did so. Possibly visitors can now move about and mix with Bondas freely and without fear, although it was hard to forget that several who had been incautious in the use of their cameras had been struck with Bonda arrows. After the effusion of so much optimism in the early chapters, can it possibly have been the same man who a few pages further on produces this depressing summation of the Bonda condition and future? 'They are no longer self-sufficient as they were in the past, and are in dire want of food and other necessities of life. Excepting a few well-to-do families, most of them need credit in the shape of foodstuff for consumption, seeds and also cash for agriculture, and domestic animals for payment of bride-price.'

Following his work with the Murias, Elwin moved on to the Bondas, contributing a chapter entitled 'The Bonda Murderers' to the encyclopaedic collection Man-in-India published in 1945. In this and later in a full-length book, *Bonda Highlanders*, he shows himself as fascinated and even perplexed by a tribal society in which homicide, often casual and seemingly unpremeditated, was perhaps the strongest cultural feature. Bonda males suffered from fits of anger provoked by the slightest of offences, or even imaginary grievances, but having killed the offender rarely bothered to cover up their traces. When arrested they co-operated readily with the police because their code of beliefs, which permitted murder, prohibited a lie. Elwin found them completely fearless, indifferent to property and devoid of sexual jealousy. They prided themselves on their stoicism. He reported an annual 'castigation ceremony' when, in the manner of North American Indian braves, they demonstrate their indifference to various tortures inflicted on them. An extraordinary village institution in the Bonda highlands was the formation by the women of a kind of feminine home-guard to prevent their menfolk from committing murders, or themselves being murdered.

Our only hope of finding beds in the Bonda hills area that night was at the Block administrative headquarters at Khairput, and we were a few miles short of this on a road winding through low hills when it occurred to Ranjan that we might discover that there was no food to be had when we got to the end of our journey. By the greatest good luck he had hardly mentioned this when the next building – the first sign of human habitation for miles – carried a notice in Sanskrit characters announcing itself to be a chicken farm. It was an extraordinary place, run by a Hindu whose business consisted in the supply to the villages of chickens for sacrificial purposes. Most of them were caught for him in the jungles by tribals – usually young boys – who imitated the cries made by chickens of either sex in search of a mate and then shot those deceived in this way with small, blunted arrows which only inflicted temporary damage. The Hindu also bred captured jungle fowl with selected domestic breeds, to produce stunningly beautiful hybrids retaining the brilliant iridescent plumage of the wild, although twice the size of birds from the jungle. For these magnificent creatures which only the richest villages could offer to their god on the occasion of the annual festival, a huge price was asked. The man, perhaps suspecting that Ranjan was acting for such a community, produced the best on offer, a truly splendid cockerel cascading multi-coloured feathers, with an autocratic expression, burning eye and a flaming spread of comb the size of my hand.

When it was brought to us the owner clasped his hands together momentarily as if in prayer. It was only through a hitch somewhere in the mechanism of its Karma, he said, that it had been born what it was and not a man. The price worked out at about £20. Ranjan told him we wanted a bird to fry up for the evening meal. The news seemed to stun the owner, and he said something about religious principles. In the end he relented to the extent of indicating a neighbouring market and we went off there and bought a run-of-the-mill chicken for the equivalent of 50p.

Khairput, despite its official prominence and its name on the map, proved to be a nothing of a place, reminding me of a war-time position of no special importance hastily abandoned in anticipation of an attack. It was formless, unkempt, deserted and a little sinister. In the optimistic assumption that we should find somewhere to put up for the night the first essential was to find someone to cook the chicken. Khairput turned out to possess the filthiest dhaba we had so far encountered, with refuse scattered everywhere over the earthen floor under investigation by a small, incontinent dog. Four tribals with obsidian faces, blanketed like Mexicans, their eyes fixed immovably upon us, occupied the next table. The unwashed and taciturn Hindu who ran the place came up as stealthily as an assassin from behind, and when Ranjan asked him to cook the cockerel he said that not only was his a vegetarian restaurant but he had never cooked a chicken in his life. Ranjan then gave him instructions how this was done and he agreed to cook the bird so long as it was eaten off the premises. An untouchable sweeper was on hand to carry out the execution, and grabbing the protesting bird from Ranjan he reached for an old ceremonial bayonet hanging on the wall, and slipped through a tattered curtain and out of sight.

Overlooking this scene was a recently published mass-production picture of Lakshmi, shown as a pleasing, fair-skinned young woman of strikingly Western appearance, who could have been a film star, extending her blessings with four arms. I waited under her indulgent gaze while the hideous outcry behind the curtain began, reached its brief crescendo, then stopped, and the sweeper reappeared, kicked the dog from under our feet, and hung up the bayonet.

We finished our tea and went out. Ranjan had been directed by the owner of the dhaba to the man who kept the keys of what were called Suites Nos. 1 and 2, where officials obliged to visit Khairput were normally lodged. He went off, shortly returning with the keys and slightly disquieting news. Next day, Sunday, the Bonda market would be held as usual about half a mile down the road from Khairput. However a recent market had been the scene of a violent incident. Outsiders – no one knew who they were, but they could have been Indians or even foreigners – had appeared in the market and begun to take photographs using flashbulbs. Possibly from fear they were under attack the Bondas had snatched up their bows and one or two of the intruders had been struck by arrows. The news was imprecise and shot through with rumour. One person said one thing, and another something quite different. Certainly, though, there had been trouble.

Suites Nos 1 and 2 were on the far side of the desolated little open space, each forming a half of a low-lying concrete barrack with a pitted front, corrugated-iron roof, shuttered windows, and a goat tearing at shreds of matting on the verandah. Suite 2, first inspected, consisted of a large, dark, tarnished room, empty except for a bed and a mattress sullied with disquieting stains. People had come here to face the night and had left, often scattering unwanted objects on the floor: screwed up election-leaflets and cinema handbills, bus-tickets, a flattened toothpaste tube, a brush that had shed most of its bristles, and the stones, kernels and skins of a variety of fruits. Large spiders had inhabited this room at a time when the rainy season had provided abundant insect prey. They had draped the gossamer voile of their webs across the windows in such a way as almost to simulate curtains of an exceptionally light material. Now, in the dearth of approaching summer, they had gone, leaving only the desiccated remains of an exceptional specimen dangling like a small overlooked article of clothing from a hook in the suite's bathroom. This cell in total darkness contained a large tub of stagnant water, and the torch revealed a swirling pattern left on its surface dust suggesting that some small animal, perhaps a gecko, might have fallen in and circulated for a while before drowning and sinking to the bottom. Beside the usual hole in the bathroom floor there were a cracked jug for ablutionary use and, fixed to the wall above, a sink. From this hung down a foot or so of piping through which any water, used say to wash the hands, would splash straight on to the floor.

The condition of Suite No. 1, to be occupied by Ranjan, was roughly the same, and the problem now arose of what to do to clear up this very considerable mess. Even in a village like Khairput where a tribal population was accustomed to keeping houses clean, the caste influence of a minority of Hindus was so strong that a kind of shadow of untouchability had developed among the tribals themselves. Ranjan rushed round the village looking for someone to sweep out the rooms, change the water in the bathrooms, and perhaps clean the windows, but although he offered more than a labourer would have been paid for ten hours of the most gruelling work, it was some time before a reluctant and sulky boy could be found to take on the job. Shortly he arrived, treating us to a baleful glance as he slunk past clutching the bunch of twigs and the filthy cloth with which the process of cleansing would be accomplished.

The chicken was delivered steaming and fragrant, and Dinesh, averting his eyes from the spectacle, scuttled away down to the dhaba for his rice with dhal. Ranjan settled to his usual evening lecture. He enjoyed speculation on the subject of the Bonda because at the end of the twentieth century, so little was known about them – in the matter of their origins, nothing at all. They were here, and, said some of the savants, had been here since palaeolithic times. But of course it was all surmise, there was no proof of anything. Their language, it was clear, belonged to the Austro-Asiatic group, which was fortunate for Ranjan, because so did the Saora language, which he spoke fairly fluently. The difference between the two tongues might have been greater than that between English and German, but when a Bonda spoke there were words here and there that Ranjan recognised, and sometimes meanings could be pieced together. The Bondas in Dr Patnaik's scientific account were as stiff and unconvincing as the woodcuts in an ancient treatise. When Ranjan spoke of them from his own experiences they came vigorously and menacingly to life, leaping, grimacing and waving their bows as they had done a year before when Ranjan had ill-advisedly pitched his tent in the shadows of a wood in Bonda country.

It turned out on that occasion they wanted food. He gave it to them and they danced round him and went away. He had been alarmed, but fascinated, too. They were different in every way. He had never encountered human beings like them before and he wanted to know more about them. He found that they carried everything to extremes. If you tried to cheat a Bonda he killed you on the spot, not because he objected to material loss, but for the lie underwriting the attempted fraud. Visitors to the Koyas were startled to hear that Koya boys of thirteen married women of thirty, but the Bonda went one better, for marriages of boys from 8–10, said Ranjan, with girls in their twenties were commonplace. Most of the tribals either approved of, or at least permitted, marriage by capture. In the case of the Bondas it became a kind of sport: they not only raided their own villages for suitable brides, but even mounted expeditions for this purpose into the territory of neighbouring tribes. This, too, Ranjan saw as a typical excess in a community never short of sexual adventure, with its courting parties of young boys going from village to village to serenade girls compelled by the rules of hospitality to take them to bed in the local dormitory.

Ranjan did not surprise me by expressing his admiration for the Bondas' intense individualism. They refused to take orders from anybody, and it was impossible to induce them to engage in communal undertakings of any kind. He was impressed by the fact that they possessed a great number of different musical instruments, and that every man played one or more of them. More remarkably, he could even find an excuse for their showing no care or concern for their parents or the old people.

What seemed to shock him – reflecting probably his position in a society ruled by strict dietetic taboos – was the fact that even at a time when game of all kinds such as pig and deer were in plentiful supply and jungle trees produced abundant fruit, the Bondas should happily eat rats, mice, crows and such insects as cicadas and ants. Yet the avoidance of such foods is largely a matter of custom and prejudice. I have never been brought to the pass of having to satisfy hunger with nutriment of this kind, but friends have done so. Marcus Colchester, when working among the Yanomami of the Orinoco, was compelled for a time to subsist on an exceptionally large genus of caterpillar. These, he said, were quite palatable so long as one remembered to discard the heads.

TWENTY-TWO

DESPITE THE EXTREME squalor of the dhaba, breakfast there at six in the morning turned out to be a pleasant and enlivening experience. The proprietor and his slatternly wife were shovelling pancakes and doughnuts into pans of boiling oil, to be served eventually with curried beans. All this was delectable. Breakfast must have been the main meal of the day, for cloths were taken down from a shelf, beaten with a stick to remove a caking of whitish dust and laid on each table. Despite the irremediable filthiness of the place it was full of the fragrance of sandalwood, intentionally created by dropping gum collected under the sal trees into the open fire.

A pudgy minor official of sorts was breakfasting at the next table. Ranjan asked him where all the Bondas had gone, and he said back to their hill villages. He was quite sure that the market was to be held as usual because tribal advance parties had come down at dawn, as they always did, to clean up and prepare the site. The police would be there to keep things under control and impound cameras that might be produced. Any Bondas in Khairput, he thought, could be found at the Lutheran Mission church, to which he directed us.

We rang the bell at the iron gate, and immediately the

pastor came out to greet us. He was a pleasant, smiling, rather portly young Indian, who in the instinctive judgement of this first meeting it would have been hard to dislike. He handed me his card: K. Devasahayam, I.M.S.T. Missionary, Khairput Post, then led the way into his church, which seemed very bare. The Hindu temple at Khairput had been decked with flowers, both artificial and real, and there were paper chains, little coloured flags, odd scraps of flowered material pinned up here and there, and a genial, rather ridiculous picture of Ganesh which had helped to bolster the light-hearted and indulgent atmosphere of the place. But God, as seen by the Protestant sects, was averse to such attempted beautifications and elected, they believed, to be worshipped in surroundings of unrelieved solemnity. To come here after the temple was to enter a kind of vacuum.

I asked the pastor about his work with what he might well have seen as the most intractable heathens of all. 'We have simple rules,' he said. 'Don't go to dormitory. Priest conducts marriage. No polygamy. Not to drink.'

'And is your rule accepted?'

'No,' he said. 'They smile and say yes. They go on as before.' It was impossible not to admire his frankness and also the good humour with which he admitted defeat. Yet I wondered why the notorious Bonda violence should have been excluded from the prohibitions, and why three out of four embargoes were connected with sex.

'Have you made many converts?'

'Seven families have come to Jesus Christ.'

'Out of a population of how many?'

'By latest census this is 5,100.'

'So it sounds like a long haul.'

'Ah yes, it is a long way to go. We are hoping. We go on trying. We are labouring in the Lord's vineyard.'

'What sort of instruction do you give your converts?'

'That also is very difficult. It is hard to make them understand and we have a language problem. I am showing them a picture of Our Lord walking on the water. This is a picture they are liking very much.'

There was a sudden small outburst from him as if a bitter truth had forced its way out. 'These people we have gathered to Our Lord are very poor. Very necessitous. To keep them we are giving concessions.'

'In what way?'

'We know they are breaking faith with us, but we are looking in the other direction. Very much they are taking drink. If we say to them this must stop, they will go.'

The mission house, Mercy College, was next door. I would have liked to see the converts and asked if they were staying there.

No, he said. One of the strange things about them was they would only live in houses they had built themselves.

'And the church?' I asked. 'Do you hold services?'

'No one will come,' he said. 'They are afraid to be seen. In Bonda country many people are afraid.'

Ranjan had gathered more up-to-date information. The main body of the Bondas, both men and women, were accustomed to take the direct route straight down to their market, but for some inscrutable reason a number of women, unaccompanied by their menfolk, preferred to reach Khairput by a circuitous approach. These came down from the hills using the same narrow and precipitous track on which, eleven years before, Bose in his jeep had been captured and briefly held prisoner. The Bonda women using this detour, said Ranjan's informant, were quite approachable, and raised no objection even to the taking of photographs.

We accordingly set out in hope and had walked only a few hundred yards when we spotted the first of the Bonda girls on their way down. It was still early morning, with the leaves whitened by a residue of mist, and the sun throwing down taut lanes of shadow from the tree-trunks ahead, and once again it was a piece of Indian theatre. The first girl tripped towards us half-obscured in dense patches of shadow, then scintillating as the sun winked on jewellery displayed as if in a garish fashion parade. Behind her, fifty yards further away, came a second girl and then a third, hardly more than a brilliant insect flashing through the sunshine at a distance of a quarter of a mile.

The first girl came close, then stopped, a tiny Ethiopian with a thin Amharic face, a touch of melancholy in the eyes and finely cut features, among the wide cheekbones of tribal India. The cautious wraith of a smile undermined a dignity abetted by ten aluminium hoops compelling her to hold her head imperiously erect.

The Bondas are traditionally a naked people, their enforced nudism being of ancient origin. It followed a curse laid upon them in the times of the Mahabharata when Rama and Sita were journeying in the Bonda hills at the time of their fourteen-year banishment. Sita, cleansing herself in a river after menstruation, provoked the laughter of Bondas who had gone there to draw water. She thereupon laid a curse on them that they should always go naked and be the object of laughter – a punishment which they never cease to resent. To laugh at a Bonda is the deadliest of insults.

It is the purpose of the neck hoops to draw the beholder's attention up and away from those parts of the body deprived by the rigidity of custom from normal concealment. This girl also wore the obligatory 100 long necklaces, a massive glittering bulk extending from the neck to cover the pubic regions. Each forearm carried silver bangles extending almost to the elbow. Sita had stipulated that Bonda heads must be shaved and the bare scalp was covered by a cap of minute beads. Bonda girls were obliged to wear jewellery instead of clothing, but a small concession of recent origin had permitted the adoption of a kilt which, to avoid irreparable breach of custom, is of insufficient width to go right round the waist and thus permits glimpses of bare buttocks.

While we were examining the great collection of ornaments passed by inheritance from mother to daughter, the other girls, one after another, came up, stopped to be admired and photographed and went on. Presently middle-aged and elderly women began to arrive, always in groups of three and four. These, seemingly, had passed beyond reach of the taboo from which their daughters suffered, as they had been allowed to cover their jewellery with a mantle of light cloth, reaching to the knees. The question was why had the young and pretty girls of the tribe chosen to walk alone in this area where marriage by capture was an everyday occurrence, while their elders, relieved by the years from such hazards, sought company for the journey, and perhaps the protection of numbers? Could it be that the village beauties who put themselves to such bother with their attire for the trip to market to barter a few pounds of rice for a bowlful of fruit were providing their admirers, well away from interference by fathers or brothers, with an opportunity for romantic violence en route?

We followed them, lurking behind at a respectful distance, down to Khairput's muddle of hutments through which, for their own mysterious reasons, they had chosen to pass on their way to the market. Somehow, on our way back to the suites and to pick up the car, I became separated from Ranjan, and then, a moment later, turning a corner came on him facing the first Bonda male I had seen, who stood in his path holding a bow with an arrow fixed to point vaguely in the direction of Ranjan's feet. After the surprise of the weapon came the surprise of the size of this man I first took to be a local urchin playing a silly prank. I came up behind and the Bonda glanced back over his shoulder showing the same long, thin Ethiopian nose as the girls we had photographed and a tight, thin-lipped mouth. He stood about 4ft 10ins with no more of a physique than an average Indian boy of twelve but nevertheless exuded a daunting firmness of purpose.

At such times the compulsion is to look round for an ally, but Khairput, empty as ever, offered no support. There was the dhaba squeezed into the edge of the field of vision ahead, but breakfast was over and everyone had gone away. It was a confrontation that lasted no more than a matter of seconds before Ranjan reached out and took the bow away. He handed me the arrow, which was very light and small, and beautifully made. I found it hard to imagine how a man like this, having the size and musculature of a child, and using a weapon which however expertly made was hardly more than a toy, could actually kill another man in the way that Bondas did.

While this was going on there was no reaction from the Bonda of any kind. He showed no sign of anger, or surprise, and no disposition to argue. Ranjan handed back the bow, but when I held out the arrow the Bonda waved it away with a gesture of rejection, leading me to suspect that I might have damaged its magic by my touch. Ranjan gave him ten rupees, and nothing changed on his face. For a moment I was reminded of the trained imperturbability of a gangster in an old American film. Perhaps what we had experienced was no more than an automatic response to any stranger's presence, to be countered only with a show of calm. A moment later he slipped away. Later we saw him briefly again, still mooching about bow in hand, looking perhaps for someone who would start a fight with him.

We found the Bonda market tame and quiet and shrunken by all accounts, concentrated under the trees a mile down the road. We had passed by a police building and the officer in charge, exuding the sinister jocularity often generated by the consciousness of absolute power, came out to chat. The Bondas had put their bows away out of sight and, apart from a certain amount of apathetic bargaining over vegetables, nothing very much was going on. It was the most dispirited of such markets we had attended and after a few moments we left, making for Kundili back in Kondh country. Here on this same day each week was held what was described as possibly the greatest tribal assemblage in eastern India, with an attendance of not less than 10,000. This was the market at which, Ranjan had promised, we should see the parasitic Dombs in action robbing and fleecing the Kondhs.

We arrived at Kundili after a four-hour drive to find a seething multitude, drawn from a number of tribes, gathered into a mile-wide dust bowl at the conjunction of the main road into Andhra Pradesh and a number of country byways leading down from the hills. Under the hard forthright midday sun it was a sight to guarantee eye-strain and eventual headaches. The sky was bleached white, with drifts in it of what appeared at first as red smoke blowing across, but which proved to be the blood-red dust, which lay a quarter-inch deep on every surface, caught up by the gusting wind. When the dust was blown across the sun it turned dark, swelled up and seemed to tremble. From all points of the market came the piercing glitter of metal articles for sale, from sheets of corrugated iron, pots and pans, and above all from the rows of polished aluminium receptacles containing alcohol for sale.

Desia Kondh girls dispensed the alcohol. The Desias are the branch of the Kondhs inhabiting lowland villages which are in close contact with the Hindus, thus they are influenced by Hindu culture to the extent of abstaining from eating the meat of cows. Visits by travelling Hindu film shows have also brought about changes in Kondh fashion, and these girls, although covering themselves with jewellery made by their own silversmiths, and with nose-rings so large as to cover most of the top lip, had taken to wearing saris of strident colours produced in the factories of Bombay. The girls squatted in rows in the red dust, arms linked together, supposedly to impede unwanted abductions. Additional security was provided in the case of each group by a huge, somnolent dog. In front of each girl stood a two-gallon container of alcohol which, although nowadays of aluminium, surprisingly retained the classic shape of the old pots long since thrown away. Drinks were served in aluminium pint beakers after the red dust had been scrupulously wiped from their rims. Sales were brisk and productive of much antic behaviour by drunken exhibitionists. One of the customers mentioned to Ranjan that he had walked all night carrying a small pig to market on his shoulders. 'Now I have a right to get drunk,' he said, 'and it is my intention to do so.'

Such terrific journeys at night – always with the risk of attack by animals – produced extremely low monetary reward. A government report published a few years ago said that goods brought to market in this way fetched an average selling price of 1.50 rupees per person, and even now allowing for inflation this figure is unlikely to have increased more than four or five times. Besides selling their alcohol, Ranjan said it was generally accepted that these girls were here to place themselves on display. He drew attention to lurking Kondh boys who had renounced tribal loin-cloths in favour of Hindu dhotis. They would spend the day going round the market studying all the girls, and when a boy saw a girl he fancied he would offer her a bracelet, which while keeping a stony face she was obliged by custom to accept. If the girl was to be seen wearing the bracelet when she appeared at the next week's market it was an indication that the suit might be pursued. In nine cases out of ten – probably more – Ranjan said, she threw the bracelet away as soon as the donor's back was turned. She was choosy, and could afford to be. Only the most eligible of the Desia Kondh girls sold liquor in the market and their bride-price was a stiff one. To stand any chance of success the boy would have to satisfy Hindu rather than tribal standards by having a lighter skin than average, and thinnish nose and lips. It was an ideal difficult to approach by a Dravidian Kondh. Difficult, too, was the growing of a Mexican-style moustache, now all the rage since its popularisation by the famous actor Hemamalin, although little suited to the tribal face.

The bracelets were of plastic, more appreciated in these days than the metal variety, and the red earth in the vicinity of the liquor sales ladies had been imprinted with a patterning composed of hundreds and perhaps thousands of plastic fragments, in evidence of sexual overtures refused.

The market at Kundili offered a huge range of merchandise: sugar sold by the yard in bamboo tubes, specially treated rice for the making of instant alcohol, corrugated iron roofing, chicken wire, parrots and argus pheasants, herbal remedies in abundance for all known and imagined ailments, medicines to delay – and even hasten! – the menopause, arrow poison, ground hornbill beaks to promote unnatural strength, a sap which painted on the skin ensured invisibility against tigers, charms guaranteed to procure the growth of a serpent in an enemy's intestines or encourage an invasion of his house by hornets, jungle fruit juices to lighten Dravidian skin, philtres to spread or extinguish the fires of love.

All these were no more than the mercantile trimmings: mere fair-ground embellishments along with the thorn-surgeons, barbers, fortune-tellers and the dozen or so handsome and strapping transvestites – many of whom have been castrated – who are a feature of all the great markets and festivals of India. The real business at Kundili was the buying and selling of animals, cereals and dried fish, and this was the trade that attracted Dombs, whose hold upon the tribal population was so implacable that hardly a sale could be made without their taking a profit.

The Dombs had set up two high wooden tripods supporting their scales along every road at the approaches to the market. Each of these posts was manned by three Dombs: tall men of athletic appearance and dressed in Hindu style. Peasants bringing in their grain or animals such as goats, or baskets of hens, would be stopped at the first post about a hundred yards from the market pitches, and an attempt made by the most aggressive kind of bargaining to acquire what they had for sale. Those who refused to sell found a further and more vigorous attack at the second post, fifty yards further on, where reluctance to be subjected to an enforced sale was countered by every degree of physical persuasion short of outright assault, with Dombs wresting sacks of grain from the tribesmen's hands, tipping the contents into their scales, thrusting a few rupees into their victim's hands and waving them away.

Three or four tribesmen travelling together might have been expected to put up a struggle, and thus escape molestation. Solitary individuals, even couples, were inevitably accosted and, weighted down with their bundles, found it impossible to escape the Dombs, who sprinted after them bellowing blandishments and threats, and waving their arms like great birds labouring to take off.

No woman could escape, and it amazed us that they risked journeying alone. Within minutes of placing ourselves in a position where we could watch operations at one of the scales a woman appeared in sight, saw what was happening, and succeeded despite her load of grain in making a wide detour to avoid the first Domb scales, only to be caught at the second. After a brief and hopeless struggle and mewing protest she gave in, her rice was weighed and she was paid what Ranjan said would normally be about half the market price. All this happened within sight of a number of people who did not attempt to intervene.

How could it be that the Kondhs, who were at the market by the thousand, could have tolerated such spectacular robbery, which had been going on for decades, had been continually denounced in the press, prohibited by an act of Parliament, yet continued unchecked as before? A Domb had deprived a man of his goat, tearing the lead from his hand and running away with it, but somehow the man had got the goat back. Now he told Ranjan that the market price of a large goat such as this was 400 rupees but the Domb had refused to pay more than 220 rupees under the pretext that by the new health regulations only Dombs could sell goats in the market. When it came to grain, he said, the Dombs scored on two counts, for they not only grossly underpaid for whatever they bought but, as everybody knew, used false weights.

Why didn't the Kondhs get together and put up a fight? Ranjan asked.

'The Dombs pay gangsters to look after them.'

'Even so, there must be ten times the number of Kondhs in the market.'

'If anyone starts a big fight the police will be called in. They'd call it a riot and bring their guns along. The police are in the Dombs' pay, too.'

'So there's nothing you can do?'

'Nothing. They can do what they like with us.'

TWENTY-THREE

THE NEAREST APPROACH of modern times to Kangrapada happened when an earth-moving machine sent in
error by officials employed on a tribal micro-project
trundled to within a mile or so of the village, chewed a
few cubic yards of earth out of a bank, broke down, and
was withdrawn. Thereafter the village had been left alone
to defend itself by self-sufficiency. A patchwork quilt of
vegetables had been spread in the sun at its entrance.
These the villagers ate themselves, as they did a meagre
harvest of dry rice, and a few rabbits hunted in the
jungle. They kept cows for their milk, and from their
own silk worms they spun silk, which the girls made into
elegant dresses. Not even the silk was for sale. The
Parajas and Godbas sharing the village of Kangrapada
took nothing from the outside world. They were modest
drinkers of one of the better versions of alcohol made
from the flowers of marua. In this way moneylenders
were kept out, and if one succeeded in worming his way
in he might be induced by a warning arrow to curtail his
stay. As the villagers incurred no debts there were no
bankruptcies, no fields seized in lieu of payment, no
contractors offering debt bondage as the only solution.
Fifty miles away we had seen girls of fourteen and fifteen

working as labourers in the road. None of them would have been from Kangrapada.

This was Ranjan's Eden, everything at first glance as it had been exactly a year before when he had spent a quite pleasurable day bargaining with the headman and his advisers, as well as making friends with the villagers before being required to mollify the village goddess for a supposed offence by the offering of a cockerel. The village was a cool place. Kondh and Saora villagers we had seen scored their partial victories over the sun by living on verandahs sheltered by a tremendous over-hang of thatched roofs. The Parajas and Godbas were spared such measures by their good luck in living in a patch of jungle in which they had spaced out the trees so as to leave no part of the village uncovered by dappled shade. Yet so cleverly had the use of shade been exploited that not a corner of the village was gloomy or dark.

As elsewhere in our travels we found that here too it was the season of leisurely relaxation – the social art-form, Ranjan said, at which these people were past masters. The village notables were gossiping, much as he had left them, within earshot of the Earth Mother. People, dressed in their best, were walking up and down chatting to each other. A few were taking naps on their verandahs. One or two women were occupy-ing themselves with silk-making processes in an uncommitted way – children were playing a game like hop-scotch. An occasional male appeared to be inoffen-sively drunk.

Two things disturbed Ranjan slightly. The first was that as he now remembered the only outsider to have stayed any length of time in Kangrapada had been an anthropologist, who having done field-work there returned to Bhubaneswar to stage an exhibition. For this a party of Godbas had agreed to build a replica of one of their unique round houses, and this – built, as Ranjan remembered, in five days – had produced excited comment from visitors who could not understand how primitive tribals could produce anything having so great an appeal for what were sometimes called 'normal people'.

This was something that had drawn attention to Kangrapada for the first time and there had been articles in the local papers about it. The second matter for concern was that despite the admiration evoked in the city by the Godbas' circular house they were falling out of favour in Kangrapada, where a Godba couple with the assistance of Paraja neighbours had built themselves a rectangular house in Paraja style which in Ranjan's opinion was 'a box with a verandah'. Ranjan's informant, one of the tribal elders with whom he had been involved in the negotiations over his breach of custom in the previous year, said something to the effect that 'we all have to move with the times'. When Ranjan complained that the Paraja houses were less comfortable, the man replied, 'Sometimes we may sacrifice comfort for appearance.'

The lure of modernity had also touched the Godba girls. Ranjan had been relieved to find that the older women still wore the great, solid silver necklaces passed down from generation to generation and which could only be removed by the silversmith after death. At the time of our arrival he was a little surprised to find the girls parading in their best dresses, as if for a festival, although nobody had mentioned one. All the dresses were identical, almost as if uniforms, and made of cream-coloured cotton cloth into which were woven a series of wide diagonal stripes; three of them red alternating with one black. Despite the influence of the Hindu sari the general effect was Western rather than oriental, with nothing about it that we would have labelled 'ethnic'. What was different was that the enormous silver hoop earrings, six inches in diameter, which the girls had worn dangling on their shoulders at the time of his previous visit, had been replaced by a standard factory product supplied by a pedlar. When we spoke to the Godba girls about this, they said that that change had come about through unanimous decision. They objected, they said, to the discomfort. For special occasions they would wear the earrings hooped over their ears, but not suspended from the lobes. I found them all very beautiful, but somewhat reserved and unsmiling. They would be dancing later that morning, they said, and then they would wear the traditional earrings.

The strikingly wrapped sweets bought in Jeypore were now doled out, to the children first – engagingly shy when pushed to the forefront of a respectful encirclement – then the adults of both sexes. There followed a brief demonstration in the method of removing the wrappers, certain to be carefully conserved without damaging them in any way. Within a few minutes half the population of Kangrapada was sucking sweets.

'Nice people,' Ranjan said. 'Very reasonable. I just asked if it was all right to park the car where it is and the old headman said, "You have been introduced to the goddess, and you offered her a cockerel. There is no problem. You are one of the family now."'

'They're very poor,' I said.

'We may feel this as poverty, which for us it will be.

For them it is not poverty, it is living their life. They feed themselves. They are happy. What else, they will ask, is important? A moneylender who comes here must wear mourning. To lend money he will be asking for a security, and what security can he find? If he asks for a field it must grow rice, and there is no water for this purpose. A field for growing chillies is no use to him. As yet the buses are not coming and that is good . . . '

By now every corner of the village had been explored and greeting exchanged with Ranjan's acquaintances of old for the second and third time. The village was full of cordial little pigs with long snouts whose ancestors would have been wild boars. 'They are saying a pig has been killed to be cooked,' Ranjan said. 'They do not know why.' We turned back for another tour of the neighbouring collection of houses. 'We are walking,' Ranjan said, 'because I am looking for that girl.'

'Don't you know where she lives?'

'I know where she lives but I do not understand their customs in this way of visiting, and am not wanting to put my foot in it as has happened before.' He was referring to his misadventure in the Bhunjia country, when the out-house containing a family shrine had had to be burned down after he had blundered into it out of mere curiosity. 'They were very understanding. No one blamed me for my mistakes. Something like that could happen to me here if I am not careful. This is to be avoided.'

'I agree with you,' I told him. 'Better to play for safety.'

'Soon her friends will go to tell her I am here,' he said, 'and she will come out.'

Somewhere over on the further side of the village

drumming had started. We stopped to listen. 'Does that mean they're dancing?' I asked.

'This is certainly the case. In Kangrapada always there are celebrations going on. For the birth of a child they are celebrating, and then again for the first cutting of hair. When the rain comes and when it stops there is a very big dancing. If a man recovers from a sickness all his friends must dance with him. If they cannot find a reason for celebrating they are doing so for no reason at all. In this village there is dancing with any excuse.'

We strolled in the direction of these celebratory sounds, finding ourselves shortly in an open space shaded by splendid old trees in which a man hammering on a drum was being accompanied by another on an exceedingly shrill flute. Nine Godba maidens, arms linked, advanced, retreated, advanced and kicked, almost in chorus-girl style. With a change in the music's tempo they formed a single file to follow their leader waving a broom in a capering circle round the musicians. Crouching in a shady corner of this scene was a bearded Westerner in shorts, a video camera held to his eye. A second Westerner, clean-shaven, also in shorts, was doing his best to direct the action of the dancers and confine this within the camera's field of vision.

'Those are the girls we were talking to just now. Seems as though they're putting on a performance,' I said.

'For money,' Ranjan said, 'someone is paying them money.'

'It's something you have to expect.'

'In Kangrapada no one is given money to do such things. Money is not necessary. They are dancing all the time for the pleasure of dancing.'

'Our friends have no way of knowing that. Apart from Kangrapada that's the way things are done.'

'But there is an Indian with them. He should tell them.'

At that moment a young Indian dressed in town style in shirt and slacks had come into view from behind the car that had brought the filming party. 'This is something you have to accept,' I said. 'Even Kangrapada will have to come to terms with money.'

Variations had to be introduced into the dance routine to accommodate the camera's requirements. The girls were halted and called back led by the broom-waver for several repetitions of their dance. The music was slowed down to give each girl time to provide a separate dead-pan close-up before moving back into line. They had stiffened up. Spontaneity wilted.

'This is not Godba dancing,' Ranjan said. 'When the Godbas dance they are not going for walks. They are staying in one place.'

'I expect the photographer wanted more action, and this is the best they can do.'

'Yes, that may be so. They are accustomed to dance in their own way.'

'Does it matter if it's not authentic? They're trying hard. The man with the camera is getting what he wants. After all, this is not for local consumption.'

'The village has changed. Now everything will be bought with money.'

'Eventually, yes. It was bound to happen. The change has come sooner than expected, that's all. After all one single video camera in a thousand miles isn't too bad.'

The drum thumped out its subtle complexities that had left the dancing-to-order so far behind, and as the flute squealed untamed ecstasy the Godba girls traipsed conscientiously up and down and backwards and forwards. The photographer's assistant gestured to the girl with the broom to wave it more vigorously, and she did so. He pulled at the corners of his mouth, producing a grimace meant to represent a smile, but the girls did not understand. Ranjan had said of another such village, in illustration of tribal temperament, 'When they are dancing no one is knowing when it will end. While they are happy this dancing must go on.' The pity in this case was that it all depended on the running time of the film which at that moment seemed to have come to an end. The cameraman held up his hand and it was all over. The music wailed through a showering cascade of half-tones to silence. The drummer let fall his sticks. The girls, dismissed by the Indian boy's gesture, shuffled off into the background. Their leader threw the broom away, and the crows that had taken refuge from this disturbance in overhanging branches now unfolded their wings and dropped about us from the trees.

'No one came to watch the dancing,' I said.

'They do not come to watch dancing, they come to dance. That is why no one came.'

It was one of the small misadventures of travel, an abrupt debasement of the coinage of experience that I suspected neither of us would forget. The day had flagged. Watched by the village elders with amiable somnolence we recovered the car for a final tour of the village. After a few minutes, and with no sign of disappointment, Ranjan said that we might as well go, and we had reached the last of the houses when he spotted the Paraja girl he had come to see, standing among a group of friends at the top of a slope from which they could keep the road under observation.

We stopped and waited, sitting in the car. The Paraja girl detached herself from her friends and came down the slope, bent down to the window and she and Ranjan began what sounded like a casual chat. She was a pretty, lively girl with a gentle smile. Ranjan had mentioned that, as usual, none of the villagers of Kangrapada knew their ages. I would have put her as being seventeen. Despite the immense effort taken in all these tribal villages to prevent interbreeding there was a recognisable form of beauty shared by these girls, whether Parajas or Godbas. Why should the Parajas smile, I wondered, whereas the Godbas remained straightfaced? The foreigners had chosen badly, the Parajas should have danced for them.

The soft-voiced discussion through the car window ought to have betrayed traces of excitement even if under control – but there was none. 'When I am with these people,' Ranjan said, 'I watch them and I try to behave as they do. Always I play for safety.' This was in reply to my comment that I never remembered seeing a Paraja who was not actually smiling, or who failed to convey the impression that he or she was about to smile. But perhaps this was all part of the protocol of concealment of feeling. The Paraja stiff upper-lip. Slowly I was coming to the realisation that for all the apparent free loving and living of the so-called primitives they were in reality wanderers under watchful eyes in the labyrinth of custom. Now Ranjan and the girl appeared to be joking together, but I remembered the implacable joking and no-joking relationship imposed by the Kondh and the Bonda. Perhaps this, too, was a ritual prescribed for such an occasion. Perhaps, even, it was all played according to the rules, including the antics at the Paraja drunken wedding we had attended.

Could it even be that this encounter and this setting had been contrived in advance? I had heard Ranjan's story of his proposed marriage with the Paraja girl in which the father had taken the unheard-of initiative of renouncing the bride-price, besides consenting to her union with a caste-member from the city. The question was how had the village taken this? Ranjan may have been deceived by an assumed complacency. He seemed never to have considered the possibility of opposition, yet surely there must have been a minority of dissenters in a community ruled by a cabal of ancient conservatives under the all-seeing and assuredly critical eye of the Earth Mother in her heap of stones?

At the top of the slope seven Paraja girls, all identical from this distance, the same earrings, nose-rings, bracelets, anklets and smiles, stood in a motionless row to watch what was going on. Were they part of an essential audience? Now I realised that other onlookers had silently placed themselves within the frame of vision: a man with an archaic stringed instrument wearing a long old-fashioned loin-cloth, whom I saw here for the first time, a man carrying a single peacock's feather held like a staff of office, a man leading a white dog on a length of rope. There was a planned formation in this setting, like that of a scene from *Antigone* when the Fates are about to enter their part of the drama.

The exchange of words faltered, was breached by small silences, which in turn were filled in by what I suspected were repetitions. It was the familiar climate of partings, when there is nothing new to be said. Heads were rocked in Indian fashion gently from side to side to signify acceptance, agreement, conclusion. The Paraja girl straightened herself and moved back; Ranjan touched the driver on the shoulder, and the car began to draw away. Ranjan continued to look straight ahead but after a few yards I twisted round to watch the Paraja girl climb the slope to join her friends, still facing us and in line. The few onlookers had begun to drift away.

TWENTY-FOUR

WE MADE AN early start next morning on the road back to Bhubaneswar, taking a short cut through north-eastern Andhra Pradesh which extends a closed hand in profile with the index finger pointed northwards along the coast in the direction of distant Calcutta.

I was in no hurry to arrive. As in the case of most pleasurable experiences, time had speeded up, and what was left of the journey was slipping away too fast. When we stopped for tea I got out the local, amateurish large-scale map which tore a little more at the folds every time I opened it, and for which despite its inaccuracies in the matter of place names and distances I had developed an affection. It was full of signs and symbols and little conventional drawings of temples, hot springs, rock inscriptions and paintings, images of Vishnu sleeping under an umbrella, of Buddhist antiquities, and 'Scenic Picturesque Picnic-spots', of forests furnished with tigers and crocodiles in an aggressive stance, and a single sinister ideogram denoted a hydro-electric project with its dam, at the head of a tragically flooded valley.

What I was looking for was excuse for delay, a short detour back into the vanished hinterland, a post-ponement of the moment when I would face the engrimed Super-Fast ready on the dot to pull out from Bhubaneswar station, a final truancy to prepare for and soften the impact of anti-climax.

But all roads from this point on led to Bhubaneswar, and from the moment of crossing the state border of Andhra Pradesh an instant change was to be felt. South Orissa had been peopled by thin men; here there were fat men too. Their faces, demeanour and even their walk were different. People you saw in these streets were going about their business; no one carried musical instruments. In Orissa we had sometimes driven all day without passing another car. In this right-hand top corner of Andhra Pradesh fed by National Highway NH5, rampaging legions of lorries filled the road. In the small countryfied towns and the vast emptiness we had come through the police had been spread thin. Here they were everywhere, watching, questioning, poking among the fearful carnage of road-accidents waiting to be cleared away, manning check-points through which vehicles preferring to pass without inspection could do so in payment of a standard fifty-rupee bribe. I saw something I had never seen in Orissa, a whole roadside village of wonderfully woven beehive huts occupied by untouchables, with neat and pretty untouchable girls crawling in and out of them. Ranjan said that they had been ordered to build their houses in this way to assist caste differentiation. Further on there were labour gangs of girls of about fifteen or sixteen, supplied by this community to haul stones broken up with hammers into position for road repairing steam-rollers.

There was a different pulse of life here; different inducements, different goals. Luxury advertisements had appeared to encourage the circulation of money. Film stars displayed their Westernised good looks from every wall, otherwise covered with a scrofula of misleading appeals by candidates for election. The whiff of development and prosperity fostered lapses of taste. An up-to-date temple with parking offered facilities for the better class of traveller. Three over-large factory-produced images of Saraswati, Krishna and Ganesh, sharing local adulation, had been unappealingly sprayed in shiny black enamel, and one could sit in comfortable chairs and sip superb tea served by the lady attendants while exchanging stares with these. A little way down the road a retired admiral had built a villa in the shape of the front half of a warship, painted in undulations of grey-green camouflage with portholes for windows and a stone five-pounder threatening the surroundings from its deck.

Hereabouts we suffered the first tyre trouble for well over 1,000 miles, an occurrence that sparked off a small mutiny in our driver who complained that this was due to our not paying our respects at another shrine which we had overshot, after which Ranjan had refused to turn back. Up until this we had been travelling in the main through the spheres of influence of easy-going tribal deities, but now we were in the territory of Kali, who, as the driver assured us, was less likely to overlook such offences. With that, almost, the tyre went down, calling for an awkward repair. Our hope had been to spend the night at the Ashram of Shiva about sixty miles further on. ('The priestess will not even question your religion,' Ranjan said. 'If she is not minding, why should you?') Now, with the onset of darkness, this would not be comfortably possible. We decided to find beds in the local metropolis Srikakulam, thrusting its flood-lit towers into a sky in which – as if in presage of what was to come – a single rocket exploded to spread a glittering, slowly falling trail.

Srikakulam had half a ring-road, a one-way traffic system, white taxis and the first traffic lights I had seen since leaving Calcutta. At the moment of our arrival the lights were stuck at red, and the biggest and most unruly herd of buffaloes I had ever seen were stampeding, like a scene from a western round-up, in the wrong direction down the one-way main street, and carrying all before them. Srikakulam, too, was in the throes of its many weddings, with fireworks now exploding all round and insoluble tussles for precedence at the lights between the processions and distraught buffaloes separated from their herd. The Hemamalin Film Star Hotel was bursting at the seams with fantastically attired wedding guests, and marooned among these were a number of regulars, some extremely fat, and one asprawl in an arm-chair being fanned by one middle-aged woman and massaged by another. There were no rooms, said the reception clerk, adding in a voice that held a suspicion of triumph that we would not find any in the town. Nor, he added, was there any food. Drinks could only be served to guests in their cars, but this – and we agreed with him – was impossible in a street which at that moment was glutted with panicking cattle. He then handed us a leaflet about a local cobra festival to be held in November, for which hotel reservations were required well in advance.

With the buffalo stampede at an end, somebody directed us to a last-chance hotel in the less fashionable part of the town, and we drove there under a sky speckled with small explosions and the surroundings fitfully lit by a descending parachute flare as if in preparation for military assault. The General Lodging, as it was called, reminded me of a prison in Madrid where I had once visited a prisoner detained for political reasons. It occupied in this case a floor of an unfinished building long since abandoned. A passage accessible through an iron gate led to a dozen small rooms: well-swept, adequate cells, free of mosquitoes and devoid of dark recesses in which venomous spiders might have lurked, each with a clean sink, small barred windows, and a naked bulb that dispensed waxing and waning light. I had come very much to like the people who owned or ran such places and the roadside dhabas; unsmiling as a whole, the practitioners of extreme if distant courtesy, and free of ingratitude or pretence. I was happy to be where we were rather than at the Film Star Hotel.

The problem of food arose, and it was a little more complicated than usual. On the whole we were committed, like it or not, to a diet of rice and dalh, which suited our vegetarian driver very well. We were directed to the Military Meals Restaurant, a flashy sort of place, where after taking one look at us the doorman pointed at a side entrance leading to an upstairs area set aside for patrons in search of a discreet ambience in which to drink whisky and eat meat. To ensure privacy and anonymity diners were served in booths like oversize telephone boxes, so faintly lit that they must have had to grope for their food.

Dinesh would have none of this. The waiter assured us that pure and unadulterated vegetarian food was served on the ground floor, but the driver raised the objection that the ladles used for the rice might have been contaminated by meat, and made a bolt for the door. Left to ourselves we chose the relatively well-lit main restaurant, simple food and good Indian beer.

Back in the General Lodging I took up position to enjoy the view over the low wall of our passageway, which also served as a communal balcony. The building occupied half of a substantial crater, possibly fifty yards across, from which it was to be supposed that sand and gravel had once been extracted leaving a wilderness of a special kind, deeply eroded and fissured, and an occasional small cavern among little pyramids of building materials in its bottom. This, by Indian standards, was a valuable site, since it provided shelter of a basic kind for those who could not afford a roof and walls, and in most cases not even rent. A flight of steps had been cut into the crater's side and these joined at the bottom with a path leading to a settlement improvised in the foundations of the General Lodging itself. This appeared to be occupied by citizens in regular work, who arrived home in some instances carrying briefcases. Tucked away in a far corner of the crater and only partially visible by leaning over the wall was an encampment made from plastic sheeting stretched over a wooden frame, of the kind put up in a single day to accommodate labourers working in the neighbourhood. It was early enough for the shops still to be open in the street running along the top of the crater wall, from which a certain amount of light penetrated into the cavity. Smears of torchlight showed in the interiors of the black plastic shacks, but it was likely that the labourers and their wives had already gone to bed, for there was nothing of them to be seen. Nevertheless their children, still up and about, continued a joyous and jubilant exploration of the crater's fairyland.

Ranjan joined me to enjoy the view, followed by the owner of the place, who had the face of a wolf but who was very kind, bringing us tea. Something in the air made me feel Ranjan's mood had changed. It was hard not to be soothed in this environment. Not a word had been said about Kangrapada since leaving it, and I had found it significant that he had not even marked the village's position on a sketch map of our journey I had asked him to make. Now he suddenly brought up the filming of which he had shown such disapproval, news of which had reached a contact in Jeypore where we had spent the last night. 'These men were Americans,' he said. 'The Indians who took them told them the people were not asking for money. Instead they gave them a pig.'

Since the matter was now in the open, I asked a question. 'Any further thoughts on the subject of marriage?'

'Yes,' he said. 'This has been settled in my mind. I am thinking it will be an arranged one.'

'Traditional style,' I said.

'That is the meaning of an arranged marriage. It means I am saying yes to tradition.'

It came as a disappointment. I would have preferred this romantic adventure and my tiny involvement to have ended on a different note.

This he seemed to have sensed, and there was a touch of consolation in his laugh. 'Unless minds are changing,' he said. 'That is always possible.'

After a moment of failure the town's lights had all come on again, and we sipped our tea and enjoyed the prospect. A night market was held along the road across the crater with the leaves of the shade trees turned to coral by its cooking fires. Shoppers piled their bundles into the rickshaws and struggled to help the pullers drag them up the slope to where the road levelled out. Below us the labourers' children screamed unflagging delight; a husband back from work came scrambling down the crater waving his briefcase to a wife positioned somewhere out of sight beneath. Film theme-music from distant sources had been blended by an ocean of air into a sweet Eastern droning. For me it was the best of India. It was a scene to be included in the album of the journey's memorabilia along with the sad aquatints of Bihar, the blossoming night skies of the steel towns, and the ghostly Australia of the mountains where tribals danced upon metallic ores.

In this context of the immediate past a gallery of faces were called to mind, all of which had made an appearance, however brief, in this experience: Mr Chawra, enraptured at Patna by the balloon, the genial and helpful Mr Singh who liked humanity on the whole but was depressed at the prevalence of insurance fraud, Devi with his swaggering Japanese car fraternising cautiously with his casteless driver – even the Debjon's manager who was cordiality itself and rewarded me on my departure with two additional Christmas cards, one inscribed 'Well come. Any time to drop in.' Finally there was Ranjan, lapsed Brahmin, and a prey to romantic impulse, but otherwise a man of extraordinary perception who showed me his country in a new light, and with whom I would have asked nothing better than to travel on uncovering together hidden pleasures of India.

He had gone off with the General Lodging's owner and was back with more tea. 'What time in the morning?' he asked. 'Six?'

'Let's make it later,' I said. 'There's no hurry.'

I wondered what the few miles along the coastal road had to offer. 'How long is it to the ashram?' I asked.

'Two hours.'

'I suppose we could stay there if it came to the push?'

'They will be welcoming us, but better it is to stay only a short time. This is a very quiet place. There is very little to catch the eye or occupy the interest.'

'In that case there's nothing for it,' I said. 'It's on to Bhubaneswar.'

Index